Limerick Soviet 1919

'We must look at life in all its aspects from the point of view of the *Bottom Dog* – the oppressed – be it nation, class or sex'

Limerick Soviet 1919
The Revolt of the Bottom Dog

Dominic Haugh

Thomond Publishing
Shannon

Thomond Publishing
Tullyvarraga, Shannon, Co. Clare, Ireland.

© 2019 Dominic Haugh

ISBN: 978-1-9160909-0-3

First published 2019

The publisher has no responsibility for the persistence or accuracy of URLs for any external or third-party internet websites referred to in this book and does not guarantee that any content on such websites is, or will remain, accurate or appropriate.

For Stephanie

Contents

Images

Cover Image: Painting by 'Jason Brannigan, anarchist', based on the iconic photograph of the Bruree Soviet, 1921.

https://www.facebook.com/jasonbranniganart/

Back cover image: the logo of the Limerick Soviet Centenary Committee.

http://limericksoviet100.ie/

Abbreviations

ASE	Amalgamated Society of Engineers
ASRS	Amalgamated Society of Railway Servants
CPI	Communist Party of Ireland
DLF	Irish Democratic Trade and Labour Federation
DW&WR	Dublin, Wicklow and Wexford Railway
GS&WR	Great Southern and Western Railway
IALU	Irish Agricultural Labourers Union
IADMU	Irish Automobile Drivers and Mechanics Union
ICWU	Irish Commercial Workers Union
ILIU	Irish Labour and Industrial Union
ILLA	Irish Land and Labour Association
ILPTUC	Irish Labour Party and Trade Union Congress
IPP	Irish Parliamentary Party
IRA	Irish Republican Army
IRB	Irish Republican Brotherhood
ITGWU	Irish Transport and General Workers Union
ITUC	Irish Trade Union Congress
IWWU	Irish Women Workers Union
LAA	Limerick Amnesty Association
LFLC	Limerick Federated Labour Council
LUTLC	Limerick United Trades and Labour Council
NSFU	National Sailors' and Firemen's Union
NUDL	National Union of Dock Labourers
NUR	National Union of Railwaymen
PLG	Poor Law Guardians
RIC	Royal Irish Constabulary
RSP	Revolutionary Socialist Party
W&CR	Waterford and Central Line Rail Company
W&LR	Waterford and Limerick Railway
WFA	Waterford Farmers Association

Reference is made in the text to old English currency

12 pence (d) = 1 shilling (s)

20 shillings = 1 pound (£)

Acknowledgements

The book is the culmination of many years of intermittent research that has finally come to fruition. Over the years I have had significant help from many sources including the staff of the National Archives of Ireland, the National Library of Ireland, the staff of Limerick City and County libraries and my PhD supervisor, John Cunningham.

I would also like to thank my wife Mary Lehane for her patience and support and her unstinting efforts to correct the typographical errors that I insisted on repeatedly making. A thank you is also due to Dave Vallely for his advice and to Joe Higgins for writing the foreword.

Lastly, I would like to thank Jason Brannigan for allowing the use of his fantastic painting for the cover of the book and the Limerick Soviet Centenary Committee for the use of their logo.

FOREWORD

'Limerick Soviet 1919 - The Revolt of the Bottom Dog' deals of course with the dramatic events in Limerick in April 1919 but crucially analyses these events against the background of the turbulent years before and after, as well as chronicling the development of the organised labour movement in Ireland over the previous century. The book will stand out for the meticulous research that informs it, based on the use of primary, contemporaneous sources but most especially for its unique Marxist analysis of the forces which shaped the events in question and their outcomes.

'The history of all hitherto existing society is the history of class struggles'.

Beginning Chapter 1 with the famous quote from Karl Marx and Friedrich Engels, the author validates its essential truth with a comprehensive overview of the struggles of the working class and rural poor in Limerick and further afield, reaching back to the first large scale strike in the city which was by journeymen tradesmen in May 1806. This and the next two chapters give a fascinating account of the unceasing efforts of workers to organise and act in defence of their class during the course of the 19th Century. Organisation and strike action by groups such as the rail and dockworkers were mirrored by, and often interlinked with, the struggles of farm labourers and the rural poor for whom life was an endless battle for mere survival.

This history is unknown to most people. In schools, the history of 19th Century Ireland boils mainly down to Daniel O'Connell and Catholic Emancipation, the tragedy of the Famine, Fenianism and the Parnellite campaign for Home Rule with the Land League also featuring. However, how many know that within the Land League movement itself there were bitter conflicts between the tenant farmers who were pitted against the big landlord class and the impoverished farm labourers who were insistent on justice for themselves and their impoverished families?

On January 21st, 1919 the first Dáil met in Dublin comprised of deputies elected under the Sinn Féin banner in the December 1918 General Election who refused to take their seats in Westminster in order to establish an Irish Parliament. On that same day also a group of Republican activists staged an unauthorised ambush at Soloheadbeg in Tipperary killing two members of the Royal Irish Constabulary, an event that kicked off what developed into a guerrilla conflict between Sinn Féin and the IRA and the forces of British Imperialism.

Three months later the working class of Limerick exploded onto the national - and international - stage in reaction to repressive measures by the British army in the city. Showing the powerful impact of the world's first successful workers' revolution in Russia only 18 months previously, the organised workers of Limerick established their own 'Soviet' or workers' council and took all vital areas of life in the city into democratic control.

The chapter on the general strike/Soviet illustrates the power and remarkable organisation of the workers and debunks the theory often advanced that this was merely an adjunct to the nationalist strategy of Sinn Féin. The following three chapters show how the next four years were marked by waves of struggle by urban and rural workers in defence of already meagre living standards which were under sustained attack. This covered the tumultuous period of guerrilla warfare, the formation of the Irish Free State, Civil War and the consolidation of Cumann na nGael in power, representing capital and the big farming class.

The book graphically illustrates the bitter conflict that developed between the two major social forces that asserted themselves in the first months of 1919 - Sinn Féin and its military wing representing essentially the nascent Irish capitalist class and the urban and rural workers organised in the trade unions. It shows how this was not a period when all classes in Irish society were in a happy coalition against a 'foreign invader'.

Referring to Irish nationalists, James Connolly wrote in *Socialism Made Easy*, 'After Ireland is free, says the patriot who won't touch socialism . . . if you won't pay your rent you will be evicted same as now. But the evicting party will wear green uniforms and the Harp without the Crown, and the warrant turning you out on the roadside will be stamped with the arms the Irish Republic.' This book shows how the foreboding of Connolly was borne out as it graphically illustrates how the 'patriots' in Sinn Féin ruthlessly imposed the same exploitative control of capital over workers as existed under British rule. Even as it imploded into civil war from July 1922, both the pro- and anti-Treaty wings of Sinn Féin and the IRA brutally repressed workers' strikes and did literally evict them from their occupations and broke up their Soviets. With ample, well researched examples, the author shows the real nature of the Sinn Féin of that time which the political party of the same name today aspires to emulate.

The economic and social plight of the working class, including the rural poor, was acute but their willingness to struggle for a better life undeniable. *The Limerick Soviet 1919 -The Revolt of the Bottom Dog* shows how in struggle after struggle they were betrayed by the national leadership of their own movement, the Irish Labour Party, Trade Union Congress (ILPTUC). Documented with unrelenting rigour, the conservatism, cowardice and treacherous class collaboration with the representatives of native Irish capital is laid bare. The harshest of lights is cast on figures such as Tom Johnson and William O'Brien, leader of the Irish Transport and General Words Union.

This book deepens the thesis of the Socialist Party in Ireland as outlined in *Ireland's Lost Revolution: 1916-1923* that, in the decade following the crushing of the 1916 Rising, the organised working class in city, town and countryside demonstrated again and again its power and the strength of its organisation. At several junctures it could have taken the leadership of the national struggle and thereby made it a struggle, not just for independence from imperialism but for social emancipation from capitalism and landlordism and the achievement of socialism in a Workers' Republic. This would have cut across the alienation of the Protestant working class in the north east of the country as they saw how a future Irish government would be dominated by the Catholic Church and would not hesitate to use divide and rule to divert from economic crisis and use them as a minority scapegoat.

Unfortunately, there was not a political organisation in the mould of the Bolshevik Party that led the mighty Russian Revolution in October 1917 which could have given the political programme and organisational methods that would have been necessary to achieve success.

A new dimension which the book develops was the crucial role of key trade union activists at local level who were strongly influenced by Marxist ideas and had a revolutionary outlook. The heroic role of the organisers of strikes, occupations and soviets like Sean Dowling, Jack McGrath and Jack Hedley is unsung and largely undocumented in establishment history while the names of IRA activists like Dan Breen, one of the authors of the Soloheadbeg ambush and later a right-wing Fianna Fail politician, are prominently cited in every history of the period.

Had the courage and dedication of these activists, and working class people generally, been emulated by the national leadership, the eventual outcome of the huge range of struggles which they led could have seen a very different Ireland emerge. Before the Free State was established, Johnson and O'Brien asserted that it was necessary to let the nationalists win independence before the political power of the working class could be demonstrated independently. This was shown in their abject capitulation in not fighting the 1918 General Election. Equally shameful betrayals continued, however, after independence as evidenced by their betrayal of the national post office workers strike in September 1922 and their contemptible abandonment of the Waterford farm labourers in the summer of 1923 as they faced a full frontal assault from the Specials set up by the Free State government as organised strike breakers using semi fascist methods.

In the concluding chapter of the book Dominic Haugh powerfully illustrates the real nature of the new State under the leadership of Irish nationalists in the example of the construction of the Ardnacrusha hydro power station on the banks of the River Shannon. The Free State government actively connived with giant multinational Siemens to impose a low wage regime to accompany outrageously squalid living conditions in which many workers, and even their families in some cases, were forced to exist. Even the horrific exploitation on Irish construction sites by the multinational, Gama Construction, and outed by its Turkish workers and the Socialist Party in 2005, would seem relatively benign by comparison!

This book is essential reading for all those who want to gain an understanding of how the tumultuous decade currently being marked by centenary events resulted in the creation of two poverty ridden, sectarian states on this island rather the new Ireland of freedom and plenty for all which workers and the poor would have aspired to. It is a rich store of original research and will be an invaluable asset to socialist activists putting forward a Marxist analysis of the period in question. It is a fitting tribute to the thousands of men and women workers who fought so hard to raise the conditions of their class in the teeth of the enormous obstacles raised against them.

Most especially it adds further significant evidence to the unique analysis of the Socialist Party on how the unresolved National Question in Ireland can be resolved based on the unity of the working class - Protestant, Catholic, Agnostic, Atheist, North and South - and on the struggle for the socialist transformation of society. And it demonstrates how this can only be achieved with the development of a new mass party of the working class with a socialist analysis and programme, and a revolutionary leadership.

Joe Higgins is a former Socialist Party City Councillor, Teachta Dála (Member of the Irish Parliament) and Member of the European Parliament.

INTRODUCTION

*'not a trade dispute, not a strike against the military, but purely a
labour demonstration of bolshevism served out with a flavour of
Sinn Fein'*
*—Report to the United States Secretary of State on the nature of
the Limerick Soviet. 1919*

The refrain 'labour must wait' has been a constant element of the dialogue of nationalist politicians and the native capitalist class since long before independence and it has continued right up until the present day. The second quarter of the nineteenth century saw the monster meetings of Daniel O'Connell's Repeal Movement where the message was pitched that we are all in this together and everything would be better if only there was a parliament controlled by the Irish Catholic landlord and business classes. The latter half of the nineteenth century saw the development of the Land War when landless labourers were promised that if only the native Catholic tenant farmers could get security of tenure and a fair rent, then the cause of the labouring classes would be fought by the entire nationalist movement. Then we had the 1918 general election when the Irish labour movement, with the assistance of its leadership, was browbeaten by Sinn Fein into not standing in order to give the Irish electorate 'a clear choice' between Home Rule and full Independence. This refrain has continued right up to the present day with recent comments like Enda Kenny's 'we all partied' during the property bubble, Brian Lenihan's 'we all have to pull on the green jersey' as he piled austerity on the backs of working class people and Leo Varadkar and Micheál Martin constantly using the refrain of the 'national interest' when in reality they mean the interests of the Irish capitalist class.

Of course, the real intention of the native bourgeois classes during the revolutionary period, as it is today, was to promote the interests of the native Irish capitalism. The nationalist movement developed around a focal point of the revolutionary period in Ireland and ultimately the emergence of the Free State. It is into this context that the Limerick Soviet must be viewed – a stark reminder for the establishment in Ireland of the power of the labour movement and the ability of the working classes to manage and run their affairs.

The Limerick Soviet took place during a period internationally of widespread social upheaval in the aftermath of the Russian Revolution. While the imperialist powers were arguing over the carve up of the empires of the defeated world powers, the working class in country after country were engaged in revolutionary movements campaigning for the social, political and economic emancipation of the working class.

Ireland was not immune to these developments. In February 1918, more than 10,000 people packed the Mansion House in Dublin to celebrate the Russian Revolution. After the meeting, thousands marched through the streets of Dublin singing *The Red Flag*. Subsequently the *Irish Times* warned of the dangers of Bolshevism stating: 'They have invaded Ireland, and if the democracies do not keep their heads, they may extend to other countries in Europe. The infection of Ireland by the anarchy of Bolshevism is one of those phenomena which, though almost incredible to reason and experience, are made intelligible by the accidents of fortune or human folly'.[1] This is a demonstration of the impact that international developments were having on the class consciousness of the Irish working class.

For ten days in April 1919 the workers of Limerick took over the city and organised all aspects of city life. From the production of necessities, to the distribution of food, to policing, to transport, workers committees were active in ensuring the working class of the city were catered for. This event became known as the Limerick Soviet and is one of the most important events in the history of the labour movement in this country, a history that has been systematically buried by the political and academic establishment since the foundation of the state.

Ultimately the Soviet ended after ten days as a result of the failure of the leadership of the Irish Labour Party and Trade Union Congress (ILPTUC) to act in support of the Soviet. However, the impact of the Soviet did not go unnoticed at the time. Constance Markewicz warned the Sinn Fein leadership that 'Labour will swamp Sinn Fein'.[2] The London *Times* commented that 'the collapse did not come before it demonstrated the power of labour to an impressive degree'.[3] A report to the United States Secretary of State office was even more stark in their pronouncements, stating that the Soviet was 'not a trade dispute, not a strike against the military, but purely a labour demonstration of bolshevism served out with a flavour of Sinn Fein'.[4]

The reality is that the Limerick Soviet occurred at a critical juncture during the revolutionary period in Ireland. It demonstrated the power of the working class that prompted large-scale strike action in Ireland over the following four years. The Soviet also provided an example of workers control that was to inspire the workplace soviets, numbering up to two hundred, that took place between 1920-1922. The 'Soviets of Ireland' culminated with the Munster Soviets which resulted in the occupation of more than one hundred workplaces, with more extensive control exercised over many towns and villages, as part of the widespread industrial and social unrest operated in parallel to the developing civil war between the two wings of Irish nationalism.

Given that this year is the centenary of the Limerick Soviet we are likely to see public commentary on the subject over the coming period. The history of the revolutionary period in Ireland is dominated by two perspectives, primarily determined by the civil war in Ireland which split Irish nationalism down the middle. On one side there is the overtly republican/nationalist perspective and on the other the general anti-republican 'revisionist' historiography of the political and academic establishment. The pre-existing commentary on the Limerick Soviet generally falls into these two perspectives.

Examples of this narrative are demonstrated by the claim from Sinn Fein's Aengus O Snodaigh TD that 'The militancy which was associated with the Irish labour movement was gone and with it the belief that civil disobedience or protest could dislodge the British. The IRA was now seen as the only credible opposition to the British'.[5] From academic historians we have claims, like that from *Foster*, that Irish nationalism 'not only absorbed pre-war social radicalism, but... negated it'.[6] For *Foster* the social radicalism was a pre-war phenomenon and did not exist during the revolutionary period in Ireland. Others have suggested that the Limerick Soviet was only allowed to continue existing through the 'toleration of the British Army'[7] and there is a generalised minimising of the Soviet and its impact.[8] As will be demonstrated, none of these narratives are substantiated by historical evidence.

There is a third perspective, a perspective that has been systematically swept under the carpet as the establishment have moved to create a nationalist hegemony about the revolutionary period. The perspective of the Irish working class during the revolutionary period has consistently and consciously been ignored. This work will look at the developments in Limerick and throughout the country during the revolutionary period from a working class perspective.

The Limerick Soviet was not the first time workers in Ireland moved to establish limited workers control, nor was it to be the last. It was a microcosm of the evolving revolutionary period in Ireland. The general strike in Limerick was to play a pivotal role in the following three years. It gave a clear demonstration of workers power coupled with an example of the ability of workers to manage the affairs of the entire city in the interests of working class people. The Limerick Soviet proved to be the catalyst for an escalating class struggle, leading to widespread workplace occupations, land seizures and large-scale strike action throughout the period of the War of Independence and the Civil War.

Many of the later actions by workers were driven by Marxist elements within the Limerick labour movement who played a pivotal role in many of the key events over the following years. As the conflict continued the mass of the working class operated outside the official structures of the trade union movement, engaging in struggle to defend jobs and working conditions and challenging both British Imperialism and the Irish capitalist class.

The Soviet holds important lessons for the workers movement and for left activists. From the process that led to the emergence of the Soviet, through to the role of the leaders of the ILPTUC and the attitude of the nationalist movement. It presented an opportunity, one of many during the revolutionary period, for the leadership of the ILPTUC to place the Irish labour movement at the head of the struggle for national self-determination. This would have required them to confront not only British Imperialism, but the nationalist movement in Ireland and the native capitalist class, a task the leadership of the ILPTUC were unwilling and unable to lead. It would have also required the workers movement to look beyond national liberation to full social, political and economic emancipation and the establishment of a democratic workers republic.

The Limerick Soviet also demonstrated the impact that of a lack of a revolutionary party of the working class can have on events. While many Marxist organisers emerged during the revolutionary period, they failed to develop an understanding of the necessity for a revolutionary party rooted in the ideas and methods of Marxism to take the workers movement forward. Parties based on Marxist ideas did exist during the revolutionary period in Ireland but the predominant outlook of the left in Ireland was based on the ideas of syndicalism. Rather than building a mass political party of the working class, activists focused on the development of the trade union movement – the creation of One Big Union – that would organise a general strike and lead the working class to take power. These methods, ultimately, were to prove a failure as the opportunity for a workers' revolution was replaced by two reactionary and repressive regimes North and South in the post-independence period.

Nationalism and Socialism

The significant religious division in Ireland dates to the plantation policy of the English monarchy in Ireland during the sixteenth and seventeenth centuries, a policy designed at the time to sow division and implement control through a tactic of divide and rule. Efforts by the United Irishmen, and later the plebeian revolutionary movement of Robert Emmet, to throw off the yoke of sectarian division during the revolutionary upheavals at the end of the eighteenth century were ultimately defeated. Throughout the nineteenth century, British Imperialism repeatedly whipped up sectarian tensions as a mechanism for maintaining British rule of the island.

Outlining an approach to defeat sectarianism, James Connolly explained that 'the pressure of a common exploitation can make enthusiastic rebels out of the Protestant working class, earnest champions of religious and civil liberties out of Catholics, and out of both a united Social democracy.'[9] Connolly saw the emergence of an organised working class, with workers from both Catholic and Protestant backgrounds organised in common trade unions, as key to defeating sectarianism. When British Imperialism proposed the division of Ireland through partition Connolly issued an emphatic warning that partition 'would mean a carnival of reaction both North and South, would set back the wheels of progress, would destroy the oncoming unity of the Irish labour movement and paralyse all advanced movements while it endured.'[10] As well as campaigning for self-determination and a socialist republic in Ireland, Connolly recognised the fears of the Protestant working class towards Home Rule, promising that 'on the day a Home Rule government goes into power the socialist movement in Ireland will go into opposition.'[11] Connolly's prediction of a carnival of reaction was to be realised as two sectarian states, North and South emerged after the revolutionary period in Ireland.

The national question and the emergence of the working class in Ireland as an organised force were the key and interconnected factors that dominated early twentieth century Ireland.[12] The cornerstone of the national question was the national, political, social and economic oppression of the mass of the population in Ireland, Catholic and Protestant, by British Imperialism and capitalism.

The nationalist narrative of the revolutionary period in Ireland suggests that you either supported national liberation or socialist revolution, but support for both was not possible. Connolly's assertion that partition would 'paralyse all advanced movements while it endured' has been used to claim that a socialist revolution would not be possible without the resolution of the national question. In addressing the revolutionary period in Ireland, it is crucial to recognise that the interests of the working class lay in the national emancipation as well as the political, social and economic emancipation. The real question was whether it would be the nationalist movement or the labour movement that would lead the struggle for national liberation.

Previously published work on the Limerick Soviet

The current writings on the Limerick Soviet are limited. Furthermore, the existing material is based on limited research. The first recorded commentary on the Limerick Soviet dates from an RTE radio documentary in 1974. It was this work that formulated the proposition that Robert Byrne 'was a prominent trade unionist' as asserted by Jim Kemmy.[13] This documentary was followed up two years later by an article on the Limerick Soviet by Kemmy in *Saothar*, the journal of the Irish Labour

History Society. The article followed similar lines of the RTE documentary and, like the documentary, failed to address the impact and fallout of the Soviet.[14]

The initial written piece on the Soviet dates from 1979 with the first edition of O'Connor Lysaght's *The Story of the Limerick Soviet,* published by the Limerick branch of People's Democracy. This work furthered the claim that Byrne was a prominent trade unionist asserting that he was 'a member of the trades council, who had lost his job as a telegraph operator for his part in organising his colleagues in his union'.[15] This pamphlet was limited in approach, failing to place the Soviet into the wider context of national and international developments and engaged in a very limited analysis of the aftermath of the Soviet. The is little evidence to support the assertion of Robert Byrne's trade union credentials. While he was a delegate to the Trades Council, in the previous eighteen months before his death he only attended one meeting of the Trades Council, a meeting that discussed his sacking from his job in the post office. Furthermore, the reason for his sacking was almost certainly down to his activities as an IRA member rather than any trade union activity.

A five-page article in the Old Limerick Journal by *Jim Kemmy* was published in 1980.[16] This was basically a reprint from the *Saothar* article several years earlier. What has been regarded as the seminal work on the Limerick Soviet was published in 1990, Liam Cahill's *Forgotten Revolution*.[17] Most of the subsequent writings on the Limerick Soviet rely heavily on Cahill's book, and its approach, including the academic material and much of the left-wing political commentary like the Workers Solidarity Movement in Ireland and Militant in England.[18] However, like much of the other commentary on the Limerick Soviet from this period, *Cahill's* book is limited in terms of research and specifically fails to put the Soviet in a wider context of developments or analyse the impact of the Soviet and its aftermath. Even the most recent published works on the Soviet add little to the previous commentary.[19] *Queally* describes the Limerick Soviet as 'an anomaly' and suggests the strike 'was not politically inspired'.[20] If looking at the Limerick Soviet from a nationalist perspective the it would be correct to assert that the Limerick Soviet received little or no political inspiration from the nationalist movement. In fact, the nationalist movement were hurtled into a state of panic by the strike. However, from a class perspective the Limerick Soviet most definitely had political undertones and was inspired by the event in Bolshevik Russia.

One of the key features of all of these works is the emphasis on the role of John Cronin as leader of the Soviet and that of the other two leading figures of the Trades Council, James Casey and James Carr. Yet none of the published material on the Limerick Soviet mention the role of the key trade union activist in Limerick during this period, Sean Dowling, Industrial Organiser for the Irish Transport and General Workers Union (ITGWU). Dowling, a Marxist, was described as the 'philosophical begetter' of the Limerick Soviet.[21] In the period following the general strike against conscription in April 1918, Dowling and several other Marxist industrial organisers in the ITGWU drafted a blueprint for localised general strikes and occupations to be implemented if the British Government attempted to introduce localised conscription. It was this blueprint that was used to organise the work of the Limerick Soviet. As we shall see, Dowling and the ITGWU were to play a key role in the Limerick Soviet, organising the work of the Soviet and implementing its proclamations. As with other works on the Limerick Soviet, *Queally* fails to recognise the tensions that existed within Limerick United Trades and Labour Council (LUTLC – referred to as the Trades Council in the text) and the more radical approach of Sean Dowling and the ITGWU to the conservative approach of Cronin, Casey and Carr.

The following work adopts a Marxist approach to the analysis of the Limerick Soviet, its impact and aftermath. It will place the Limerick Soviet in the context to the wider revolutionary upheavals occurring during this period as well as within the traditions of struggle of the Limerick working classes. As with all historical writings, the purpose is to interpret and analyse the historical evidence to develop a better understanding of this historical epoch and learn the lessons of history. This work will attempt to draw out the lessons of the Limerick Soviet and its place in the wider period and provide a platform for the labour movement and the wider working class to gain a better understanding of the history of Irish labour.

Divided into four parts, this work will first look at the history and traditions of the struggle of the Limerick working classes, urban and rural, during the nineteenth century. This will encompass the efforts first by the craft unions and later the general unions to organise, the class conflict in rural areas between the landless labourers and tenant farmers, along with the struggle by the masses of poor to survive during the famine.

The second part deals with the labour council elected in 1899, before looking at the establishment of the ITGWU in Limerick in September 1917, a development that was to drive the radicalisation of the Limerick labour movement in the period up to the Soviet in April 1919.

The events of the Limerick Soviet are addressed in the third section. Also included is an assessment of the role of the different sections of society – the trade unions, locally and nationally, Sinn Fein, the Catholic hierarchy, the Chamber of Commerce and the British military authorities.

The last section of this work examines the fallout from the Soviet. Included is a review of the justification by the leadership of the ILPTUC for not calling a general strike in support of the Limerick Soviet. More importantly, this part addresses the impact of the Soviet on future local and national developments, including the large number of workplace soviets established over the following three years, the land seizures throughout the country and the crucially important farm labourers strikes that took place locally and further afield. The organisational blueprint of the Limerick Soviet was to form the template for the workplace soviets and many of the land seizures. The radicalisation and the growth in class consciousness that flowed from the Limerick Soviet drove the militancy of farm labourers.

The history of the Limerick Soviet is part of the buried history of the Irish labour movement and the Irish working class. This was a conscious decision of the Irish establishment in the new Free State to manufacture an Irish nationalist hegemony which required the elimination of all traces of class conflict in the revolutionary period, a hegemony that has only being challenged in recent times as labour historians look to uncover the deep and rich history of class struggle on the island of Ireland.

---

[1] Colm Bryce, 'Ireland and the Russian Revolution', *Irish Marxist Review,* Volume 6, Number 17, (2017), p. 42

[2] Ruth Russell, *What's the Matter With Ireland?* (New York, 1920), p. 98.

[3] *The Times*, 2 May 1919.

[4] Arthur Mitchell, *Revolutionary Government in Ireland*, (Dublin, 1995), p. 180.

[5] Aengus O Snodaigh, 'The Limerick Soviet', *An Phoblacht,* 29 April 1999

[6] R. F. Foster, *Modern Ireland, 1600-1972,* (London, 1989), p. 446

[7] John O'Callaghan, *Revolutionary Limerick, The Republican Campaign for Independence in Limerick, 1913-1921*, (Dublin, 2010), p. 120

[8] Sharon Slater, *The Limerick Soviet – Two Weeks of Self Rule,* [Available online at: http://limerickslife.com] (Accessed on 10 March 2019)

[9] James Connolly, *Labour in Ireland*, (Dublin, 1940), p. 168

[10] *Irish Worker*, 14 March 1914

[11] *Forward*, 23 August 1913.

[12] Laura Fitzgerald & Kevin McLoughlin, 'A Stand Against Imperialism and War', in Cillian Gillespie (ed.), *Ireland's Lost Revolution 1916-1923,* (London, 2016), p. 55

[13] The documentary is available as a podcast here: https://www.rte.ie/radio1/doconone/2012/0703/647122-documentary-podcast-limerick-soviet-workers/

[14] Jim Kemmy, 'The Limerick Soviet', *Saothar,* (Volume 2, 1976), pp. 45-52

[15] D. R. O'Connor Lysaght, *The Story of the Limerick Soviet,* (Limerick, 1983).

[16] Jim Kemmy, 'The General Strike 1919', *Old Limerick Journal,* (Volume 2, March 1980), pp. 26-31

[17] Liam Cahill, *Forgotten Revolution, Limerick Soviet 1919: A Threat to British Power in Ireland,* (Dublin, 1990)

[18] Workers Solidarity Movement, *Limerick Soviet 1919,* [Available at: http://www.wsm.ie/c/limerick-soviet-1919-notes] & Michael O'Connell, *Remember Limerick 1919,* (London, 1994). Militant is now known as the Socialist Party of England and Wales.

[19] Included here would be: Nicola Queally, *Rebellion, Resistance and the Irish Working Class: The Case of the Limerick Soviet,* (Cambridge, 2010) & Mike McNamara, *The Limerick Soviet: When Limerick took on an Empire,* (Limerick, 2017).

[20] Queally, pp. 3 & 5

[21] C. Desmond Greaves, *The Irish Transport and General Workers Union – The Formative Years,* (Dublin, 1982), p. 236

THE RISE OF THE LIMERICK LABOUR MOVEMENT

'The history of all hitherto existing society is the history of class struggles.'
—Karl Marx and Frederick Engels[1]

The narrative of nineteenth century and early twentieth century Irish history is told from a nationalist perspective to the almost complete exclusion of the history of class struggle in Ireland during the period. This is particularly the case during the period of centenaries spanning the revolutionary period in Ireland from 1916-1923, a period of intense class struggle.

Limerick during the nineteenth century was a city with major social divisions with the social strata comprising of a small Protestant elite, a rising Catholic middle class benefitting primarily from the trade in provisions and the masses of trades and labouring poor. By 1830 an estimated 90% of Limerick's middle class was Catholic and most of the remaining 10% were Quakers.[2]

The social divisions were clear to see, from the overcrowded tenements on Kings Island to the Georgian splendour of Newtown Perry. In one of the tenement houses at the rear of where Barrington's Hospital now stands, no less than 176 inhabitants resided, some rooms containing three families. In such cases the diet consisted mainly of oatmeal, and all three families shared the one saucepan for cooking and had to wait their turn accordingly. High mortality resulted firstly from malnutrition and its related ailments, and secondly from the spread of infection through the lack of proper housing and sanitary conditions.

For the mass of the population the threat of starvation and death from fever was a constant feature right throughout the first half of the nineteenth century. Working class people reacted to rising food prices by regularly engaging in food riots to force the local establishment to reduce the cost of food and provide some relief from rampant unemployment. At the same time large quantities of food were being exported from Limerick Port. General James Duff commented that "many rich Individuals" were "employed in the Monopoly of Grain" at Limerick. Throughout the period from 1750-1845 Limerick exported vast amounts of corn and provisions from the fertile hinterland in North Munster.

The outbreak of 'fever' was a constant threat.[29] The atrocious housing conditions, poor diet and lack of proper sanitary services created an ideal environment for the spread of disease. Generally, the local establishment paid little heed to the plight of the poorer classes until the spread of disease threatened their own wellbeing.

The Trades of Limerick

The early nineteenth century saw the decline of the trade guilds as master tradesmen and journeymen came into conflict over wages and conditions. Striving to increase profits the master tradesmen attempted to drive down wages and increase the number of semi-skilled workers and apprentices carrying out the work of tradesmen. When confronted with opposition from the journeymen, the masters attempted to use non-unionised, often migrant labour, to break the local societies of organised journeymen.

As a result of the pace of change in manufacturing being brought about by the Industrial Revolution in Britain, large-scale unemployment had emerged among many of the trades in the city at the beginning of 1801. Some trades, mainly in the construction sector, were able to maintain their position in society but the impact of cheap imports from Britain undermined the standing of most of the city's trades. One of the most severely hit was the weaving trade. Almost all the stuff weavers in Limerick were out of work,[3] due to declining demand for textiles resulting from the availability of cheap products from the industrialised mills of England.[4]

Unlike in Britain where urban workers were part of an expanding economy, Irish workers, following the economic depression in the aftermath of the Napoleonic Wars, were faced with a contracting or at best a stagnant economy.[5] Regularly, charges were laid against Irish workers that their wage demands, and restrictive practices, were responsible for the failures of Irish industry. From the perspective of the emerging Irish capitalist class, workers should have been prepared to accept lower wages and poorer working conditions and to submit to the dilution of the skilled workforce through the greater use of semi-skilled workers and non-unionised workers.[6]

The Combination Laws banned strikes and imposed severe penalties on workers who 'combined' to defend their interests. The first large-scale strike in the history of Limerick began at the beginning of May 1804. By the middle of May widespread strike action was taking place involving the city's journeymen tradesmen. The business class responded in a ruthless fashion. The *Limerick Chronicle* commented that "the licentiousness of the Journeymen in this city, should be refuted by every citizen interested in the progress of the extensive improvements now going forward". The Mayor and Magistrates were called on "to inflict heavy and severe punishment" on anyone engaged in combination and "to convict such persons in a summary way" with penalties of up to six months in jail. In particular, the journeymen carpenters were targeted for being involved in the strike.[7] Widespread repression was implemented by the Unionist establishment who controlled the Corporation, supported by the Catholic merchants. On 30 May four journeymen carpenters were arrested, charged with combination by Sheriff Carroll and subsequently jailed.[8]

The repression implemented by the city's establishment was repeated with regularity. The years that followed saw the growth of trade union organisation. The crest of Limerick Trades Council indicates that the Trades Council was formed in 1810. Certainly by 1812, at the latest, there was a citywide body of workers known as the 'United Trades' representing workers across the city's industries and services. The Trades Council had a haphazard existence throughout the nineteenth century, emerging into activity during periods of industrial conflict while retreating into inactivity during lulls in the class struggle.[9]

The most intense period of class conflict in the city occurred in from 1819-1821. With strikes being illegal, violence was a constant feature of industrial conflict. Workers in the city and rural labourers now began engaging in joint activity against employers and tenant farmers. At the end of April, 1820, a riot took place in Irishtown and threatening notices were appearing in rural areas in support of striking workers signed with the name of "Captain Moonlight".[10] This was followed at the end of May by a large crowd of city and rural labourers parading in a disciplined fashion in support of striking workers in the city.[11]

Workplace picketing was banned under the combination laws, so the main focus of the striking workers was on preventing the 'colts'[12] from scabbing on strikes. Members of one union would engage in acts of violence on behalf of another union engaged in strike action to reduce the risk of recognition or conviction.[13] The strike wave of 1820 was violent and intense, resulting in several deaths, as employers and workers fought to gain the upper-hand in the conflict. Street riots became a regular occurrence with the British military and the local police playing the role of protectors of property and the judiciary imposing imprisonment on an indiscriminate basis in an attempt to suppress the strikes.

In October 1820 a new Recorder[14] was appointed in the city. Addressing the Grand Jury, the new judge stated that he was "aware of the disturbed nature of your city, and of those nocturnal depredations, that disgrace it'. Smyth pledged himself to discharge his duties 'with resolution and impartiality and to inflict the severest punishment, the law allows, upon those persons that shall be convicted of the crimes I allude to".[15]

The strike wave reached a high point in January 1821 culminating in the brutal murder of a journeyman tailor named John Roughan. Roughan was scabbing on a strike by tailors when he was attacked on his way home as he walked through Denmark Street.[16] The ferocity of the attack on Roughan shocked all sections of society in Limerick. The strike wave dissipated and the city's elites, Protestant Ascendancy and Catholic merchant alike, used the retreat to impose vicious cuts to jobs and wages. Despite these defeats, workers struggle did break out on a regular basis throughout the rest of the 1820s.[17]

Unusually for this period and demonstrating a developing class consciousness among the most downtrodden of workers, a General Union for labourers emerged in the city by the middle of 1819, existing possibly up until the new Combination Act that was introduced in 1825.[18] Attempts to organise labourers unsurprisingly brought opposition from the Chamber of Commerce. The Chamber minutes for the 22 October 1819 state:

> 'The Committee of directors of the Chamber of Commerce having been credibly informed that certain Oaths have been administered to different Salters & Labourers, employed in the Merchants stores in this City in the curing of provisions and being determined to discountenance all such illegal acts do hereby offer a reward of £50 to any person or persons who will prosecute to conviction within two month from this date any three of the offenders or a proportional sum for a lesser number. [19]

The Chamber of Commerce went on to instruct its members not to employ any salter or labourer who had engaged in combination.[20]

Class struggle and the rural poor.

Class struggle was not confined to the city. Throughout the first quarter of the nineteenth century rural Co. Limerick was riven with class conflict. Emerging in 1806, the Caravat/Shanavest conflict seriously disrupted large areas of Waterford, Kilkenny, Cork, Tipperary and Limerick.[21] The Caravats comprised mainly of agricultural labourers and cottiers[22] and defined their message as unity of the poor against the 'middle class'. The tenant farmers established the Shanavests who invoked elements of 1798 nationalism to forge their class unity and legitimise their counter-terrorism against the Caravats.[23] The conflict between the two groups was unusually violent, even by Irish standards[24] with both groups operating in a clandestine fashion.[25]

In response to the emergence of the Caravats, an Insurrection Act was introduced in the House of Commons on 9 July 1807 by Sir Arthur Wellesley,[26] with a special view to the disturbances in Limerick.[27] Much of the conflict originated in the extreme poverty that existed among the landless labourers and the cottiers, the contrast of the fertility of the rich soil with the wretchedness of their cabins clothes and food.[28]

While efforts were being made countrywide to generate support for a petition in support of Catholic Emancipation it was receiving little echo in Co. Limerick. During 1813 the Lord Lieutenant indicated that 'Roman Catholics in Limerick take no concern in the event of the question of R.C. Emancipation'[29] and that the lower orders feel no concern in the Catholic petition and refuse to sign it at the different chapels – 'where there were one hundred signatures last petition I don't believe there are five now'.[30] The rural poor had more pressing matters on their minds.

By 1815 the local political establishment were becoming increasingly concerned that the landless labourers and cottiers were gaining the upper hand in the Caravat/Shanavest conflict. Tenant farmers were abandoning their farms following threats from night-time bands of attackers and leaving their landlords with unpaid rents.[31] Local magistrates began encouraging retaliation by tenant farmers and 'recommended and encouraged a spirit of combination and exertion among a better sort of farmers.' This change of strategy resulted in tenant farmers, knowing they had the backing of the local Protestant establishment, becoming more confrontational and engaging in widespread reprisals against the rural labourers.[32] Large-scale repression in 1816 ultimately defeated the Caravats and the conflict petered out. During a debate on the Irish Insurrection Bill in May 1817, Mr Leslie Foster MP declared 'the aggressors and the victims of outrage were all Catholics alike'.[33]

The Rockite Rebellion

By 1819 a new movement emerged that became known as the Rockite Rebellion. The collapse in agricultural prices in the post-Napoleonic period caused widespread unemployment amongst farm labourers fuelling the discontent on which the Rockite movement thrived and grew to maturity.[34] The Rockite disturbances were of the scale usually associated with a major regional movement.[35] For a period the Rockite Rebellion took on a semi-insurrectional character.

This rural movement was class based and was neither infused by Catholic consciousness nor nationalism but was a major force in the politicisation of the rural poor and reflected the primacy of economic factors. A study of the agrarian activity in Co. Limerick reveals that well over half the outrages involved labourers pitted against tenant farmers.[36] Similar to the Caravat/Shanavest conflict, Rockites were associated with farm labourers while the tenant farmers organised themselves as Whiteboys.[37] Direct confrontation between these two conflicting social groups culminated in a gun battle on 6 October 1821 which erupted on the Racecourse three miles outside Limerick city. Police reports indicate that thousands had assembled on either side armed with pistols and swords. Four detachments of Dragoons were sent and managed to intervene and disperse the crowd.[38]

Rockite notices were commonplace with threats against farmers over the price of provisions, the cost of potato ground and the hiring of migrant labour.[39] By the end of February 1822 many of the attacks were directed at the residences of landlords or large farmers and motivated by the hiring of migrant labour intended to break the activism of local labourers. If these attacks were repelled, the insurgents would move to burn the local church.[40] A bumper corn harvest in the Autumn of 1822 contributed to the reduced levels of violence as there was a plentiful supply of food and the cost of provisions fell.[41]

During a debate on the state of Ireland in the House of Commons in June 1823 the Earl of Liverpool was reported as stating:

> "Amidst all the disturbances which had taken place in Limerick last year, he had good authority for saying, that if the king had appeared in Limerick at that time, he would have been received with as much enthusiasm as he had been in Dublin. It was not a combination against the government, but against property in general, whether in the hands of Protestants or Catholics and he believed, that the exasperation of the people of Ireland against Catholic proprietors was, in many instances, even greater than against Protestant proprietors".[42]

By 1823 the Rockite Rebellion petered out. There was a resurgence of violence in 1825 in a more pronounced sectarian character and with the prevalence of attacks by Catholic tenant farmers on Protestant landlords.

Rural Limerick during the period 1825-1844 was characterised by low-level conflict between different sections of the rural population that was occasionally punctuated with short periods of more intense violence. This conflict generally broke down along class lines, with disputes between tenant farmers and landlords and also between landless labourers and cottiers on one side and the tenant farmers on the other. By the 1830s the graziers of Limerick were among the wealthiest Irish farmers in the country.[43]

The Terry Alt Rebellion

The conflict between farmers and labourers, coupled with anti-tithe agitation escalated quite dramatically in November 1830 with the first incidents of serious conflict being reported in County Clare.[44] The election of Daniel O'Connell in Clare in 1828 has raised expectations about improvements in the social and economic conditions facing the poorest sections of society. These raised expectations gave rise to simmering tensions. By the beginning of 1831 the Terry Alt Rebellion was to escalate into open conflict involving landless labourers and cottiers. The Terry Alts were initially a clandestine group modelled on other secret societies like the Caravats and Rockites.[45] However, as the movement developed it emerged as a more open and conscious mass movement of the poor involving tens of thousands of landless labourers and cottiers.

The shift from tillage to pasture farming in the aftermath of the Napoleonic Wars had a profound impact on the position of the agricultural labourer in Irish society. Farmers were intent on cutting jobs and wages. It was this shift from tillage to pasture coupled with the loss of potato land that ignited the Terry Alt Rebellion.

In 1831 there were 80,000 landless labourers and 80,000 cottiers in Co. Clare. Labourers were paid 8d per week for irregular work.[46] The cottiers had too little land to produce enough provisions capable of paying rent.[47] While occasionally involving attacks on the police, arms raids and assaults on migrant labourers and labourers working for prescribed employers, the main focus of the Terry Alts was the digging up of pasture. Emphasising the need for rural employment, hundreds and occasionally thousands of labourers participated in digging up fields and even entire farms rendering them useless for pasture farming.

Initially this digging up of pasture land occurred in a clandestine fashion at night time, but as the Terry Alts became more emboldened, participants would march in military fashion in day time with their shovels presented over their shoulders, led by a band and cheered on by hundreds of supporters as they proceeded to dig up the pasture land in defiance of the landlords, farmers, local clergy and the police who were impotent to stop the activities.[48] *William Pare* in reference to the activities of the Terry Alts, stated "the peasantry armed with their farm implements declared war on pasture land."[49] Potentially up to twenty per cent of the adult population participated in the Terry Alt Rebellion.

The Terry Alts were just as prone to attack Catholic as well as Protestant farmers and landowners.[50] Occasionally attacks were even carried out on the clergy and Catholic churches. Following the robbery of a firearm from a policeman in Clarecastle the local parish priest retrieved the gun. A few days later the church was broken into and the pews and seats smashed in a warning to the priest not to interfere with the activities of the Terry Alts.[51]

By the middle of 1831 the Terry Alts were in virtual control of the entire of County Clare. Not surprisingly Daniel O'Connell condemned those involved in the outrages in the county, sending his chief lieutenant, Thomas Steele,[52] to attempt to suppress support for the rebellion.[53] Steele declared on posters displayed in Ennis "Unless you desist, I denounce you as traitors to the cause of liberty in Ireland. I leave you to the Government and the fire and bayonets of the military. Your blood be upon your own souls."[54] Improving harvests in 1831 and 1832 led to a dissipation of the Terry Alt movement as prices for provisions dropped and more employment was available during harvest time.

Food Riots

Food riots were common in the eighteenth and nineteenth century, with the mass of the poor taking to the streets and forcing concessions from the ruling establishment. Riotous assemblies by the 'mob' were triggered by soaring prices, malpractice among dealers or by hunger.[55] Food riots in Limerick during the first half of the nineteenth century followed a complex pattern with unemployment also playing a role in the riots, particularly in the second quarter of the nineteenth century.

The bulk of the population were small consumers dependent on a cheap and plentiful supply of bread.[56] They expected that corn should be consumed in the region it was grown, especially in times of scarcity.[57] However, from the beginning of the nineteenth century the exportation of corn from Limerick was to be a major focal point of class conflict. Regularly, during periods of scarcity, food provisions intended for export were targeted by the mob. The first recorded food riot in Limerick occurred on 12 May 1772 when a starving crowd rioted outside the Lock Mills seeking food.[58] Subsequently, riots are recorded as having occurred in 1786,[59] 1791,[60] and in 1800 and 1801.[61]

May 1817 saw full-scale rioting continuing for more than a week as the mass of the poor battled with the military and police in response to high prices and food shortages. The Unionist establishment and the Catholic merchants were at sixes and sevens over how to respond to the widespread protest,[62] ultimately making large quantities of provisions available at subsidised prices.[63] While this measure paused the process for a day or two, rioting broke out again and continued until 11 June when more than 14,000 people were supplied with oatmeal at largely subsidised cost.[64] In an effort to ensure that there was no repeat of the rioting, the city's establishment continued to subsidise food provisions into September 1817.[65]

Further incidents occurred, in 1826 there were large-scale protests in Rathkeale[66] and in 1827 protests occurred at Limerick's Potato Market to prevent the export of potatoes from the Market.[67] The food riots in 1830 were particularly noted for the prominent role played by women.[68] The riots were eventually diffused again by the subsidising of food prices.[69] Further episodes of rioting occurred in 1837[70] and 1839.[71]

The high point and most extensive food rioting in Limerick occurred at the beginning of June 1840 when several days of full-scale rioting and the raiding of food stores involved large numbers of the poor of the city affected by rising food prices. It followed a well-worn pattern of previous years. With the urban and rural poor living on a day-to-day basis any increases in the price of food was generally met with rising social unrest that occasionally spilled out into full-scale rioting and the looting of food stores. The local establishment and food merchants regularly initiated the supply of food at subsidised prices in an attempt to divert social unrest but often it was too little and too late to prevent rioting occurring.

The rioting that did occur was not indiscriminate but planned by the working classes who organised and participated in food rioting en-masse. Mass meetings took place across the city to plan the raiding of merchant stores and to combat the actions by local police and military to suppress the riots. The rioters would separate into several different groupings and spread out across the city in order to spread the forces opposing them as thinly as possible and would engage in hit and run tactics on food stores looting as much food as possible before police or military arrived. The rioters then returned to the tenements where distribution centres were established to distribute the plundered provisions among the mass of the poor in each district.[72] For more than a week intense rioting impacted on the city only to be eventually suppressed through a combination of widespread repression and the subsidising of food prices.[73]

---

[1] Karl Marx, & Frederick Engels, *Manifesto of the Communist Party,* (Moscow, 1969), p. 14

[2] Matthew Potter, *The Government and the People of Limerick, The History of Limerick Corporation / City Council 1197-2006,* (Limerick 2006), p.251.

[3] The stuff weavers produced a thick woven cloth. It is claimed that the number of weavers in Limerick dropped from approximately 1,000 to less than 100 between 1800-1840.

[4] Roger Wells, 'The Irish Famine of 1799-1801: Market Culture, Moral Economies and Social Protest', in Adrian Randall & Andrew Charlesworth (eds) *Markets, Market Culture and Popular Protest in Eighteenth Century Britain and Ireland,* (Liverpool, 1996), p.167-168 (pp. 163-194).

[5] John W. Boyle, *The Irish Labour Movement in the Nineteenth Century,* (Washington, 1988), p. 3.

[6] Ibid, p. 4.

[7] *Limerick Chronicle* 16 May 1804.

[8] *Limerick Chronicle* 2 June 1804.

[9] Robert Herbert, The Trade Guilds of Limerick, *North Munster Antiquarian Journal, 2/3* (1941), p. 130 & Limerick Chamber of Commerce Meeting 9 October 1812, *Limerick Chamber of Commerce Minute Book May 1807-1813,* p. 340-341, Limerick City Archives.

[10] *Limerick Chronicle* 26 April 1820.

[11] *Limerick Chronicle* 31 May 1820.

[12] The term 'colt' was used to describe a worker who was not a member of a trade union. Colts were usually migrant workers who were employed at reduced pay rates in an effort to undermine local wages and conditions and trade union organisation. The unions focussed on attempting to recruit the 'colts' into unions and violence flared when this was unsuccessful.

[13] Emmet O'Connor, *A Labour History of Ireland 1824-1960* (Dublin 1992), p. 12

[14] The Recorder was a magistrate having the highest civil and criminal jurisdiction in the city. The appointed Recorder was Carew Smyth.

[15] *Limerick Chronicle* 25 October 1820.

[16] *Limerick Chronicle* 17 January 1821.

[17] Coopers took strike action in January 1823 and tailors in September 1823. A strike by butchers in 1825 led to large-scale rioting throughout the city.

[18] Boyle, *The Irish Labour Movement in the Nineteenth Century*, p. 33.

[19] Limerick Chamber of Commerce Meeting 22 October 1819, *Limerick Chamber of Commerce Minute Book 23 June 1815-28 April 1820,* p. 303-304, Limerick City Archives.

[20] Limerick Chamber of Commerce Meeting 22 October 1819, *Limerick Chamber of Commerce Minute Book 23 June 1815-28 April 1820,* p. 303-304, Limerick City Archives.

[21] Paul E.W. Roberts, Caravats and Shanavests: Whiteboyism and faction fighting in East Munster 1802-1811, in Samuel Clark and James S. Donnelly Jr. (eds) *Irish Peasants Violence and Political Unread 1780-1914,* (Wisconsin, 1986), p.66.

[22] Edmund Burke (Ed.), *The Annual Register or a View of the History, Politics and Literature for the Year 1811,* (London, 1825), p. 21

[23] Emmet O'Connor, 'Labour and Politics, 1830–1945: Colonisation and Mental Colonisation', in Donal Ó Drisceoil, Fintan Lane (eds), *Politics and the Irish Working Class, 1830–1945,* (Basingstoke, 2005), p. 41

[24] Ted Margadant,' Commentary on Charles Tilly's "Social Movements"', *Theory and Society*, Vol. 27, No. 4, (Aug., 1998), p. 485-486

[25] Roberts, p.94.

[26] Sir Arthur Wellesley is better known as the Duke of Wellington

[27] Geoffrey Locker-Lampson, *A Consideration of the State of Ireland in the Nineteenth Century* (London, 1907).

[28] Maurice Lenihan, *Limerick; Its History and Antiquities,* (Cork, 1866), p. 425

[29] *State of the Country Papers,* 28 January 1813, SOC 1544/18, National Archives, Dublin.

[30] *State of the Country Papers,* 25 December 1813, SOC 1540/17, National Archives, Dublin.

[31] *State of the Country Papers,* 4 November 1814, SOC 1556/37, National Archives, Dublin.

[32] *State of the Country Papers,* 3 June 1815, SOC 1717/15, National Archives, Dublin.

[33] *House of Commons Debates,* 23 May 1817, Volume 36, cc835-42

[34] James S. Donnelly, Jr., *Captain Rock, The Irish Agrarian Rebellion 1821-1824,* (Wisconsin, 2009), p.330

[35] Roberts, p.95.

[36] Pat Feeley, 'Whiteboys and Ribbonmen', *The Old Limerick Journal,* No. 4, September 1980. p. 26.

[37] Ibid, p.24.

[38] *State of the Country Papers,* 7 October 1821, SOC 431/2296/17, National Archives, Dublin.

[39] *State of the Country Papers,* November 1821, SOC 431/2296/47, National Archives, Dublin.

[40] *State of the Country Papers,* 28 February 1822, SOC 2350/94, National Archives, Dublin.

[41] *Limerick Chronicle* 28 August 1822.

[42] *House of Commons Debates,* 19 June 1823, Volume 9, cc1033-72

[43] Margaret MacCurtain, 'Pre-Famine Peasantry in Ireland: Definition and Theme', *Irish University Review,* Vol. 4, No. 2, (Autumn, 1974), p. 193

[44] *Limerick Chronicle* 10 November 1830.

[45] Flan Enright, *Pre-Famine Clare-Society in Crisis* [http://www.clarelibrary.ie/eolas/coclare/history/prefamine_clare.htm]

[46] R. G. Garnett, *Co-operation and the Owenite Socialist Communities in Britain 1825-1845,* (Manchester, 1972), p.104

[47] Alf MacLochlainn, 'Social Life in County Clare', *Irish University Review,* Vol. 2, No. 1

(Spring, 1972), p.60

[48] James S. Donnelly Jr, 'The Terry Alt Movement 1829-31', *History Ireland,* Vol. 2, Issue 4, (Winter 1994)

[49] William Pare, *Co-operative Agriculture: A Solution of the Land Question, As Exemplified in the History of the Ralahine Cooperative Agricultural Association, County Clare, Ireland,* (London, 1870), p. 5

[50] *The Times*; London, 12 April 1831

[51] Joe Power, 'Terry Alt and Lady Clare', *The Other Clare,* Volume 10 March 1986, p. 16.

[52] Thomas Steele was a landlord in Co. Clare who became the Chief Pacificator for Daniel O'Connell. In effect Steele was O'Connell's chief enforcer in the mid-West whose job was to suppress any potential opposition to O'Connell's political agenda in the region.

[53] *Limerick Chronicle* 18 May 1831.

[54] *Ennis Advertiser,* 16 April 1831

[55] E. P. Thompson, 'The Moral Economy and the English Crowd in the Eighteenth Century', *Past and Present,* Volume 50, (February 1971), p.78

[56] George Rudé, *The Crowd in History,* (London 1999), p.36

[57] Thompson, 'The Moral Economy, p.98

[58] Jim Kemmy, 'The Seige of Lock Mills', in Jim Kemmy (ed.), *Limerick Anthology,* (Dublin, 1996), p.236.

[59] *Limerick Chronicle* 23 January 1786.

[60] Boyle, *The Irish Labour Movement in the Nineteenth Century*, p. 18.

[61] Wells, 'The Irish Famine of 1799-1801', p.182 & *Limerick Chronicle* 14 January 1801.

[62] *State of the Country Papers*, 24 May 1817, SOC 1836/10, National Archives, Dublin, Limerick Chamber of Commerce Meeting 28 May 1817, *Limerick Chamber of Commerce Minute Book 23 June 1815-28 April 1820*, p. 127-128, Limerick City Archives.

[63] *Limerick Chronicle* 31 May 1817

[64] Limerick Chamber of Commerce Meeting 13 June 1817, *Limerick Chamber of Commerce Minute Book 23 June 1815-28 April 1820*, p. 131-132, Limerick City Archives.

[65] Limerick Chamber of Commerce Meeting 5 September 1817, *Limerick Chamber of Commerce Minute Book 23 June 1815-28 April 1820,* p. 144, Limerick City Archives.

[66] *Limerick Chronicle* 12 August 1826.

[67] *State of the Country Papers*, 26 March 1827, SOC 2853/18, National Archives, Dublin

[68] *Limerick Chronicle* 26 June 1830. Rioting also occurred in Askeaton where a large mob plundered the entire stock of the mills of Mr. Paul Erson.

[69] *Limerick Chronicle* 30 June 1830.

[70] *Limerick Chronicle* 10 June 1837.

[71] *Limerick Chronicle* 3 July 1939.

[72] 1 June 1840, 17/10539, *Outrage Papers, County Limerick,* 1840, National Archives, Dublin & 2 June 1840, 17/10541, *Outrage Papers, County Limerick,* 1840, National Archives, Dublin. & 2 June 1840, copy, no reference number, *Outrage Papers, County Limerick,* 1840, National Archives, Dublin & *Limerick Chronicle* 3 June 1840, 1 June 1840

[73] *Limerick Chronicle* 13 June 1840.

STRUGGLE, ORGANISATION AND SOLIDARITY

'we meant to coerce'
— Activist Dan Peters to the owners of the railway companies in
Ireland when they accused the railway workers of trying to coerce
them by going on strike. 1877

Limerick during the Famine

Many local history articles have been written about the course of the famine and its impact on Limerick city and county. What is noticeable about this commentary is the lack of reference to the social struggle that took place in the region. For example, the Limerick Corporation produced a *Famine Commemorative Edition* pamphlet in 1997 that only mentions the resistance of the masses in passing and does so in the context of 'crime'.[1] *The Old Limerick Journal* produced a Famine Edition in 1995.[2] The title of the editorial, 'Blight, Starvation and Flight'[3] was to demonstrate the approach of the journal to the topic.[4] Where conflict and struggle is mentioned it is only as something that was of little consequence. With the exception of *Eriksson*,[5] what is noticeably absent from discussion on the famine in Limerick is the class conflict between tenant farmers and the landless labourers and cottiers in rural areas and class conflict in urban areas between the workers and the business classes.

By 1845 the ruling elites in Limerick were the Catholic merchant class who had overthrown the Protestant Ascendancy elite as a result of the enactment of the Irish Municipal Corporations Act.[6]

The year began with a spate of clandestine attacks in rural areas. During January a large number of tenant farmers met in Toomevara to demand action by the police to suppress the night-time attacks on farmers in East Limerick and North Tipperary.[7] Landless labourers were attempting to prevent rising rents for conacre potato ground. *The Landlord and Tenant Commission* had previously put the blame for rising conacre rent firmly on the tenant farmers, claiming that the practice of landlords renting to middlemen was now non-existent with their role of renting conacre to landless labourers being taken up by tenant farmers.[8] The clandestine attacks were followed by agricultural labourers demanding wage rises to compensate for the rising conacre rent.[9]

The second half of 1845 saw a major upsurge in struggle by labourers in response to increasing food prices. Notices were posted by activists around Castleconnell warning labourers not to work for less than 1s per day.[10] A week later labourers working in the city's corn stores struck demanding wages of 9s a week.[11] Mass protests by hundreds of labourers forced the contractors constructing the Waterford-Limerick railway line to immediately employ seventy five workers with promises that more would be employed in the immediate future.[12] When the contractor reneged on his promise, the Mayor mobilised 100 police from rural areas to confront the demonstrators. The stand-off lasted for several days.[13]

The protests in rural areas around conacre demonstrated that the landless labourers were engaging in a conscious measure of collective action.[14] In the run-up to Christmas the attacks continued, grain stores of farmers were raided, and the local clergy joined with the tenant farmers in condemning the labourers for the 'whiteboy' activities.[15]

One incident demonstrated the attitude of the tenant farmers. In early December a landlord in Sixmilebridge, David Wilson, distributed some land on his estate to labourers who had been evicted by his tenant farmers. In response the farmers threatened Wilson, forcing him to withdraw the offer to the evicted labourers and to distribute any available land to the tenant farmers instead.[16]

Mass protest did force concessions. On 14 January 1846 a mass mobilisation of up to 1,500 people occupied 49 houses on the estate Sir Capel Molyneaux at Castleconnell to prevent the eviction of farm labourers. Thousands more gathered on the surrounding hills in support. The military commander read the Riot Act on several occasions but backed off open confrontation with the assembled crowd. After the threat of the evictions was lifted the crowd dispersed.[17] The mass mobilisation to prevent the evictions rapidly led to escalating violence with widespread attacks taking place in the district around Castleconnell. Threats were made against landlords' stewards ordering them not to employ migrant labour and against workers for working for less than the expected wage rate.[18]

Defending Jobs and Wages

Violence erupted on the outskirts of the city when rural labourers were employed to scab on a strike by workers constructing the Waterford-Limerick railway line. Large numbers of police were deployed to protect the scabs.[19] At the same time a series of demonstrations took place between Limerick and Cratloe demanding employment.[20]

In March 1846 landlord Sir David Roche was shot at after being accused of hoarding food, with the *Chronicle* commenting that 'no man is safe when an intimate friend of O'Connell can be attacked'.[21] The attack on Roche led to utter panic among the local establishment. Within days, meetings were held in city and county areas to discuss an expansion of public works and the purchase of Indian meal.[22]

The local clergy condemned labourers in Adare and Croom who attempted to organise mass meetings to campaign against unemployment.[23] Three days later a meeting of more than 2,000 labourers took place in defiance of the clergy. The assembled labourers chanted 'all we want is work, we can't starve' as the Rev. James O'Shea demanded that the assembled crowd 'respect their clergy' and only assemble when it was lawful to do so. O'Shea was drowned out by chants of 'we want work' when he pleaded with the labourers not to 'disconnect from their clergy or from the tenant farmers' and he claimed the landlords were doing all they could.[24]

By the end of March 1846 protest began to focus on the relief schemes. Complaints emerged about the way employment was being distributed on the schemes with it being claimed that the contractors 'generally employ their own families and servants'.[25] Many protests occurred in anticipation of workers being discharged.[26] To lose your place on an outdoor relief scheme meant that you didn't have money for food. In May the labourers on the Relief Schemes staged a one-day strike throughout the city.[27]

The social unrest that now prevailed across the entire city and county was manifest in a demonstration organised to welcome the maverick nationalist MP, William Smith O'Brien.[28] On 13 June 1846 more than 30,000 people attended a demonstration organised by the Trades Council.[29] Demonstrations of such size were not unusual, particularly when Daniel O'Connell was in attendance, but this demonstration was of a different social character. The *Chronicle* noted that the participants were exclusively made up of the working classes stating that 'The procession was marked by the absence of all the gentry. In wealth, station and character it was totally deficient.'[30]

There was uproar when the Chamber of Commerce demanded an end to the importation of Indian meal because it was depressing prices in the city.[31] The middle and upper classes campaigned against the relief schemes, stating that they had the undesirable effects of increasing labour militancy and social unrest.[32] Landlords and tenant farmers indiscriminately evicting labourers and then tearing down their cottages to force them into the city were common.[33]

Constant police patrols were maintained, with the military kept on stand-by. Sporting and other events that would attract large crowds were postponed in order to avoid the mobilisation of large numbers and the consequent potential for disorder to occur.[34] Police were placed on guard at food stores in the city and in several rural towns to prevent plunder by the starving masses.[35]

From the perspective of the establishment these protests were getting out of control. Cartloads of provisions on their way to markets in Limerick were attacked and plundered. Mass meetings of unemployed labourers took place and demands for employment grew. The local Catholic clergy continued to condemn the protests and the plunder of provisions. On the last Sunday in September Thomas Steele, O'Connell's Chief Pacificator, used the pulpit at mass at Bridgetown to warn labourers not to 'join any confederacy against the laws'. Steele went on to defend the local millers who had been hiking up the price of flour.[36]

While the urban working classes and the rural poor continued to starve, other sections of society were benefitting from the crisis. The *Chronicle* commented on the fact that the local banks had never been as busy handling deposits from local tenant farmers who were making significant profits from the scarcity of food.[37]

By October 1846 the plunder of provisions in the city took on an organised and systematic fashion, with a network existing in the working-class tenements to distribute the plundered food. As the month progressed the protests became increasingly violent. Those plundering cartloads of supplies resorted to shooting the horses to prevent the drivers galloping off. The frequency of shooting incidents increased, and relief scheme workers regularly supported the plunder of provisions by forming a cordon to stop police and troops who were trying to prevent the food supplies being carried off. Protestors were now acting in open defiance of the clergy and the Repeal politicians. There was a dramatic drop in attendance at Repeal Association meetings as O'Connell and his allies condemn the protests.[38] The public works schemes served as the platform for organisation by workers. Protests against the export of provisions was almost always planned and plotted by the labourers on public works schemes, who then took time off to riot.

Apart from sporadic periods of organised protest in 1847, as the famine period progressed, food riots and attempts at plunder continued in a more haphazard and disorganised fashion. The military were capable of dispersing rioters with greater efficiency while the destitution and starvation of the poor led to a dramatic rise in vagrancy and begging.[39] The increased disorganisation and destitution among the poor allowed the ruling elites to deal with opposition with greater repression.[40]

The changing character of protest coincided with a significant increase in the numbers being struck down by fever, with Bruff and Hospital being particularly badly affected.[41] In an act of conscious sacrifice, the poor suffering from fever in Hospital sought shelter in the ruins of the old Dominican priory so as not to infect members of their families and their neighbours.[42] A local doctor, Morgan O'Connell, noted that this was '...particularly a poor man's question... His health is his property – and health gone, house and land, income and credit, tools, furniture, clothing and independence and, too often, honesty, all follow and go with it'. Dr. O'Connell was to add 'the wealthier can always take care of themselves.'[43]

The Struggle to Survive

1848 and 1849 saw a major subsidence of social conflict with the outrage that did occur being largely confined to petty crime.[44] Many turned their attention to escaping the crisis through emigration. During 1848 a total of 9,401 people emigrated on ships from Limerick.[45] The one thing that the Guardians were willing, even enthusiastic, to do was subsidise the cost of emigration. Their objective was to solve the problem of feeding the destitute by getting them out of the city through emigration.[46]

The easing of the crisis in 1850 did lead to some renewal of social conflict. In February of that year a series of street protests involving hundreds of workhouse inmates marched through the city streets chanting 'Bread or Blood' and resulted in the plunder of food stores.[47] Several mass protests by labourers demanding employment occurred at road works on Ashbourne Road leading to confrontations with the local police.[48] In May there was an outbreak of fighting between soldiers and locals in the city.[49] This was followed at the end of May by a full-scale riot involving up to 5,000 paupers in the city as they fought running battles with the police and plundered food stores.[50] Further rioting occurred in the workhouse at the end of June[51] and in July[52] but by September the *Chronicle* was reporting that the city was "gutted with foreign breadstuffs".[53]

After five years of famine some semblance of normality was returning to the city and county. The death, disease and emigration had led to a drop in population in the city and county from 330,029 in 1841 to 262,132 in 1851.[54] Given the estimated increases of the pre-famine period[55] it is likely that the population of Limerick at the start of the famine was significantly higher than the 1841 figure.[56] Even taking the 1841 figure there was still a drop of more than one in five of the population.[57]

After the Famine – A New Phase of Class Struggle.

The nature of class struggle in Limerick city and county changed in the post-famine period. Demands from rural workers shifted from the provision of potato ground to demands for secure employment and increased wages. For urban workers the focus was on building trade unions and fighting for recognition from employers. In particular, semi-skilled and unskilled workers demonstrated a developing a class consciousness, fighting for union recognition.

One of the key groups of workers to fight to build their union were the dock-workers in Limerick. The Limerick Dock Labourers Society was formed in 1863[58] and over the following forty years the dock labourers fought an unrelenting battle against the Harbour Board and the city's merchants for decent jobs and wages, and for union recognition. The Limerick dock labourers also became synonymous with working class solidarity, regularly supporting other workers in struggle.

The first recorded strike action by dock labourers occurred in 1866. The basis of the strike was a demand for a weekly wage for the dock workers rather than a daily rate. The dock labourers rejected a day rate of three shillings instead demanding a weekly wage of twelve shillings.[59] The dock labourers were day-labourers who did not know if they would have work from one day to the next. This issue of a weekly wage was to be one of the main motivating factors in subsequent efforts to build union organisation among the dock workers and the main source of confrontation in future years. While strikes were fought out over pay rates, the notion of dock workers being permanently employed on a weekly wage was always in the background of any dispute.

The dock labourers regularly engaged in strike action from the 1860s onwards. The strikes oscillated between offensive actions over wages and defensive actions against wage cuts or the use of non-union labour at lower rates of pay. There was a constant to and fro struggle between the dock workers and the employers during this period.

A month long strike beginning in February 1868 forced the concession of a weekly wage of ten shillings for a ten hour day.[60] Another major strike erupted on the docks in July 1870 which resulted in the employers agreeing to pay labourers a day rate of three shillings per day or a weekly rate for permanent labourers of twelve shillings.[61] This was the first agreement that led to permanent labourers on the docks that were paid a weekly rate.

The scale and outcome of the strike action on the docks was determined by the balance of class forces between the dock workers and the merchants, and within the city as a whole. The use of the police and repression against striking workers was also a major factor in determining the outcome in many of the strikes.

A strike that broke out in July 1887 demonstrated a regular pattern of industrial conflict on the docks. The use of steam winches was to be the catalyst for the strike and was part of a plan by the Harbour Board and the city's merchants to again bring about the destruction of the Dock Labourers Union and ensure the use of steam winches on the docks.[62] On 26 July the dock labourers went on strike when steam winches were used to unload the Ardnamult.[63]

The Harbour Board had formed a sub-committee charged with the task of drawing up a strategy to break the union by hiring scabs to break strikes. The intent was to bring scabs in from Scotland and house them on board ships in the docks under police protection.[64] Initially scabs were brought in from Tralee and Waterford and on the night of 27 July the striking dock labourers rushed the police cordon at the dock gates and broke through leading to a full-scale riot on the docks. Showers of stones were pelted at the police as they baton charged the striking workers.

Several policemen were injured, including two seriously, and four of the strikers also ended up in hospital. Seven strikers in total were arrested for rioting. Subsequent to the riot the magistrates held a private meeting and requested the intervention of the military to break the strike.[65]

The dock labourers were receiving widespread support across the city. The magistrates appealed for the redeployment of an extra two hundred police to Limerick and banned the playing of marching bands on demonstrations through the streets of the city at night for the duration of the strike. The newly deployed police promptly arrived and heavy police patrols were organised on the docks and the streets of Limerick. A scab was attacked and beaten up on Patrick Street and when the police arrested his attacker a large crowd surrounded the police demanding his release. Under pressure from the growing crowd the police released their prisoner who was promptly spirited away by the crowd.[66]

The strike was proving effective. The crew of the Ardnamult abandoned their ship when asked to unload the cargo and joined the strike and the scab labour brought in from Tralee and Waterford also joined the strike.[67] As the strike continued the Harbour Board sent those workers home to Tralee and Waterford to avoid a situation where they became active participants in the dispute. Coal merchants were now exploiting the strike by raising the price of coal by three shillings per ton. Further ships were diverted to Waterford and the cargo sent by rail to Limerick.[68]

The Harbour Board once again attempted to use scabs to unload cargo on the docks. Twenty-five labourers were brought in from Waterford under police protection to unload the Arranmore. The attempt to use scab labour provoked a major riot on the docks. A large demonstration, including a band, pushing a lighted tar barrel arrived at the docks where the ship was tied up. As the protestors arrived they began to shower the police lines with stones forcing them inside the dock gates. The demonstrators now launched a full scale attack on the dock gate on St. Alphonsus Street. Several of the policemen climbed up on the wall but were driven off by showers of stones. At this point the workers on the Arranmore walked off and joined the protest. Rocks, stones, bottles and other debris were flung in volleys over the wall into the docks. The blazing tar barrel that had been rolled to the dock gates was also thrown over the wall. The windows of the Clyde Shipping Company offices were smashed and some of the protestors managed to break through the gates but were surrounded by the police who managed to force the rest of the crowd back and close the gates. Several striking workers were arrested and charged with riotous assembly and assaulting the police.[69]

As the strike continued into a fifth week the Harbour Board was coming under increasing pressure from the merchants and shipping companies to sack the striking workers and from that point forward to use the steam winches to unload ships at the docks.[70] The strike ended when the workers agreed to the use of winches to unload coal but not any other products.[71]

Strike action continued throughout the rest of the 1880s and into the 1890s. Three strikes are recorded as having occurred on the docks in Limerick in 1890.[72] It is clear that the impetus for these developments, and the strikes in other ports around the country, came from the successful strike by dock workers in London.[73] This period was an intense period of class conflict in Ireland. More than thirty unions were formed between 1889-1891 many catering for semi-skilled and unskilled workers.[74] Among the most prominent of these was the National Union of Dock Labourers (NUDL) formed in Glasgow in 1889.[75]

The first Irish branch of the NDUL was established in Belfast in July 1891 following the arrival of Michael McKeown from Liverpool.[76] McKeown did not confine his activities to Belfast. In early August 1890 he travelled to Wexford to organise dock workers in the town.[77] By the end of the year the NUDL had established fourteen branches around the country.[78] Greaves asserted that the NUDL established a branch in Limerick in 1890.[79] It is possible this is the case. 'New Unionism' did spread to Limerick. In January 1891 workers at the Condensed Milk Factory in Landsdowne joined the London based Gas Workers and General Labourers Society[80] and staged a strike for union recognition.[81] There is no evidence that the Limerick dock labourers joined the NUDL.

Workers on the docks in Limerick launched a concerted effort in 1890 to force concessions from the Harbour Board and the merchants who operated on the quays. In August, during the course of the widespread railway strike, the carters on the docks struck against the employment of non-union labour hired to cart coal from a steamer, owned by Mullocks, on the docks.[82] As the strike continued the dock labourers came out in early September in support of the carters.[83] The solidarity of the dock labourers forced the hand of the merchants bringing the dispute to an end.

Membership of the Limerick Dock Labourers Society is recorded at one hundred in 1892 with an increase to one hundred and fifty for 1893 and 1894.[84] In June 1894 they staged a successful strike against the use of non-union labour on the docks with the implemention of a closed shop[85] and in 1898 were two hundred strong.[86]

The dock workers of Limerick proved to be the backbone of the Limerick labour movement in the latter half of the nineteenth century. They fought an ongoing battle with employers for union recognition with decent rates of pay and working conditions. On a regular basis they faced attempts to break their union and undermine union solidarity on the docks. Occasionally they suffered setbacks, but regularly returned to strike action when conditions favoured their cause to regain any concessions they gave. The dock workers were regularly confronted by the use of the state forces during industrial disputes. Violence was a common feature of strikes on the docks, with riots breaking out, attacks on scabs and court cases. The traditions laid down by the dock workers were to continue into the twentieth century. The Dock Labourers Society affiliated to the ITGWU at the beginning of 1918[87] and provided the mainstay for the development of the ITGWU in Limerick in subsequent years.

Railway workers and the Struggle for Recognition

While the Limerick Dock Labourers Society was a local labourers union, the railway workers in Limerick were part of a nationwide campaign to establish a national trade union on the railways. The first construction of railways in Ireland occurred in 1833-34 with the building of the Dublin – Kingstown line but it wasn't until 1845 that the building boom in railway construction really took off. In 1847 and 1848 up to 40,000 workers were employed on the construction of the railway network and continued at a level of 10,000 – 15,000 throughout the 1850s.[88]

By 1855 there were 5,672 men employed across twenty-one separate railway companies.[89] Initially companies employed English engine drivers and boilermen but as local workers were trained the English men were repatriated. The Waterford and Limerick Railway (W&LR) began repatriating their English engine and boilermen in the early 1850s.[90] In 1856 the Great Southern & Western Railway line (GS&WR) which ran several lines into Limerick was the largest employer on the railways with 1,749 employees. At the same time the W&LR employed 414 workers, largely based in Limerick.[91]

The first major strike on the railway network occurred in September 1877. The strike was started by milesmen who carried out repairs on the GS&WR. Beginning in Cork, within two days the strike encompassed Cork, Kerry, Limerick, Tipperary, Carlow and Kilkenny and spread along the line to Dublin involving more than 700 workers.[92] Eighty men marched from Charleville to Limerick along the line with all the workers along the way joining the march. The workers held a mass meeting in Limerick station to organise the strike action.[93]

The initial successes led to a growing confidence among the workers. The Waterford and Central Line Rail Company (W&CR) agreed to the strikers wage demands [94] In order to avoid being dragged into the strike action W&LR issued a statement that they would not accept bookings for passengers or goods for transfer to other companies and would only accept bookings for their own line on the basis that they would not be held responsible for any delays.[95]

Local strike committees sent delegates to at least two national meetings in Thurles. These meetings were one of the first indications that the workers were looking for wider union organisation than their own local societies.[96] Strike committee delegates travelled up and down the line to keep the local strike committees informed of developments.[97] The *Freemans Journal* reported that while no national organisation of striking workers has been established yet, strike committees were set up on every line with the headquarters for the strike in Templemore. The strike received significant support from the local communities. A strike fund was established but the strikers made a point of rejecting donations from local businesses.[98]

By the middle of October, the strike began taking its toll on the workers. Workers on some of the smaller branch lines and in Dublin began drifting back to work. On 13 October 1877 a closed meeting of the representatives of the strike committees in the fourth, fifth and sixth divisions of the Railway company was held in Hayes Hotel, Thurles.[99]

A delegation of forty striking workers led by Dan Peters met the employers in the Boardroom at Kingsbridge. The delegation consisted of gangers and milesmen from the Limerick Junction district. The workers from this district were selected because the company considered that the strike had its roots in this region. The Chairman, Colville, stated that he couldn't understand why they were on strike because it would take two years for them to get back the wages they had lost during the strike. Colville stated that 'to try and coerce the company into acceding the wage demands is not the appropriate way' to which Peters replied, 'that is the meaning of the word "strike"'. Peters continued saying that 'we meant to coerce'. At this point Colville pleaded that it was not the intention of the company to coerce the workers to which Peters replied, 'I maintain that the men who struck meant to coerce you'.[100]

However, despite the efforts of Peters and the other strike leaders, the strike was now crumbling. With no prospect of compromise from the Company workers in Tullamore, around Roscrea, on the GS&WR south of Limerick Junction, at Newbridge and on the Athlone and Portarlington branch lines all abandoned the strike.[101]

Despite the collapse of the strike, the workers set down a marker that would prove to be important for the future organisation of trade unions in Ireland. The strike laid the foundations for the intent to build a nationally organised trade union among railway workers. It was to take many years before a national organisation for railway workers came into existence. It was to face resistance from other sections of the trade union movement and lukewarm support from union officials, but the 1877 strike on the GS&WR provided the framework for the struggle to build national trade union structures.

Solidarity among Workers and the Sympathetic Strikes

In December 1889 there was the beginning of a series of strikes across the railway network, including Limerick.[102] This period also saw an increasing frequency of workers engaging in sympathetic strike action in support of striking workers. On the back of this dispute the British based Amalgamated Society of Railway Servants (ASRS) began extending their base among the railway workers. Having established a branch in Belfast in 1885[103], after the 1889 strike the union succeeded in establishing a branch in Dublin.[104] The period demonstrated the effectiveness of solidarity action and the threat of cross-network strikes.

The ASRS emerged in England in 1871 following a controversy over the working conditions of railwaymen involving Michael Thomas Bass, Member of Parliament for Derby, and the chairman of the Midland Railway. There was widespread public sympathy for the railwaymen and Bass encouraged the formation of the ASRS. By 1873 the ASRS had grown to 17,000 members, The ASRS was generally opposed to strike action and did not establish a strike fund until 1880. The hesitancy of the leadership of the ASRS to sanction strike action and distance itself from unofficial action when it occurred was to be a feature that inhibited the building of the union in Ireland.

At the beginning of April 1890, a strike began at two flour millers in Cork, McMillans and Furlongs. When two railway workers refused to handle strikebound goods brought by scabs to Cork railway station they were sacked. The strike spread rapidly as did solidarity action and was to be one of the key workers disputes at the end of the nineteenth century. GS&WR workers in Limerick went on strike after receiving a telegram from the Cork strike committee and the workers on the W&LR in Limerick refused to handle any diverted goods.[105] In Cork 150 dock workers went on strike in solidarity with the railwaymen. Workers on the Dublin, Wicklow and Wexford Railway (DW&WR) were locked out when they engaged in a solidarity strike.[106]

The solidarity action provoked a response from the conservative leadership of Cork Trades Council. At a general meeting of dock-workers a Trades Council representative argued that because the railway and shipping companies were in direct competition then the best way to force the railways to back down was to load the goods onto the ships. However, the dock workers were determined to maintain the solidarity action and rejected the demand to return to work.[107]

On 16 June William Foreman,[108] of the ASRS, organised a meeting of railway porters in Cork. Foreman claimed at the meeting that ninety per cent of the GS&WR employees had already joined the ASRS around the country. Fifty of the workers in Cork joined the ASRS at the end of the meeting.[109] A week later Foreman addressed a similar meeting of GS&WR workers in Limerick. Foreman adopted an approach that was common for the rest of his time as Irish Secretary of the ASRS when he denied that the union was responsible for a recent strike on the GS&WR in Dublin. He warned that the union would offer little help in a strike situation, stating that the ASRS was 'democratic' and each section of the union had a right to take strike action on its own. Foreman outlined that the 'society' would only come to their aid in emergency situations. Despite the lack of commitment by Foreman to support workers in struggle, the workers themselves demonstrated their instincts for the necessity for national organisation and unanimously accepted a proposal to establish a branch of the ASRS in Limerick.[110] By the end of June 1890 the ASRS was making significant inroads in recruiting workers. The strike ended in a major victory for the workers. So effective was the strike action that food supplies dwindled to crisis levels across the southern half of the country ultimately forcing the employers to cave in and re-instate all the workers who had been dismissed. The railway owners even made concessions on union recognition, although immediately looked for opportunities to act against the new-found organisation of the railway workers.

Three further strikes were to impact on union organisation on the railways, which were to lead to significant delays in consolidating the nationwide union structures on the railways. The first in Limerick in July 1890 began when about 250 fitters, smiths, carpenters, engineers and labourers at the new constructed locomotive workshops in Limerick, members of the Waterford and Limerick Railway Trade Union and the ASE, went on strike.[111] The porters, guards and other members of the recently formed ASRS branch met and committed to striking in solidarity with the locomotive works strikers if the company hired people to scab on the strike.[112]

While the workers at the Limerick locomotive works were on strike, the ASRS in Dublin issued strike notice on the DW&WR over the dismissal of two workers.[113] After four weeks on strike ASRS representative, D'Alton, proposed to a mass meeting of striking workers to submit their claim to arbitration. The workers rejected his intervention.[114]

On 9 August the striking members of the ASRS appealed to the Waterford and Limerick Railway Trade Union to call all their members out on strike to force the company's hand.[115] However, when William Foreman arrived in Limerick he advised the workers to submit their claims to arbitration and outside of verbal support he offered nothing to assist the workers in winning their demands.[116] Foreman then wrote to Spaight,[117] chairman of the W&LR, to deny he was responsible for the strike in the Limerick locomotive works.[118]

While the strike in Limerick continued the management of the DW&WR sacked 250 workers they had previously locked out and hired scabs to run the trains. As a result of the lack of action from Foreman, it took a number of years before the ASRS were again able to recruit on the DW&WR.

The strike ended in a compromise. The agreement granted nothing more than some small increases to the lowest paid workers, but it did force a reversal of the plan by the company for redundancies.[119] Foreman returned to Limerick following the settlement and claimed the resolution of the dispute as a 'great victory'. He then went on to call on the men to form a branch of a national trade union to assist them in organising in the future, but his pleas fell on deaf ears.[120]

It was 1893 before the ASRS was established in Limerick. P.J. Tevenan, the new Irish Secretary of the ASRS, stated that he 'did not know a body of men that needed combination more than the men of the Waterford and Limerick Railway'. Tevenan argued that if the workers had been members of the ASRS then the strike in 1891 would not have needed to have taken place and the workers would have achieved their demands. Thirty workers joined on the night and the membership was fifty within a few days.[121]

Railway workers in Limerick repeatedly demonstrated a determination to defend their jobs and working conditions. The workers understood the need for being part of a national organisation and the importance of engaging in solidarity action with other workers engaged in strike action. Repeatedly the workers were promised support by the ASRS which failed to emerge. Despite this, the workers did maintain their intent to organise and ultimately became part of a nationwide union organisation and reinforced their intent to defend their interests when necessary.

[1] Limerick Corporation Commemorative Edition, *Limerick City and The Great Hunger,* (Limerick 1997) p.54.

[2] *The Old Limerick Journal Famine Edition,* Volume 32, (Winter 1995).

[3] *The Old Limerick Journal Famine Edition,* Volume 32, (Winter 1995), p. 3

[4] Thomas P. O'Neill, 'The Great Irish Famine 1845-1852', *The Old Limerick Journal Famine Edition,* Volume 32, (Winter 1995), pp. 16-20 & Kevin Hannan, 'The Famine in Limerick, *The Old Limerick Journal Famine Edition,* Volume 32, (Winter 1995), pp. 21-24, Mark Tierney, 'The Great Famine in Murroe', *The Old Limerick Journal Famine Edition,* Volume 32, (Winter 1995), pp. 75-83

[5] Andrés Eiríksson, 'Food Supplies and Food Riots', in Cormac Ó Gráda (ed), *Famine 150: Commemorative Lecture Series,* (Dublin 1997) pp. 67-94

[6] The Irish Municipal Corporations Act of 1840 opened the door for the Catholic bourgeois class to gain control of local government in Ireland.

[7] *Limerick Chronicle,* 11 January 1845

[8] *Her Majesty's Commission of Inquiry into the State of the Law and Practice With Respect to the Occupation of Land in Ireland,* (Dublin,1847), p. 1100 & *Limerick Chronicle,* 22 February 1845

[9] *Limerick Chronicle,* 3 May 1845

[10] *Limerick Chronicle,* 22 October 1845

[11] *Limerick Chronicle,* 29 October 1845

[12] *Limerick Chronicle,* 5 November 1845

[13] *Limerick Chronicle,* 12 November 1845

[14] John Cunningham, "'Tis Hard to Argue Starvation into the Quiet': Protest ad Resistance 1846-1847", in Enda Delaney & Brendán Mac Suibhne (eds), *Ireland's Great Famine and Popular Politics,* (London, 2016) p. 13

[15] *Limerick Chronicle,* 13, 17 and 20 December 1845

[16] *Limerick Chronicle,* 13 December 1845

[17] *Limerick Chronicle,* 14 January 1846

[18] *Limerick Chronicle,* 31 January 1846

[19] *Limerick Chronicle,* 21 February 1846

[20] *Limerick Chronicle,* 25 February 1846

[21] *Limerick Chronicle,* 4 March 1846

[22] *Limerick Chronicle,* 14 March, 18 March, 21 March, 1 April 1846.

[23] *Limerick Chronicle,* 8 April 1846

[24] *Limerick Chronicle,* 11 April 1846

[25] *Weekly Reports of Scarcity Commission showing Progress of Disease in Potatoes, Complaints and Applications for Relief,* March - April 1846, p. 7

[26] Eiríksson, 'Food Supplies and Food Riots', p. 78

[27] *Limerick Chronicle,* 9 May 1846

[28] Conflict between the Young and Old Irelanders was reaching a climax and heading towards a split. Smith O'Brien, being a leading figure in the Young Irelanders, attracted much support from the labouring classes at this time.

[29] *Limerick Chronicle,* 13 June 1846

[30] *Limerick Chronicle,* 17 June 1846

[31] *Limerick Chronicle,* 17 June 1846

[32] Eiríksson, p. 89

[33] *Eighth Report from the Select Committee on the Poor Laws (Ireland),* 1849, p.50 - 53

[34] *Limerick Chronicle,* 12 September & 16 September 1846

[35] *Limerick Chronicle,* 16 September 1846

[36] *Limerick Chronicle,* 28 September 1846

[37] *Limerick Chronicle,* 3 October 1846

[38] *Limerick Chronicle,* 21 October 1846

[39] *Limerick Chronicle,* 13 January 1847

[40] *Limerick Chronicle,* 16 January 1847

[41] *Limerick Chronicle,* 29 May 1847

[42] Mainchín Seoighe, 'Aspects of the Famine in Limerick', *North Munster Antiquarian Journal,* Volume 49, (2009), p. 81

[43] *Minute Book of the Kilmallock Union,* quoted in Seoighe, 'Aspects of the Famine in Limerick', p. 81

[44] *Limerick Chronicle,* 24 February 1849

[45] *Limerick Chronicle,* 3 January 1849

[46] *Eighth Report from the Select Committee on the Poor Laws (Ireland),* 1849, p. 74

[47] *Limerick Chronicle,* 16 February 1850

[48] *Limerick Chronicle,* 3 April 1850

[49] *Limerick Chronicle,* 11 May 1850

[50] *Limerick Chronicle,* 1 June 1850

[51] *Limerick Chronicle,* 26 June 1850

[52] *Limerick Chronicle,* 24 July 1850

[53] *Limerick Chronicle,* 11 September 1850

[54] Limerick's Life, *Limerick Population Changes* [Available online at http://limerickslife.com/limerick-population/] (Accessed on 4/4/2015)

[55] The percentage increase from 1831-1841 was 4.65%

[56] Tom Ryan, 'The 1841 Census', *Old Limerick Journal* (Winter Edition 1996), p.25

[57] Limerick's Life, *Limerick Population Changes,* (Accessed on 4/4/2015)

[58] John B. Smethurst & Peter Carter, *Historical Directory of Trade Unions, Volume 6,* (Farnham, 2009), p.170

[59] *Freemans Journal,* 17 August 1866

[60] *Limerick Chronicle,* 11 February, 18 February & 10 March 1868

[61] *Freemans Journal,* 22 July 1870

[62] *Irish Times,* 1 August 1887

[63] *Irish Times,* 27 July 1887

[64] *Freemans Journal,* 27 July 1887

[65] *Irish Times,* 30 July 1887

[66] *Freemans Journal,* 27 July 1887

[67] *Freemans Journal,* 27 July 1887

[68] *Irish Times,* 1 August 1887

[69] *Irish Times,* 15 August 1887

[70] *Freemans Journal,* 29 August 1887

[71] *Irish Times,* 2 October 1887

[72] *Report on the Strikes and Lock-Outs of 1890,* p. 14

[73] *Limerick Chronicle,* 8 November 1890 – The London dock strike 1889 was one of the pivotal struggles in the establishment of the trade union movement in Britain and ended in complete victory for the dock workers and the establishment of a strong Dock, Wharf, Riverside and General Labourers Union.

[74] O'Connor, *A Labour History of Ireland 1824-2000,* p. 51-52

[75] Boyle, *The Irish Labour Movement in the Nineteenth Century,* p. 107-108. For information on the formation of the NUDL and the Irish influence in the formation of the union see: William Kenefick, 'Irish Dockers and Trade Unionism on Clydeside', *Irish Studies Review,* Volume 5, Number 19, (1997), pp. 22-29. For information on the history of the NUDL see: Eric Taplin, *The Dockers' Union: A Study of the National Union of Dock Labourers, 1889-1922,* (Leicester, 1986).

[76] John Gray, *City in Revolt: James Larkin & the Belfast Dock Strike of 1907,* (Belfast, 1985), p. 24. McKeown was originally from Drumintee, Co. Antrim, before emigrating to Birkenhead. He joined the NUDL when he got a job on the docks and was secretary of the Birkenhead branch during the Liverpool dock strike in 1889. For more information see: Laurence Marley, 'Michael McKeown', in Emmet O'Connor & John Cunningham (eds), *Studies in Irish Radical Leadership,* (Manchester, 2016), pp. 71-84

[77] Marley, 'Michael McKeown', pp. 74

[78] Gray, *City in Revolt,* p. 24. *O'Connor* and *Boyle* stated that the NUDL was organised in fifteen ports with 2,000 members by mid-1891. O'Connor, *A Labour History of Ireland 1824-2000,* p. 53 & Boyle, *The Irish Labour Movement in the Nineteenth Century,* p. 108

[79] Greaves, *The Irish Transport and General Workers Union,* p. 5

[80] *Limerick Chronicle,* 20 January 1891

[81] *Report on the Strikes and Lock-Outs of 1891,* p. 168. The strike lasted from 19 January 1891 until 15 February. Many of the striking workers were replaced and attempts to gain union recognition failed.

[82] *Report on the Strikes and Lock-Outs of 1890,* p. 90, *Limerick Chronicle,* 14 August 1890 & *Freemans Journal,* 15 August 1890.

[83] *Limerick Chronicle,* 11 September 1890 & *Freemans Journal,* 12 September 1890

[84] *Nineth Annual Report by The Chief Labour Correspondent on Trade Unions (1896),* p. 99

[85] *Report on the Strikes and Lock-Outs of 1894,* p. 170-171

[86] *Report by The Chief Labour Correspondent to the Board of Trade on Trade Unions in 1898,* p. 73

[87] For more information see: Dominic Haugh, 'The ITGWU in Limerick 1917-1922', *Saothar* (Volume 31, 2006), p. 29

[88] Joseph Lee, 'Railway Labour in Ireland, 1833-1856', *Saothar,* Volume 5, (1979) pp. 9-10

[89] Ibid., p. 13

[90] Ibid., p. 14

[91] Ibid., p. 15

[92] *Irish Times*, 20 September 1877

[93] *Irish Times*, 22 September 1877

[94] *Irish Times*, 25 September 1877

[95] *Irish Times*, 26 September 1877

[96] *Irish Times*, 28 September 1877 & 13 October 1877

[97] *Irish Times*, 25 September 1877

[98] *Freemans Journal*, 27 September 1877

[99] *Irish Times*, 13 October 1877

[100] *Irish Times*, 20 October 1877

[101] *Irish Times*, 20 October 1877

[102] *Limerick Chronicle*, 10 December 1889.

[103] Joseph J. Leckey, 'The Railway Servants Strike in Co. Cork, 1898', *Saothar*, Volume 2, (1976) p.40

[104] *Limerick Chronicle*, 31 December 1889

[105] *Irish Times*, 23 April 1890

[106] *Freemans Journal*, 23 April 1890

[107] *Freemans Journal*, 23 April 1890

[108] Foreman was a former sub-editor of the ASRS journal before he became the Irish secretary of ASRS. He died in Dublin on 12 December 1892 at the age of thirty-seven of 'congestion of the lungs'.

[109] *Irish Times*, 16 June 1890

[110] *Limerick Chronicle*, 24 June 1890

[111] *Irish Times*, 28 July 1890 & *Limerick Chronicle*, 26 July 1890

[112] *Irish Times*, 29 July 1890

[113] *Limerick Chronicle*, 26 July 1890

[114] *Limerick Chronicle*, 2 August 1890

[115] *Irish Times*, 9 August 1890

[116] *Limerick Chronicle*, 28 August 1890 & *Freemans Journal*, 28 August 1890

[117] Spaight was a prominent Limerick merchant

[118] *Limerick Chronicle*, 4 September 1890 & *Freemans Journal*, 5 September 1890

[119] *Freemans Journal*, 20 September 1890

[120] *Limerick Chronicle*, 28 September 1890

[121] *Limerick Chronicle*, 15 August 1893 & *Freemans Journal*, 15 August 1893

THE RISE OF RURAL LABOUR

'we demand our rights and happy homes'
—Banner of the Labourers League,
Shanagolden, Co. Limerick, 1881

The Irish Agricultural Labourers Union

The first serious attempt to mobilise in the interest of the labourers came from the milieu of the Fenian-influenced amnesty agitation.[1] This agitation led to the emergence of the Irish Agricultural Labourers Union (IALU) in August 1873. From the outset the main mover of this union, P.F. Johnson from Kanturk, used his influence to ensure the participation of Isaac Butt and another prominent nationalist M.P., P.J. Smyth. Delegates attended from Cork city, the Munster counties of Limerick, Kerry, Tipperary and Clare, and from Queen's County in Leinster.[2] During 1873 and 1874 the IALU had some limited success in forming branches in Munster and Leinster, but it never became a truly national union and by 1875 had all but disappeared.[3]

The first recorded meeting of farmers in Limerick in the period of the Land War occurred in September 1879. Addressing the meeting the Catholic priest chairing stated that he hoped they 'would be able to effect a reformation or a modification of the land laws so that no tenant farmer should be deprived of the results of their labour... they did not want anything at all connected with Communism or with international societies, the principles of which were repugnant to the Catholic people of Ireland'.[4] Almost immediately tensions arose between farmers and labourers. Labourers criticised the farmers for ignoring the plight of the labourers, bringing an angry response from farmers who claimed that the criticisms were an attempt by agitators to create 'disunity between the labourers and their best friends the farmers'.[5] These tensions between the labourers and farmers in Limerick were to be a constant feature of the Land War.

A 'Land' meeting in Ardagh on 3 October 1880 saw the labourers to the fore with demands for 'the land for the landless people' and declarations proposed by P.F.

Johnson deploring 'the present conditions of the agrilabourers'.[6] The Clare and Limerick Farmers Club responded by establishing a branch of the Land League at a meeting in Slattery's, Thomas Street.[7]

A refrain that was first to emerge during O'Connell's Repeal movement, 'Labour Must Wait', was to become a mainstay of agitation by tenant farmers, the clergy and the nationalist movement during the Land War. The demands of the working class for economic, social and political emancipation were to constantly be demoted, not only to a secondary position, but cast into the far distant future.

In response to the establishment of the Limerick Land League by tenant farmers, a week later a Labourers League was formed in Ardagh. The labourers rejected the argument that the farmers' problems had to be settled first.[8]

Throughout 1881 the competing interests of labourers and farmers were a constant feature at public meetings, gatherings and demonstrations. In April at a Land League meeting in Ardagh, several local labour leagues attended calling for a rejection of the Land Bill because it 'did nothing to assist the labouring classes'.[9] A few days later a spate of agrarian outrages lasting more than a week occurred in Abbeyfeale when the homes of tenant farmers were attacked and the farmers warned to reduce the rent for conacre.[10]

A Land League Conference in Limerick on 21 April rejected any discussion about the plight of labourers.[11] Nationalist interests began pressurising the Labourers Leagues to abandon their campaign and row in behind the Land League. On 2 May a large meeting of labourers took place in Feenagh. The secretary of the Labourers League wrote a report on the meeting outlining that while the Labourers League supported the objectives of the Land League, the meeting stressed the necessity for the Labourers League to remain separate and distinct from the Land League to represent the interests of labourers. On the same day a meeting of the Land League in Athea rejected any debate on the plight of the labourers. There followed a night of attacks on farmers' houses in the area around Newcastle West.[12]

However, the pressure was mounting on the Land League. Some of the more progressive elements held a meeting in Thomas Street Limerick to push the cause of the labourers, which they claimed had been 'hitherto all but neglected'.[13] However, the nationalist interests and the clergy decided it was time to act. At a Land League meeting in Limerick on 16 May a decision was taken to send a Land League delegation to a planned Labourers Convention on 19 May. The delegation was to carry a message from Fr. Ryan who stated that the labourers should be guided by advice from the Land League delegation and condemned them for organising separately from the Land League. At the Monday meeting Ryan warned the Land League that allowing the labourers to organise separately could result in the labourers' organisations being 'a source of trouble in the future'.[14]

Over 300 delegates representing Labourers Associations from Clare and Limerick attended the Labourers' Convention in the Town Hall in Limerick which led to the establishment of the Munster Labour League.[15] Several members of the local clergy attended and attempted to dictate the agenda of the Convention. Delegates made widespread criticism of the treatment of labourers by tenant farmers with numerous examples of exploitation being outlined. A proposal was put to the Convention not to accept any land reform that excluded addressing the concerns of labourers. The clergy opposed the resolution on the basis that it would prevent farmers gaining their rights and argued that labourers should support land reform and then, when that was achieved, agitate for labourers' rights. Rev. Maher of Newport condemned labourers' agitation because it was driving capital out of the country and causing divisions between labourers and farmers. Maher said that the labourers could enjoy 'prosperity and comfort' like the peasantry in France if only they backed up the farmers. He then went on to criticise the notion of nationalising land and said that free trade in land was in the interests of the labourer. Despite this the delegates unanimously adopted the resolution.

A further resolution condemning Limerick Corporation for the failure to build labourers' cottages was unanimously adopted, as was one calling for the election franchise to be expanded to labourers. One resolution of note was accepted expressing support for the idea of working class unity north and south with support being offered for 'orangemen' who faced similar problems to labourers in Limerick.

The final resolution debated at the Convention called for the establishment of a National Labour League with delegates stating that they 'would no more entrust a labourer to the power of the farmer than...into that of Old Nick'. Rev Sheedy of Kilmallock attacked the resolution and called for unity between farmer and labourer but the delegates carried the resolution.[16]

This pattern was repeated over the following weeks. At a Land League meeting in Abbeyfeale, Mr Hishion of the Shanagolden Labourers' League warned that there would be 'no settlement of the land question from a government that refuses their (labourers) rights'.[17] At a Land League meeting in Shanagolden the Labourer's League paraded with a banner inscribed 'we demand our rights and happy homes'. When Rev. Mulqueen stated that the 'interests or farmers and labourers... are identical', McCoy, the Vice-President of the Labourers League responded 'landlords labourers are better paid, fed and housed than farmers' labourers'.[18] At a Labourers meeting in Ballingarry in July the Chair gave the apologies of the parish priest who was unable to attend stating that 'the people could not do without the priest'. This resulted in heckling and cat-calls and shouts of 'we don't want him'. The meeting called for the establishment of a nationwide organisation of labour.[19]

At this stage farmers began resorting to violence. Widespread intimidation of labourers occurred to enforce the boycott of landlords.[20] Labourers were attacked in

Birdhill and Ardagh for breaking the boycott.[21] However, the pressure on the leaders of the Labourers Leagues was starting to have an impact. A number of Labourers delegations attended the National Land League Convention in Limerick on 17 September. At the Convention the Labourers delegates agreed to abide by the Land League's instructions concerning labourers rights.[22] This provoked a further backlash from labourers. Groups of protesters carried out coordinated attacks on several churches during Sunday mass,[23] soldiers were assaulted on George's Street by a large mob[24] and sporadic attacks occurred on soldiers during the following few days.[25] As large numbers were brought before the courts for rioting there was another outbreak of violence.[26]

On Sunday 16 October another riot broke out near City Hall. Troops opened fire on the mob wounding one man and dispersing the crowd. The military imposed martial law and cleared the streets. At dusk the crowds began to re-assemble and engage in running battles with police for several hours before the police cleared the streets using considerable violence. The following day large crowds assembled while those arrested the previous day were brought to court. Rioting broke out again as prisoners were transferred to city gaol, with troops opening fire on rioters. The police were given orders to open fire on anyone who threw a stone or in the direction that a stone was thrown from.[27]

Sporadic rioting continued for the remainder of the year with outbreaks in Bruff,[28] at the Munster Assizes,[29] after a court case which convicted some of the rioters,[30] and in Doon.[31] A planned Labourers meeting in Doon was abandoned after widespread intimidation by the military and local farmers.[32]

Following the suppression of the Land League many of the local leaders turned their attention to the Labour Leagues. Moves soon began to create a national labourers' organisation that would be more firmly under the control of the Land Leaguers.[33] There was, not surprisingly, stiff resistance from the labourers to this development. Despite the suppression of the Land League the Labour Leagues continued and grew. By the summer of 1882 labour leagues and herds associations had spread throughout Munster, Leinster and into significant parts of Connacht.[34] This led to Parnell supporting the establishment of the Irish Labour and Industrial Union (ILIU). With Parnell as president, the ILIU adopted more extensive labourers' demands, facilitating Parnellite control of the labour agitation that was now widespread in the country. From the perspective of the nationalist leadership, if the rural labour movement was allowed to continued to grow it had the potential to cause a severe split along class lines in nationalist Ireland.[35]

Parnell's National League was formed in October and proved to be the death knell of the ILIU. Branches of the ILIU were instructed to transform into NL branches which most did. The rural labour movement was subsumed by the Parnellites and effectively neutralised.[36]

On Sunday night 25 June 1882 thousands of farm labourers attend a mass meeting at Bruff. Different localities brought banners as they marched to the meeting. Extra police and military were drafted into the locality and rumours were widespread that the police would ban the meeting. At the meeting a tenant farmer named Hartigan was proposed as chair and the speakers included several Poor Law Guardians (PLG). Hartigan said that he was always on the side of the labourer and, even though there were few farmers at the meeting, the best of farmers would always support the labourers' cause. This resulted in loud heckling from the assembled labourers. Many of the labourers demonstrated their hostility to the farmers by heckling that they would not pay rent to the farmers. A speaker named Osborne asked what happens to 'the farmer who does not give half an acre of land' – the crowd shouted he's 'a dead man'.[37] A week later a similar meeting was held in Kilteely with more than 5.000 in attendance and the reports of the meeting indicate widespread heckling of any speaker supporting farmers, with condemnation of the farmers prominent throughout the meeting.[38]

Painstakingly, the Parnellites strangled each attempt by farm labourers to exercise any independent action. At meetings in Croom,[39] Patrickswell,[40] Bruff,[41] and Rathkeale[42] the agenda and speeches were tightly controlled to manage the expectations of and promises to the labourers in attendance. By 1883 the rural labour movement was almost fully incorporated into the National League, with the remaining labourers' groups lacking any sense of national cohesion.[43]

A mass meeting of labourers was held in Croom on Sunday 2 March 1884. The meeting was to agitate for employment and the implementation of the Labourers Act.[44] A large contingent attended from Bruff under the leadership of prominent labour advocate Patrick Osborne. Those in attendance condemned the landlords and tenant farmers in equal measure for acting against the interests of the labourers. When a solitary farmer attempted to address the crowd from the platform he was thrown off the platform by angry labourers with shouts of 'we want no farmers here... they gave us nothing'. Osborne attacked the failure to implement the Labourers Act and criticised Parnell and 'his little band of patriots' for their failure to defend the interests of labourers in the House of Commons.[45]

Two weeks later another labourers meeting was held in Bruree with an increased attendance The *Limerick Chronicle* commented that the plight of the labourers was finding little support among the local Catholic clergy. The paper quoted Rev. Enright who stated that it was the first time since his arrival in Bruree that he 'was not at the head of his flock'. Addressing the labourers meeting, Maurice Murphy stated that even though they did not have the support of the farmers or the clergy, they had the support of millions of labourers in England and across the Atlantic. Murphy called for all labourers to 'bond themselves together'. Several other speakers called on all labourers to unite and not to regard the farmers as their allies.[46]

Slowly the opposition of the rural labourers was worn down and it wasn't until 1890 that there was some movement towards the re-emergence of militancy by labourers. At this time leading nationalists were ensuring that they maintained an element of control over the direction of the labourers movement. The Irish Democratic Trade and Labour Federation (DLF) was initiated in Kanturk and promoted by Michael Davitt in Cork.[47] This new movement was led predominantly by leading nationalists.[48]

Following the Federation's founding convention in Cork it spread throughout Munster. The first reports of DLF branches in Limerick date from August 1890 with a meeting in Bruff. The meeting was attended by large numbers of labourers from the town and surrounding area and there were several bands present. The burning issue at the meeting was an outbreak of potato blight that was causing severe hardship locally and the meeting called on the PLG to implement a programme of public works. Speakers called on all working classes to join together in the Federation and 'pressurise the Irish Party to ensure labourers cottages are built'. It was clear from the meeting that the leaders of the DLF were intent on ensuring that it was subservient to the nationalist movement.[49]

However, as the DLF expanded, it was clear that the labourers displayed a growing class consciousness through the expanding nature of demands being made. By October the Federation had spread to Clare and a large demonstration as held in Kildysert. Banners with the messages 'Labour, being the producer of the wealth of nations, must be respected' and 'We only ask reward proportioned to our labour' were displayed in the town. The meeting also demanded changes to the voting laws to allow labourers vote in elections to the Poor Law Unions and other Boards on the basis of 'one man, one vote'. Further resolutions demanding that the British government and the Irish Party implement free education for children were passed.[50]

Local MPs attended a massive DLF meeting in Kilfinane at the beginning of November 1890. The MPs made platitudes about the rights of labour and attempted to steer the discussion into support of the Irish Party. However, the labourers in attendance wanted a more radical approach and endorsed the demands of the Kildysert meeting the previous month.[51] The new movement, now growing rapidly faced a new crisis with the Parnellite split resulting in the same divisions that was faced by both nationalist and labour organisations.[52] The potential of the Irish Democratic and Labour Federation dissipated in the Parnellite feuding after 1890. It took another four years before the next initiative managed to gain a foothold with the founding of the Irish Land and Labour Association.

The Irish Land and Labour Association

The Irish Land and Labour Association (ILLA) was established on 15 August 1894. The intent was for Nationalist politicians to use the rural labourers as a pressure group as they campaigned for Home Rule.[53] However, at least in the initial stages, the ILLA presented a more radical and class based political outlook driven by the labourers themselves.

The drive for the establishment of the ILLA came from a number of different labourers' organisations from around Munster and parts of Leinster.[54] These organisations attempted to create a group that was a radical independent voice for rural labourers. While it did eventually succumb to control by nationalist politicians that neutered its militancy, this did not happen before a prolonged battle between the class interests of the labourers and the representatives of nationalist Ireland.

A number of Nationalist MPs attended the founding conference of the ILLA and were clearly shocked at the radical nature of the political programme debated at the conference. The stated objective of the conference was to consider the best means of 'securing to the labourer the just rewards of his labour'. The conference condemned the exclusion of labourers from voting in local government as a 'scandalous injustice'. Delegates continued by claiming that until this 'corrupt and fraudulent system' was fixed, labourers would continue to protest 'against any measures dealing with Irish labour interests being entrusted to Grand Juries, Presentment Sessions or Poor Law Boards'.

However, in defiance of the MPs present, the delegates at the ILLA conference went much further in their demands. The conference called for magistrates to be elected, with land agents and military personnel banned from being magistrates, and paid jurors drawn from the body of the whole people without distinction. Public officials, employing direct labour at a fair wage and fair time principle rather than through contractors, should carry out all public work. The conference called for the English allotment system to be extended to Ireland as well as the Labourers Acts to be extended to include all artisans, labourers and fishermen in rural areas.

Reflecting some of Davitt's ideas, the conference called for an Agricultural Board to be established with powers to promote migration, to establish co-operative colonies of working agriculturalists and to give technical instruction to those having holdings. Delegates demanded that the laws affecting land tenure and local taxation should be amended so that charges are levied exclusively on the land, not on the tenants in occupation.

The conference called for the establishment of an Irish Industrial League with the objective of establishing 2,000 acre farms with 100 men to work these farms with the state compulsorily hiring the land and providing money to the labourers to cultivate it, arguing that these proposals were necessary for 'the welfare of the community at large'.

Also discussed at the conference was the opening of state municipal workshops, the nationalisation of the railways, compulsory education with a 'substantial meal' for each child, the compulsion of all able-bodied idlers 'whether aristocratic or plebeian' to engage in productive work, the repudiation of the National Debt and the abolition of the army and the navy. Finally the conference called for 'one man one vote, with elected members of parliament to be paid and election expenses to be reimbursed by the state, state pensions for the elderly, an eight-hour day and the abolition of the House of Lords'.

The political establishment, both nationalist and unionist were clearly shocked that labourers would debate such a radical programme. The *Chronicle* criticised the conference claiming that the proposals will 'not carry much weight with careful persons' and that the labour delegates should 'confine their deliberations to labour questions'.[55]

Protests were organised often in the hundreds and sometimes, involving thousands, to compel the Boards of Guardians to build labourers cottages. In an effort to diffuse the conflict the PLG's would set up inquiries, but the meetings of these inquiries did nothing more than provide another focus for demonstrations and protests. Of particular contention was the fact that the local councils were hiving off the building of labourers' cottages to private interests through the establishment of 'development companies' funded by private subscriptions to build the cottages and repay the subscriptions through the rent collected.[56]

Within days of the founding conference of the ILLA a protest involving hundreds of labourers took place at an inquiry into the building of labourers' cottages in Newcastle West.[57] Increasing employment and some movement on the issue of labourers' cottages led to an easing of tensions during the middle of the 1890s. Nationalist politicians worked tirelessly to bring the ILLA under their control. The nature of local government mitigated against the development of the ILLA. Any influence on local councils was nullified by the continued domination of farmers and landowners.[58] Ultimately the ILLA was emasculated by nationalist politicians, in many areas destroying the movement if they couldn't bring it directly under their control.[59] Once again 'labour must wait'.

The ILLA may have endured right up to the revolutionary period in Ireland, but in Limerick it had little impact after the turn of the century and ultimately succumbed to the radicalisation of the period when the ITGWU emerged and the ILLA branches, one after another, dissolved into the ITGWU as it rapidly expanded into rural Limerick in 1918 and 1919.[60]

---

[1] Fintan Lane, 'P. F. Johnson, Nationalism, and Irish Rural Labourers 1869-82', *Irish Historical Studies*, Vol. 33, No. 130 (Nov., 2002), p. 195

[2] Lane, 'P. F. Johnson, Nationalism, and Irish Rural Labourers 1869-82', p. 200

[3] Ibid., p. 202-203

[4] *Limerick Chronicle,* 2 September 1879

[5] *Limerick Chronicle,* 6 September 1879

[6] *Limerick Chronicle,* 5 October 1880

[7] *Limerick Chronicle,* 16 October 1880

[8] *Limerick Chronicle,* 23 October 1880

[9] *Limerick Chronicle,* 19 April, 23 April & 26 April 1881

[10] *Limerick Chronicle,* 21 April 1881

[11] *Limerick Chronicle,* 21 April 1881

[12] *Limerick Chronicle,* 3 May 1881

[13] *Limerick Chronicle,* 5 May 1881

[14] *Limerick Chronicle,* 17 May 1881

[15] Lane, p. 205

[16] *Limerick Chronicle,* 19 May 1881

[17] *Limerick Chronicle,* 28 May 1881

[18] *Limerick Chronicle,* 7 June 1881

[19] *Limerick Chronicle,* 26 July 1881

[20] *Limerick Chronicle,* 9 August 1881

[21] *Limerick Chronicle,* 13 August 1881

[22] *Limerick Chronicle,* 17 September 1881

[23] *Limerick Chronicle,* 20 September 1881

[24] *Limerick Chronicle,* 24 September 1881

[25] *Limerick Chronicle,* 27 September 1881

[26] *Limerick Chronicle,* 4 October, 8 October & 11 October 1881

[27] *Limerick Chronicle,* 18 October 1881

[28] *Limerick Chronicle,* 1 December 1881

[29] *Limerick Chronicle,* 13 December 1881

[30] *Limerick Chronicle,* 22 December 1881

[31] *Limerick Chronicle,* 29 December 1881

[32] *Limerick Chronicle,* 13 December 1881

[33] Lane, 'P. F. Johnson, Nationalism, and Irish Rural Labourers', 1869-82, p. 207

[34] Fintan Lane, 'Rural Labourers, Social Change and Politics in Late Nineteenth-Century Ireland', in Fintan Lane & Donal O'Driscoll (eds), *Politics and the Irish Working Class, 1830-1945,* (Basingstoke, 2005), p. 131

[35] Lane, 'Rural Labourers, Social Change and Politics', p. 132

[36] Lane, 'Rural Labourers, Social Change and Politics', p. 132

[37] *Freemans Journal,* 26 June 1882 & *Limerick Chronicle,* 27 June 1882. The *Chronicle* recorded the attendance at 10,000 and noted that only one priest was in attendance.

[38] *Limerick Chronicle,* 4 July 1882

[39] *Limerick Chronicle,* 24 October 1882

[40] *Limerick Chronicle,* 28 November 1882

[41] *Limerick Chronicle,* 5 December 1882

[42] *Limerick Chronicle,* 2 January 1883

[43] Lane, 'P. F. Johnson, Nationalism, and Irish Rural Labourers, 1869-82', p. 207

[44] The Labourers Act dictated that farmers were obliged to provide land for the building of a labourer's cottage. The farmers resisted such an imposition.

[45] *Limerick Chronicle,* 3 March 1884

[46] *Limerick Chronicle,* 18 March 1884

[47] Lane, 'Rural Labourers, Social Change and Politics', p. 133

[48] D. D. Sheehan, *Ireland Since Parnell,* (London, 1921) [Available online at: www.gutenberg.org/files/13963/13963-h/13963-h.htm] (Accessed on 16 October 2016)

[49] *Limerick Chronicle*, 16 August 1890 & Freemans Journal, 16 August 1890

[50] *Limerick Chronicle,* 14 October 1890

[51] *Limerick Chronicle*, 4 November 1890

[52] Lane, 'Rural Labourers, Social Change and Politics', p. 133

[53] O'Connor, *A Labour History of Ireland 1824-1960*, p. 53

[54] Lane, 'Rural Labourers, Social Change and Politics', p. 135

[55] *Limerick Chronicle* 16 August 1894

[56] In 1893 the Limerick Labourers Dwellings Company report a profit of £10 16s 2d for the year after paying off £38 15s of the loan. *Limerick Chronicle* 25 September 1894

[57] *Limerick Chronicle* 23 August 1894

[58] Padraig G. Lane, 'The Land and Labour Association 1894-1914', *Journal of the Cork Historical and Archaeological Society,* Volume 98, (1993), p. 91.

[59] Padraig G. Lane, 'The Land and Labour Association 1894-1914', p. 92

[60] For more details see: Dominic Haugh, 'The ITGWU in Limerick 1917-1922', *Saothar,* Volume 31, (2006), p. 33&34

OPPORTUNITY AND SETBACK

'In Dublin, the capital of Ireland—a city of a not highly industrial type, with a population of half a million—the class struggle, which permeates the whole life of capitalist society everywhere, has become accentuated to the point of class war... At the present moment the Irish nationalists (i.e., the Irish bourgeoisie) are the victors. They are buying up the lands of the English landlords; they are getting national self- government (the famous Home Rule...)... Well, this Irish nationalist bourgeoisie is celebrating its "national" victory, its maturity in "affairs of state" by declaring a war to the death on the Irish labour movement.... The Dublin events mark a turning-point in the history of the labour movement and of socialism in Ireland. Murphy has threatened to destroy the Irish trade unions. He has succeeded only in destroying the last remnants of the influence of the Irish nationalist bourgeoisie over the Irish proletariat. He has helped to steel the independent revolutionary working class movement in Ireland, which is free of nationalist prejudices.'

— Vladimir Lenin on the Dublin Lockout[1]

Politics and the Congregated Trades 1889-1900

In 1899 there was a seismic change in the political landscape in local government in Limerick. For the first time ever the mass of woking class men were entitled to vote in a local election. The voting frachise was not extended to general elections in 1918 when women over thirty and men of no property gained the vote. However, given the opportunity in 1899 the working class of Limerick uncerimoniously dumped the business class, Catholic and Protestant, who had controlled Limerick

Corporation for the previous century, out on their ear. 'Labour' candidates swept the election in large parts of the city and the 'labour' council became known as the 'People's Parliament', as the expectations of the Limerick working class resounded around the city.

The Limerick Amnesty Association (LAA) was formed in 1889[2] and from the start the Congregated Trades took an active part in the movement. The campaign in Limerick had a particular local focus on the imprisonment of prominent Limerick Fenian, member of the Irish Republican Brotherhood (IRB), John Daly. A complete maverick within the Fenian movement, Daly had been arrested in Britain on charges of possessing explosives and was sentenced to life imprisonment.[3] His antipathy towards constitutional nationalism angered the nationalist establishment in the city who attempted to isolate him within nationalist circles. John Daly also antagonised many leading Fenians. O'Donovan Rossa came to detest Daly and used the *United Irishman* newspaper to attack him.[4]

The antagonism towards Daly displayed by the nationalist establishment in Limerick coupled with the focus of the amnesty campaign around the release of Daly from prison meant that the constitutional nationalists refused to play a part in the Amnesty Association. This left the field open for the Congregated Trades to play a central role in the campaign rather being confined to the periphery of nationalist politics as had been the norm in previous decades. Furthermore, the participation of the Trades in the amnesty campaign drew the leading figures of the Trades closer to Fenianism. This was a major development as the Congregated Trades had traditionally supported conservative constitutional nationalist politics. While the Congregated Trades continued to participate in Parnellite activities their focus now shifted to the amnesty campaign.

At this stage it appears that the Congregated Trades was not a functioning body but the 'officers'portrayed a semblance of authority using the title. In March 1890 there was a major demonstration calling for Daly's release from prison led by the Pork Butchers Society and followed by other trades.[5] At the time the pork butchers were involved in a major and long running strike with the bacon factory owners, a strike that encompassed the bacon industry in Limerick, Cork and Waterford. Alongside the pork butchers strike was a major strike on the railways involving workers in Limerick and many other centres.

The labouring classes in Limerick also actively supported the amnesty campaign for Daly's release. Daly was now being held up as an anti-establishment figure. A series of strikes involving the labourers in the early 1890s saw the city's nationalist politicians exposed for attempting to undermine and suppress the strikes. Daly was seen as standing out from the pro-business nationalist leadership.

Reorganisation of the Congregated Trades appears to have started at the end of 1892 or very early in 1893. The new body was formally launched in October 1893 with the establishment of the Limerick United Trades and Labour League and became known as the Trades Council. The meeting called on 'the workingmen of Limerick to unite under the United Trades and Labour League and encourage any effort that would give employment, urging the citizens of the great necessity of giving their work to those firms who employ the regular tradesmen'.[6] At the same time a General Labourers Union was established in the city.[7] At a meeting of the Trades Council in February 1894 that was addressed by nationalist MP William Field, it was stated that the Trades Council had been in existence a little over a year and 'had 2000 members already'.[8] The growth of the Trades Council coincided with a new strike wave that had begun to hit the city.[9] In May the *Chronicle* expressed concern about the growing independence of the working classes and carried an article attacking the formation of the Independent Labour Party in Britain and warning the Limerick working classes not to cause division in the city.[10]

Throughout 1894 a series of large demonstrations took place calling for the release of Daly from prison.[11] The pressure of the LAA mounted on the nationalist establishment who were growing increasingly concerned at developments and the prominent role the working classes were taking in this movement. In an effort to cut across these developments the local National League branch proposed John Daly as the nationalist parliamentary candidate in Limerick.[12] The Trades Council took up this proposal with enthusiasm and began to campaign for Daly's nomination.[13]

Daly was elected unopposed to the British parliament but removed as MP a month later. The subsequent by-election tore any semblance of unity between the Parnellite factions apart as both nominated their own candidates. The election resulted in a major schism within nationalism in the city with allegations and rancour being hurled from both sides. The brother of Daly, James Daly, attacking the Parnellites for wanting to keep John Daly locked up.[14]

John Daly was eventually released from prison on 20 August 1896 after serving twelve and a half years and immediately threw himself into local politics in the city.[15] The release of Daly led to a flurry of political activity. Without a support base within the nationalist movement in the city, Daly courted the Trades Council. His anti-establishment profile and his maverick nature won him support from the city's working classes. Daly engaged in manipulation to ensure his personal supporters were in a position to wield greater influence within the Trades Council and took every opportunity to promote his own profile.[16]

Engaging in populist rhetoric John Daly worked to mobilise working class support for his candidacy for the local council. In August 1897 he was nominated as a candidate for the Irishtown Ward but was ruled ineligible, as his name was not listed on the Burgess Roll.[17] Regular demonstrations took place, almost exclusively populated by working class people against the city's establishment and focussed around their attempts to prevent Daly being nominated for the city council. In an effort to quell the demonstrations the Mayor attempted to prohibit bands from parading in the city after six o'clock in the evening. Daly organised a demonstration in defiance of the mayor.[18]

During 1898 a series of strikes swept through the city deepening divisions between the constitutional nationalists and the working classes. In particular a bitter strike by tailors that lasted several months caused considerable conflict.[19] Repeated demonstrations and rioting took place as groups of scabs arrived from London to try and break the tailors strike.[20] As the year drew to a close the anti-establishment populist rhetoric of Daly was getting a significant echo among the city's working class. The prospect of 'labour' candidates caused consternation amongst the city's establishment.

The change in the voting franchise caused a dramatic rise in the number of electors in Limerick. When the Burgess Rolls were revised, the electorate increased from 709 to 5,521.[21] For the first time many among the working class received the right to vote in local elections. This led to a realistic prospect of labour candidates running in the election with the potential of winning seats on the city council. In the run-up to the election the *Limerick Leader* became the cheerleader for Daly and the labour challenge. The paper openly promoted the labour candidates and called for the working classes to elect them.[22] The labour challenge was promoted as a 'solely a workingman's movement' which would rely 'entirely' on 'the workers themselves'.[23]

A series of labour meetings took place through October and early November[24] with speeches condemning the city's establishment, and nationalist politicians in particular, as 'trying to use the workers for their own ends'.[25] A representative of the coopers' union, James Kett, identified the three classes who made up the outgoing council who were regarded as the enemies of the workingman. Kett condemned 'the publican, the pawnbroker and the landlord' for taking money from workers.[26]

The *Chronicle* reported that a meeting of 'Labour delegates' who have been working with John Daly selected 32 candidates to stand in the election.[27] Daly stressed the independence of the labour candidates rejecting any affiliation to the various nationalist factions – Dillonites, Redmondites and Healyites. Given Daly's involvement it was not a surprise that Home Rule figured prominently in the election, but the labour candidates stressed the social and economic conditions facing the working classes.[28] Fenians who supported Daly coupled with leading figures on the Trades Council dominated the list of candidates. The prospect of a clear anti-establishment list of candidates being elected generated significant enthusiasm throughout the city.

Two weeks after the labour candidates were announced a major meeting of the city's merchants and traders took place, along with some of the outgoing councillors. Alderman Hall said the 'the great employers of labour had been successful in trade and these were the men they wanted on the Corporation'. Some disagreement emerged when a small number of nationalists stated that all candidates representing the business interests should support Home Rule. The response was that there are more important issues to address than Home Rule. Repeatedly it was stated that 'politics' should not enter into the selection of merchant candidates. Mr Goodbody argued that the meeting needed to select candidates based on representing merchants, traders and rate payers to avoid a three-cornered fight between unionist, nationalist and labour. Alderman Hall proposed selecting two candidates for each ward with the objective of getting both elected. The Mayor, Michael Cusack, stated that this was the beginning of a 'new era' with those 'of wealth and high ability' taking part in the administration.[29]

The Board of Guardians had a long discussion about the need for unity between the factions of the Nationalist Party. Alderman Stephen O'Mara, father of Alphonsus O'Mara the future Sinn Fein Mayor during the Limerick Soviet, said that all nationalists should be fighting a common enemy.[30] In response the labour candidates reacted with hostility, with John O'Brien, a labourer standing in the Abbey Ward, calling the merchants hypocrites and claiming that 'the large employers of the city were dragged together to hold secret conclave to intimidate the working man'. O'Brien stressed the point that 'it was the first time in 700 years that the working class had got the privilege of citizenship'.[31] A month before the election the RIC were predicting that the labour candidates would win fifteen of the forty seats on the council.[32]

It wasn't only in Limerick that significant numbers of labour candidates were nominated. The *Chronicle* reported that the workingmen of Ennis meet in the Workmen's Room and selected three labour candidates for each ward for the Urban Council.[33] Another report spoke about the election campaign in Kilrush being predominantly between labour candidates on one side and candidates nominated by the local parish priest, Fr Malone and the merchants on the other.[34] The same scenario was replicated in other cities and towns throughout the country.

As the election approached clerical opposition to the labour challenge grew with the RIC reporting that labour and the 'extreme Nationalists' were opposed by 'representatives of the merchants and large ratepayers backed up by clerical sympathy'.[35] The Redemptorist controlled Arch Confraternity 'cautioned a congregation of some 3,000 men to see that Daly and his followers would be left severely alone' in the election.[36]

On election day there were seventy-nine candidates, thirty-four of the candidates stood under the labour banner, twenty-seven were outgoing councillors supported by the merchants and the Ratepayers Association and the remaining candidates were catagorised as 'merchants' or 'large ratepayers'.[37]

A People's Parliament.

The election result was a stunning success for the labour candidates. Labour won twenty-four seats on the new council. Among those to lose their seat was the outgoing mayor Michael Cusack. Just five of the eighteen 'merchants' candidates were successful.[38] The *Chronicle* also claimed that several of the sitting councillors that were returned should be regarded as 'labour' candidates because their success was the result of being supported by Daly. As soon as they were declared elected Alderman M. McDonnell, Alderman P. McDonnell and councillors Donnelly and Carr claimed that they were 'also representatives of labour'.[39]

The first sitting of the new council elected John Daly as mayor. The *Limerick Leader* report of the council meeting was headlined 'A PEOPLE'S PARLIAMENT'.[40] The election of the labour controlled council and of Daly as mayor created enormous expectations among the working classes in the city. Huge numbers attended council meetings in the expectation that the labour councillors would introduce policies to alleviate the plight of the poor. In particular the crowds concentrated on the issues of jobs and housing.

Almost immediately a row broke out over the nominations for High Sheriff and division emerged within the labour group.[41] Divisions like this within the labour group were to become a regular feature of the new council. Daly regularly vacillated on issues and provoked consternation among the working class supporters of the labour council. The labour councillors isolated themselves for their support base. There was no democratic control exercised over the labour group by the Trades Council or the working class in general. The labour group met only among themselves to decide their approach to corporation matters, often resulting in division among the councillors and all the while ignoring the attitude of the working class. As the labour group became increasingly divided, the merchants exploited the conflict and the working classes became increasingly frustrated.

The council was now lurching from crisis to crisis. On issue after issue divisions emerged within the labour group. Meetings to discuss the amalgamation of the GS&WR and the W&LR saw large-scale protests by workers. As the crowds became increasingly hostile, Daly and other labour councillors reacted with indignation. Daly informed one council meeting that he had instructed his 'Sergeants'[42] not to admit anyone without his permission. The locked out crowd became increasingly restless and burst through the door into the now crowded public gallery. As Daly adjourned the meeting he was heckled and hissed moving through the crowd. A voice was heard shouting that the old Corporation 'never turned us out' and it was some time before the crowd dispersed with supporters of Daly confronting the large crowd of the labouring class in attendance.[43]

The Tram System Crisis

One commitment given by the labour candidates during the election was to oppose the establishment of a tram system in the city to protect the employment of jarveys, carmen and carters. In May 1899 the hackney drivers formed a trade union in an attempt to protect their jobs. [44] Subsequently the city's carmen met with Daly to remind him that he and the labour candidates had promised before the election to do everything in their power to keep trams out of Limerick. They outlined that 300 carmen, jarveys and drivers, not including the men working for various establishments in the city, would lose their livelihood if the scheme was introduced. Daly listened to their complaints but avoided giving any commitments to the union.[45] The proposal for a tramway system split the trade unions. The guild of masons supported the proposal because of the employment the masons would receive from its construction. [46] In October labourers held a series of protests in support of the tramway project. Hostility broke out between the labourers and the carmen during one of the protests when a number of jarveys attacked the crowd, before being dragged away by the police.[47] One of the labour councillors, John O'Brien, was expelled from the labour group for supporting the carmen and called on to resign his seat because he was elected 'through the influence of the Labour Electoral Association'.[48]

Large crowds assembled when the council was debating the tramway scheme with the night-watch deployed to control the crowd. Fighting broke out in the public gallery between supporters and opponents of the tramway and abuse was hurled at the councillors. The watchmen used batons to drive back the crowd outside the council chamber. Rioting broke out in Patrick Street and Rutland Street until the police eventually dispersed the crowd. Daly had to be escorted home by the night-watch, while the police attempted to control the crowd.[49]

The labour group was now split three ways with a group supporting the introduction of a full tram system, a group supporting passenger trams but opposed to freight trams and finally a group opposed to the entire project.[50] When the labour group met to discuss the issue in the Town Hall a large demonstration met them. Daly demanded that the group should vote for or against the scheme as a split on the issue 'might result in very serious consequences'. A majority supported the project but there was no agreement. Fighting later broke out amng workers in Little Catherine Street over the issue. [51]

The tramway company made a series of assurances to try and bring the controversy to an end. These included that haulage would be from the railway station to the docks and quays, carmen made redundant as a result of the scheme would receive preference in employment with the tramway and carmen who did not receive employment would be compensated. The committee voted to adopt the guarantees and bring them before the full council.[52]

These and a series of other controversies undermined the support for the labour group on the city council among the working class. The open enthusiasm and expectations of workers for the council they had elected was replaced by cynicism and despair. The labour group was riven with divisions with councillors being expelled and others resigning from the group. By the end of the year the labour group was fractured and many labour councillors were operating as independents. One of the labour councillors, Michael Joyce became nationalist MP for Limerick, holding his seat with the support of the Irish Party until 1918.

The enthusiastic support for Daly also dwindled. He was no longer seen as the radical, anti-establishment figure that led to his election as mayor. During November 1899 he attended a meeting in Limerick hosted for a speaker from the Fabian Society in London. Daly received an openly hostile reception from the workers who attended the lecture. [53] Within two years only eight of the twenty-four labour councillors elected in 1899 were still sitting on the council.[54] One of the labour candidates elected in 1904 was John Cronin, future chairman of the Trades Council during the Limerick Soviet.

Limerick Trades Council – A Bastion of Conservatism

The collapse of support for the labour group on the city council was in part the result of the remaining labour councillors becoming increasingly identified with the nationalist movement and were completely enmeshed in the workings of the corporation and the interests of the city's merchants. The conservativism demonstrated by the Trades in their approach to building the labour movement and an independent labour voice for the working classes repeatedly undermined any political advances for the working class. This was demonstrated on several occasions by the actions of Limerick delegates at conferences of the Irish Trade Union Congress. Limerick delegates opposed a motion from William Walker who proposed that the education system should be free from denominational control.[55]

Limerick Trades Council was to the fore in promoting a conservative outlook. In 1906 when John Murphy moved a Belfast motion recommending affiliation of the Irish Trade Union Congress (ITUC)[56] to the Labour Representation Committee, Murphy argued that the trade union movement should have a distinct labour party. P. Hayes from Limerick arguing against stated that 'the Irish Party is everything that labour requires... National Unity was the primary consideration...' Hayes proposed an amendment that Murphy should 'confine his scheme to the North of Ireland' as 'its representatives had in all cases voted against the interests of labour'. Seconding the amendment from Hayes, Limerick labour councillor M. Leahy suggested it might be a good plan North of the Boyne 'but any man from the South who would try to put a man purely on a labour ticket... should be inside a lunatic asylum'. Delegates who were members of Sinn Fein worked to ensure the defeat of both proposals. The amendment from Limerick was defeated by 31-17 by a combination of Belfast delegates and Sinn Fein delegates against the constitutional nationalists. The original motion from Murphy was defeated by 33-18 by a combination of Sinn Fein delegates and constitutional nationalists.[57] *Boyle* comments that, at the time, the neglect by the craft trades for the plight of labourers emphasised the weakness of trade union organisation among labourers and the unrepresentative nature of Congress.[58]

As always there were contrasting views among the Limerick delegates. At the same conference in 1906 a prominent activist from the Bakers Union in Limerick, Ben Dineen, made an unequivocal socialist address to Congress calling on all delegates to 'come join in the only battle'.[59] Dineen was later to become one of the most prominent socialist advocates within the Limerick trade union movement, establishing the *Bottom Dog* as a workers newspaper and assisting with the establishment of the ITGWU in 1917. In an attempt to cut across the racidalism of the ITGWU and the *Bottom Dog*, the conservative elements on the Trades Council attempted to establish their own newspaper, *The Worker*. Lacking the radical approach of Dineen this new newspaper failed to make any kind of an impact.[60] Unfortunately Dineen's life was cut short when he died during the flu pandemic that swept through Europe at the end of 1918. Just as the Limerick working class were entering the stage of history it was deprived of one of its most voal advocates.

The political outlook of the leaders of the Congregated Trades was rooted in a nationalist outlook. This was a reflection of a conservative approach to politics and a desire to influence nationalist opinion. This conservative approach led to a rejection of the idea of an independent approach by labour towards politics. It wasn't until mass pressure from below forced the leadership of the Trades to act that they mobilised in opposition to the nationalist establishment, although this tended to take the form of limiting the independent political demands of the labour movement and subverting them to nationalist forces. Pockets of radical opposition did exist with Connolly's Irish Socialist Republican Party having a small support base in Limerick by 1900[61] and radical socialists like Ben Dineen did emerge after the turn of the century. It was not until the emergence of the ITGWU in 1917 that a political radicalisation and a growing class consciousness of the Limerick working class occurred.

The disillusionment that resulted from the disintegration of the 'People's Parliament' had a serious impact on the labour movement in the city. For a decade and a half there was little or no industrial conflict, and what conflict did exist was largely confined to the semi-skilled and unskilled workers, in particular the dock labourers and the railway workers. A failed attempt was made to establish a branch of the ITGWU at some point in 1913, but it was not until 1917 and the subsequent establishment of ITGWU in September of that year that workers moved back into struggle.

Ireland was engulfed in a strike wave beginning in 1918 and carrying on right through the entire period of the War of Independence and Civil War. During a two-year period from 1918-1920 three national general strikes and at least eighteen local general strikes took place.[62] Much of this industrial conflict centred around the ITGWU and in particular an expanding group of radical and left-wing 'industrial organisers' who were the full-time union organisers around the country. Many of these industrial organisers were Marxists, including a number of the most prominent based in Limerick, Sean Dowling, Jack McGrath and at a later stage, English Marxist, Jack Hedley. These individuals were to play a crucial role at different times in practically every industrial dispute in Limerick city and county during the revolutionary period.

In particular, Sean Dowling was to emerge as one of the most important trade union and socialist activists in Ireland during the revolutionary period. Dowling was a key figure in the growth of the ITGWU and the emergence of Soviets in Munster during the War of Independence and into the civil war. Yet his role has been almost completely ignored by the historical works that have been written of this period, including by labour historians.

The outlook of these Marxist industrial organisers was syndicalist in nature. Syndicalism emphasised the federalist nature of workers organisations rather than central control, coupled with the view that revolutionary objectives could be achieved by building one trade union and focusing on the general strike as the primary weapon for revolutionary change. While not fully adopting a syndicalist approach to the workers movement, the Marxists in Ireland who adopted a syndicalist viewpoint failed to understand the necessity, from a Marxist viewpoint, of building a revolutionary party.[63] While Connolly, with the Irish Socialist Republican Party and the Socialist Party of Ireland, and later Dowling with the Revolutionary Socialist Party, established political groupings, none of these operated as a basis for establishing a revolutionary party.

Sean Dowling and the Irish Transport and General Workers Union in Limerick

In September 1917 M.J. O'Connor from Tralee arrived in Limerick as industrial organiser for the ITGWU.[64] O'Connor was to leave Limerick to take over as General Secretary of the Irish Automobile Drivers and Mechanics Union (IADMU) being replaced by John (Sean) Dowling from Cobh. From its establishment in September 1917 until the end of the Civil War, the ITGWU had a pivotal impact on the economic, political and social life of Limerick city and county. The ITGWU was the driving force behind the development and expansion of the Limerick labour movement, rapidly recruiting more than 3,000 workers, including women workers[65] and developing branches of the ITGWU among rural and agricultural labourers in County Limerick.

Sean Dowling was to become the key influential figure in the development and radicalisation of the Limerick labour movement during this period. He was born in Cobh on 12 May 1885[66] and became as committed Marxist at a young age joining Connolly's Irish Socialist Republican Party.[67] Dowling trained as an engine fitter in Haulbowline Dockyard[68] and in 1914 became the first worker to be sacked from his job and prohibited to reside in 'any munitions making area' as a result of campaigning against participation in World War One.[69] A week before the Easter Rising, Dowling attended a meeting in Room No.7 in Liberty Hall where he pleaded with Connolly to allow him remain in Dublin to participate in the Rising. Instead Connolly ordered Dowling out of Dublin,[70] in all likelihood to ensure he would avoid being killed or captured during the Rising.

Dowling began his work as an ITGWU industrial organiser in Tullamore at the same time O'Connor was arriving in Limerick. Within months Dowling had organised ITGWU branches throughout Laois and Offaly. In November 1917, when Dowling recruited workers in Russell's Sawmills in Portarlington the employers locked-out the workers. The lockout lasted for eight months. The striking workers received enormous support from the local community. On 6 January there was a mass picket outside the Sawmills that resulted in Dowling being arrested by the police. He was brought to Mountjoy where he was badly beaten for refusing to answer questions. Sean Dowling went on hunger strike following his arrest and was subsequently released after three days. It took Dowling a further week to recover from the injuries inflicted during his interrogation before he returned to the picket line in Portarlington.[71]

John Cronin and the Limerick United Trades and Labour Council

With the arrival of the ITGWU in Limerick the landscape for working class struggle was immediately transformed. The labour representatives on the City Council played, very much, an auxiliary role supporting the interests of the IPP representatives. Those labour representatives who succeeded in getting elected to the city council, including future Soviet Committee Chairperson John Cronin, were regularly accused by Sinn Fein of using their council membership for patronage and corruption, and not without reason.[72]

The conservative nature of the Trades Council was further emphasised by the fact that labourers unions were excluded from membership and participated in their own body, the Limerick Federated Labour Council (LFLC).[73] It was further enforced by the LUTLC's ongoing support for the Irish Parliamentary Party (IPP) and it auxiliary organisations the Town Tenants League, the United Irish League and the Irish Land

and Labour Association (ILLA) right up to early 1917. The local clergy was also allowed or invited to regularly intervene in trade union affairs.[74]

The attitude of elements within the LUTLC towards the Irish Labour Party and Trade Union Congress (ILPTUC) at this time was demonstrated during a meeting on 11 February 1916. Mr. McConkey of the Amalgamated Society of Engineers (ASE) stated that the Council should not pay any money towards the national body as it 'had departed from the original standards laid down and had become more of a socialist clique'. He was supported by, among others, John Cronin. Cronin, critical of the ILPTUC leadership, claimed that 'the movement was being run by men who never worked at any trade or labour' and 'were simply using the trade union movement for their own ends.'[75]

Workers among the trades threatened by mechanisation, facing wage cuts and job losses, and who had previously engaged in struggle formed a more radical wing on the LUTLC. The most prominent representative of this wing was the Bakers Union representative on the Trades Council, Ben Dineen. Dineen was moving in a leftward direction under the influence of Sean Dowling when he died in November 1918 during the Spanish flu pandemic that swept through Europe. He died after leading a long and difficult strike organised by the city's Bakers Society.[76] However, it was the general unions that formed the backbone of the initial upsurge in industrial action in 1917.

Strike action in Limerick in 1916 was non-existent. However, during 1917 rising prices and stagnant wages, coupled with poverty and slum housing, led to growing social and industrial unrest. Print workers started a weeklong strike on 16 March 1917 winning an immediate 4s wage increase[77] with a further 3s three months later.[78] The first of many disputes on Limerick docks began on 23 March with a strike among dock labourers that was to last until May.[79] Two hundred coalyard workers went on a weeklong strike at the beginning of April winning a 3s increase.[80] Strikes were also threatened in other industries with pay increases being granted to carpenters and joiners,[81] railway workers,[82] postal employees[83] and masons and bricklayers.[84]

The stirrings of radicalisation began affecting even the conservative layers on the LUTLC. Limerick Chamber of Commerce expressed their concern at the upsurge in strike activity[85] and calls started for the establishment of a conciliation board to arbitrate disputes,[86] an issue that was to be a continuous bone of contention between the conservative layers on the Trades Council who supported its establishment and the radical elements who preferred to win wages increases through strike action. The mood of workers in the city had altered with the willingness to engage in strike action growing. The ITGWU stepped into this developing situation in the second half of 1917.

[1] V. I. Lenin, 'Class War in Dublin', *Severnaya Pravda,* No. 23, August 29, 1913, in *Collected Works*, Volume 19, (Moscow, 1977) pages 332-336.

[2] Timothy Moloney, *Limerick Constitutional Nationalism 1898-1918: Change and Continuity,* (Newcastle-upon-Tyne, 2010) p. 30

[3] Shane Kenna, *Jeremiah O'Donovan Rossa: Unrepentant Fenian,* (Kildare, 2015) p. 195

[4] Ibid., p. 194-195

[5] *Limerick Chronicle,* 18 March 1890

[6] *Freemans Journal,* 14 October 1893

[7] In July 1891 a delegate from the Limerick General Labourers Union attended a national conference of labour unions in Dublin. *Limerick Chronicle,* 14 July 1891

[8] *Limerick Chronicle,* 18 6 February 1894

[9] In July 1894 the Trades Council held a meeting for the workers in the mineral water stores in the city to organise a union in their workplaces. *Limerick Chronicle,* 31 July 1894

[10] *Limerick Chronicle,* 3 May 1894

[11] The largest meeting took place on 6 April at the O'Connell Monument. *Limerick Chronicle,* 7 April 1894

[12] *Limerick Chronicle* 1 May 1894

[13] *Limerick Chronicle* 14 July 1894

[14] Moloney, *Limerick Constitutional Nationalism 1898-1918,* pp. 14-16

[15] Ibid., p. 29

[16] *Limerick Chronicle* 15 May 1897

[17] *Limerick Chronicle* 10 August 1897

[18] *Limerick Chronicle* 5 October 1897

[19] The tailors strike began in May 1898 and lasted until December

[20] *Limerick Chronicle* 25 October, 27 October 1898 & 29 October 1898, *Freemans Journal,* 31 October 1898, *Nenagh Guardian,* 29 October 1898

[21] *Limerick Chronicle* 20 December 1898

[22] Enda McKay, 'The Limerick Municipal Elections, January 1899', *The Old Limerick Journal,* Volume 36, (Winter 1999), p. 9

[23] *Limerick Leader* 29 September 1898

[24] McKay, p. 4

[25] *Limerick Leader* 14 October 1898

[26] *Limerick Leader* 14 October 1898

[27] *Limerick Chronicle* 22 November 1898

[28] *Limerick Chronicle* 24 November 1898

[29] *Limerick Chronicle* 8 December 1898

[30] *Limerick Chronicle* 15 December 1898

[31] *Limerick Leader* 9 December 1898

[32] McKay, p. 5

[33] *Limerick Chronicle* 20 December 1898

[34] *Limerick Chronicle* 10 January 1899

[35] McKay, p. 5

[36] Ibid., p. 7

[37] Ibid., p. 6

[38] *Limerick Chronicle* 17 January 1899.

[39] *Limerick Chronicle* 21 January 1899

[40] *Limerick Leader* 23 January 1899.

[41] *Limerick Chronicle* 24 January 1899

[42] These 'Sergeants' would have been a close group of supporters around Daly

[43] *Limerick Chronicle* 2 February & 4 February 1899

[44] *Limerick Chronicle* 25 May 1899

[45] *Limerick Chronicle* 7 September 1899

[46] *Limerick Chronicle* 21 September 1899

[47] *Limerick Chronicle* 5 October 1899

[48] *Limerick Chronicle* 7 October 1899

[49] *Limerick Chronicle* 21 October 1899

[50] *Limerick Chronicle* 24 October 1899

[51] *Limerick Chronicle* 24 October 1899

[52] *Limerick Chronicle* 26 October 1899

[53] *Limerick Chronicle* 11 November 1899

[54] David Lee and Debbie Jacobs (eds), *Limerick Municipal Elections 1841-2009*, (Limerick, 2009), p.76

[55] Boyle, *The Irish Labour Movement in the Nineteenth Century*, p.238

[56] The Irish Trade Union Congress was renamed the Irish Labour Party and Trade Union Congress after 1912

[57] Ibid., p.234-235

[58] Ibid., p.239

[59] Ibid., p.221

[60] Cahill, *Forgotten Revolution*, p. 39

[61] O'Connor, *A Labour History of Ireland 1824-1960*, p. 64

[62] Peter Hadden, *Troubled Times, The National Question in Ireland*, (Belfast, 1995), p.25

[63] For an outline of the nature of syndicalism in the Irish trade union movement during this period see: Cillian Gillespie, 'The Life and Ideas of James Connolly', in Cillian Gillespie (ed.), *Ireland's Lost Revolution 1916-1923: The Working Class and the Struggle for Socialism*, (London, 2016), pp. 17-48

[64] Greaves, *The Irish Transport and General Workers Union*, p. 190

[65] *Limerick Leader*, 14 June 1918.

[66] John Dowling baptismal record, Parish of Cobh (Accessed on 02/12/2013)

[67] Jack Hedley, 'Sean Dowling', *Irish Democrat*, February 1949.

[68] 1911 Census, [Available at http://www.census.nationalarchives.ie/reels/nai001909785/] & *Cork Examiner*, 30 November 1948.

[69] Hedley,

[70] Hedley,

[71] Greaves, *The Irish Transport and General Workers Union*, p. 192. For a more comprehensive biography of Sean Dowling see: Dominic Haugh, 'Sean Dowling', in John Cunningham & Emmet O'Connor (eds), *Radical Irish Lives* (Manchester, 2016).

[72] *The Factionalist*, 12 April 1917

[73] The LFLC had the affiliation of societies representing unskilled and semi-skilled workers, Bread Vanmen's Society, Ballast Carters Society, United Car and Storemen, Dock Labourers Society, Corporation Employees Society, Gas Workers Society, Quarrymen and Builders Labourers Society, Pork Butchers Society, Engine Drivers and Firemens Society, Hired Carmens Society and the Corporation Workmen's Trade Union.

[74] Tom Crean, *The Labour Movement in Kerry and Limerick 1914-1921, PhD Thesis*, (Trinity College Dublin, 1996), p. 135-137

[75] *Limerick Leader,* 18 February 1916.

[76] *Limerick Leader,* 14 October 1918 & 22 November 1918

[77] *Limerick Leader,* 16 March 1917.

[78] *Limerick Leader*, 23 June 1917.

[79] *Limerick Leader,* 14 May 1917.

[80] *Limerick Leader,* 16 April 1917.

[81] *Limerick Leader,* 18 April 1917.

[82] *Limerick Leader,* 25 April 1917.

[83] *Limerick Leader,* 4 May 1917.

[84] *Limerick Leader,* 30 May 1917.

[85] *Limerick Leader,* 23 April 1917.

[86] *Limerick Leader,* 14 May 1917.

THE RADICALISATION OF THE WORKING CLASS IN LIMERICK

'a free Ireland must mean freedom for Irish workers'
—John Byrne, Secretary Limerick No.3 branch, ITGWU. 1918

The establishment of the ITGWU in Limerick coincided with ongoing union organisation among asylum workers, clerks and assistants, auto drivers and mechanics and strike action or threatened action by law clerks, gas workers, electric light workers, insurance collectors, plumbers, dock workers and coal workers at Limerick Railway Station and workers at O'Donnell's Tannery.[1] Many of these workers were to affiliate to the rapidly growing ITGWU. On 9 October 1917 the ITGWU No. 1 Branch applied for affiliation to the LUTLC.[2]

Limerick docks was the scene for on-going industrial unrest, and, by the end of 1917, business interests were already recognising the potential impact of the ITGWU in the city. A strike was organised by the Dock Labourers Society, and including coal workers at the Railway Station, began on 28 December, actively supported by the ITGWU. The dispute ended on 1 January with increases of 8s for day rate and 11s for night rate being granted.[3] Subsequently the dock workers affiliated to the ITGWU and were to become the backbone of the wider labour movement in Limerick during this period, repeatedly engaging in solidarity strike action and supporting other workers in struggle.

In January the RIC Inspector General's report noted that:

> 'at Limerick the branch of the Transport Union objected to the erection of an electric crane at the docks on the grounds that it would lessen employment. The parts of the crane are lying at the railway station and the carters refuse to move them'.[4]

A further dispute arose with the refusal of coal workers at Limerick Railway Station to load coal. This led the railway companies to refuse to bring coal to Limerick. The Chamber of Commerce demanded action and the local merchants began the construction of carriages for electric cranes on the docks.[5] This led to the dock workers engaging in strike action. support given by the ITGWU was clearly having an impact amongst wider layers of the labour movement in the city.

Police reinforcements were brought in from outside the city to continue the work.[6] On the night of Wednesday 6 February, one of the crane carriages was rolled into the River Shannon[7] and on the 14 February a crowd followed, and threw stones at men carting the machinery to the docks.[8] Subsequently claims for a reduction in working hours were lodged by the ITGWU in early April.[9] The employers responded by locking-out the carters and yardmen in late May.[10] Following an arbitration hearing the arbitrator awarded significant increases to the workers involved with the carters' wages rising from 30s to 38s and granted the workers the 8.am start they sought.[11]

Rising Industrial Conflict

February 1918 also saw the beginning of a bitter dispute at Drombana creamery that lasted several months.[12] The dispute broke out following the sacking of a butter-maker. The strike was organised by Drombana Creamery Workers Society.[13] The creamery remained open as a result of scabbing by a number of farmers' sons but ran up an overdraft of £4,000 during the first two months of the strike.[14] As with the lockout on the docks, the ITGWU actively supported the strike. The workers joined the ITGWU on 3 March with a new branch being established in Drombana.[15]

The impact of the ITGWU was now being clearly felt. By the end of January 1918 three branches had been established.[16] There were also signs of the developing political consciousness among certain sections of workers. At a general meeting of the Limerick No.3 ITGWU Branch, secretary, Mr J. Byrne, said they 'were near great political changes in the country'. Byrne argued for Connolly's ideal, 'that a free Ireland must mean freedom for Irish workers'. At the same meeting M.J. O'Connor claimed that the Union was 'not merely a wage-increasing organisation' but that they wanted to 'educate the worker', and tackle the housing and food crises.[17] The raising of political issues was to create tensions between the ITGWU and the leadership of the Trades Council as the year progressed.

The *Voice of Labour* reported that 'on the whole Limerick employers with whom negotiations have been opened up have readily recognised the One Big Union'.[18] A major advance was secured by the agreement of Cleeves to operate a closed shop and book its additional staff through the Union. [19] Strikes involving the ITGWU occurred on a regular basis. Hardware employees at Spaight's were out for four days in April winning union recognition and higher wages.[20] A strike resulting from the employment of non-union labour by forage contractor Mr. J.J. Foley also ended in favour of the union.[21] Workers at Clune's Tobacco Co. went on strike on 9 August for union recognition and a wage increase.[22] Gas workers, who had joined the ITGWU two months earlier, were out on 24 August[23] and 250 workers at O'Callaghan's Tannery went on strike on 18 October.[24]

In contrast to other parts of the country where the ITGWU supported the Irish Women Workers Union (IWWU) in the recruitment of women workers, in Limerick the ITGWU recruited women directly into its newly formed women's branch. The branch actively engaged in organising women workers in the city, winning wage increases for, among others, women earning 8s per week in Cannock's.[25] The women's branch of the ITGWU affiliated to the LUTLC in June.[26]

Many of the craft representatives on the Trades Council demonstrated a chauvinistic attitude towards the women members of the ITGWU and this was to cause repeated tensions between the craft unions and the ITGWU in the following period. The LUTLC leaders refused to recognise the female members of the ITGWU as full members of the trade union movement in Limerick because they paid a lower subscription rate than male workers. Part of the reason for this attitude among the craft union leaders was because if they recognised the female ITGWU members it would have given the ITGWU increased influence on the Trades Council to the detriment of the craft unions.

The ITGWU also turned its attention to organising workers in County Limerick. Newspaper reports show that branches were quickly established in Croom and Patrickswell, Kilmallock, Newcastle West, Askeaton, Adare, Bulgaden, Effin, Ardpatrick and Dromin.[27] The expansion of the ITGWU into rural Limerick saw it come into direct conflict with the ILLA.[28] The failure of the ILLA to secure wage increases for road workers in the county saw these workers establish a separate organisation that eventually joined the ITGWU. The end result of this phase of activity was to see the virtual disappearance of the ILLA within the county.[29] As workers became increasingly radicalised the British state (with the support of nationalists) moved to curtail the activities of ITGWU activists. The RIC began raiding the homes of activists, confiscating documents and attempting to disrupt the campaigning work of the ITGWU.[30] Their efforts were in vain. By the end of 1918 the ITGWU had four large branches in Limerick City and nineteen branches in the county organising rural workers.[31]

The Conscription Crisis

The general strike against conscription in April 1918 was a key development for the Labour Movement in Ireland and in Limerick. The Conscription Crisis posed the first of a series of opportunities for the labour movement in Ireland to place itself at the head of the movement for national self-determination and engage in that struggle on a class basis. The power of the Labour Movement was demonstrated to such a degree that the British government were forced to abandon their plans for conscription in Ireland.

However, rather than adopt an independent class position on the issue of conscription, the leadership of the ILPTUC consciously engaged with and encouraged a cross-class campaign involving Sinn Fein, the Irish Parliamentary Party and the Catholic hierarchy. Only four years earlier the leadership of the IPP had called for men to join the British army and be slaughtered in the interests of British Imperialism. The ILPTUC representatives on the Anti-Conscription Committee, William O'Brien, Thomas Johnson and Maurice Egan, assured the other parties that they would ensure the labour movement would play a subservient role in the campaign. In particular, Egan, a craft worker from Cork, was a noted arch-conservative. He had previously opposed the affiliation of the ITGWU to the ILPTUC and had repeatedly attempted to get Jim Larkin expelled from the ILPTUC. Not alone were the leadership of the ILPTUC unwilling to lead an independent labour movement campaign against conscription, they consciously sabotaged it.

Under pressure from the ITGWU the Trades Council in Limerick organised protests against conscription in Limerick independent of the nationalist movement and the Catholic hierarchy. When all the forces of Irish nationalism combined, they mustered approximately 15,000 on the streets, many of them workers who attended because of the issue rather than in support of the nationalist movement. The following day a labour demonstration saw more than 25,000 on the streets of Limerick marching behind a banner emblazoned by a picture of James Connolly and the slogan 'Death Before Conscription'.[32] The speeches at the demonstration reflected the growing class consciousness among Limerick workers.

One clear example of the conservatism of the ILPTUC leadership, and their willingness to compromise with nationalism, was their failure to call workers in the North-East out in support of the general strike. Despite the enthusiastic endorsement of a general strike against conscription by 1,500 delegates at an emergency conference of the ILPTUC, O'Brien and other leaders regarded the Protestant working class as unionist in outlook.

The reality was the opposite. Despite not being called out on strike, more than 20,000 workers in Belfast participated in an anti-conscription rally organised by Belfast Trades Council, the majority of them Protestants.[33] The following Thursday there was a major demonstration against conscription in Belfast. Similar protests took place in other locations in the North. In Ballycastle, County Antrim, Catholic and Protestant workers marched together with bands playing *The Boyne Water* and *A Nation Once Again*.

This was echoed at the Mayday protest in Limerick a week later. 15,000 marched through the streets to a mass meeting around three platforms in the Market's Field sports ground. A report in the Limerick Leader indicates that class consciousness was continuing to develop, as can be seen from the fact that resolutions were passed paying tribute to 'our Russian comrades who have waged a magnificent struggle for their social and political emancipation' and a ten-point pledge that concluded with the following statement:

> "...we pledge ourselves in the name of the oppressed of every land in every age to use all means that may be deemed effective to achieve those objectives".[34]

1918 General Election

The Annual Meeting of the ILPTUC took place in Waterford in August 1918. At the conference E. O'Carroll of the Railway Clerks Association proposed the following motion that was passed unanimously:

> 'That in view of the possibility of a General Election – Parliamentary and municipal—at an early date, this Congress urges upon all organised workers and friends of Labour the absolute necessity for immediate preparation for such a contingency by the setting up of the essential Labour machinery in every municipal and Parliamentary constituency, where this is found practicable, so that the voice and voting power of Labour (which has been considerably strengthened as a result of the passing into law of the Representation of the People Act), may be effectively demonstrated in the election results'.

The proposal went on to outline the steps that should be taken to establish functioning labour parties in each area to prepare for the election.[35]

For most of the year the ILPTUC was laying plans to run candidates in the expected general election. Sinn Fein were operating on the expectation that Labour would run candidates and attempted to negotiate an agreement with the leadership of the ILPTUC. Sinn Fein wanted Labour to adopt an abstentionist policy for the election and offered to give Labour a free run in four Dublin constituencies in return.

The situation caused a major dilemma for the leadership of the ILPTUC. Accommodating Sinn Fein would undermine the position of the ILPTUC among Protestant workers. Aligning themselves with nationalism opened up the real prospect of a split in the trade union movement in the North. The leadership also felt that if they didn't back Sinn Fein they would be accused of not supporting self-determination.

The reality is that this dilemma for the leadership of the ILPTUC was of their own making. The general strike against conscription demonstrated that the ILPTUC could have taken the leadership in the struggle for the economic, social and political emancipation of the working class, leading the campaign for national self-determination on a clear class basis. Instead of adopting an independent class-based approach the ILPTUC leadership engaged in a cross-class alliance with the forces of Irish nationalism.

The 1918 General Election presented another opportunity for the leadership of the ILPTUC to forge an independent class-based approach to the struggle for self-determination. Once again, they were found wanting. At a Special Conference on 1-2 November 1918 the ILPTUC leadership, unable to square the circle of their own creation, instead of changing their outlook decided instead to just abandon their responsibility to the working class on this island and opted out of the election by deciding not to stand any candidates.

The night before the Conference the National Executive met to organise their intervention at the Conference and ensure that their planned withdrawal from the election was supported. The Conference started with an attack by Thomas Foran and William O'Brien on the National Sailors' and Firemen's Union (NSFU) who were accused of 'playing the capitalists game' – with the specific accusation that the NSFU had refused to carry Belgian social democrat, Camille Huysmans, Secretary of the Second International, to a meeting in London. The NSFU were accused by O'Brien of being 'the scabs of the movement'. The NSFU were noted for supporting the British war effort during World War One, but much of the attacks on the NSFU at the opening of the conference was couched in anti-British sentiment and designed to whip up nationalist sentiment among delegates. Ultimately the conference delegates voted to expel the NSFU delegates from the conference.[36]

Thomas Johnson, Treasurer of the ILPTUC, was given the job of managing the conference and pushing the proposal from the National Executive to withdraw from the election. The basis of the argument for withdrawal was that the ILPTUC expected the general election to be a 'war' election and the plan was to promote the notion

> 'that the Irish Republic— if such were to be the form of Government determined upon by a people guaranteed the right to choose its own sovereignty, - should be a Workers' Republic, not an imitation of those Republics of Europe and America, where political democracy is but a cloak for capitalist oligarchy'.[37]

Johnson argued that the conditions had now changed, and they were facing a 'peace' election, that

> 'The Grand Inquest about to be opened, has for a jury the nations of the world, the verdict will be given according to the weight of evidence adduced, and that will depend upon the degree of unanimity marked at the polls on the demand for self-determination... Your Executive believes that the workers of Ireland join earnestly in this desire, that

they would willingly sacrifice, for a brief period, their aspirations towards political power if thereby the fortunes of the nation can be enhanced'.[38]

Adopting an overtly nationalist position, Johnson abandoned any pretext of class politics, stating that the National Executive propose to withdraw from the election

'in the hope that the democratic demand for self-determination, to which the Irish Labour Party and its candidates give their unqualified adherence, will thereby obtain the freest chance of expression at the polls. We shall show by this action that, while each of the other political parties is prepared to divide the people in their effort to obtain power, the Labour Party is the only party which is prepared to sacrifice "party " in the interest of the Nation in this important crisis of the history of Ireland'.[39]

The abandonment of class interests by the leadership was given left cover by Thomas McPartlin, who claimed that

'because from first to last in connection with this election he was influenced solely by the good of the working classes. He had no other thought. Neither at the public meetings or the Conferences at any time did he advance any interests except those of the workers for whom he had always fought. His action that day in seconding the motion was influenced by the same motives. He had no consideration for any political party in Ireland. He was solely influenced by the amount of good it would do in keeping the workers of Ireland united for the fight that would come in the future... It was far more effective for them to have the industrial workers organised to fight the Capitalist class than to grip political power'.[40]

The reality of McPartlin's position was that the approach of the National Executive was creating division among the working class on the island, not 'keeping the workers of Ireland united'. He went on to claim that

'they would have to fight them [Sinn Fein] as they had to fight the rotten and corrupt party [the Irish Parliamentary Party] in 1914 - They would be another political mouthpiece of the capitalist class in this country. They would do probably the same as the others'.[41]

Yet McPartlin and the leadership of the ILPTUC were willing to give this 'political mouthpiece of the capitalist class' a free run in the elections just over a year after the victorious Russian Revolution.

D.R. Campbell from Belfast Trades Council, a delegate by no means on the left politically, questioned the distinction between a 'war' election and a 'peace' election, arguing that the Labour Party was a political party, but now the National Executive wanted to withdraw the party from politics. Campbell argued that such an approach was a rejection of their policy to stick to a workers party and run candidates against all comers. Emphasising the dangers of withdrawing from the election, Campbell pointed out that by giving Sinn Fein a free run in the South they were also giving the Unionists a free run in the Northern counties. He criticised the idea that

'the national question so much transcended all other questions at the particular moment that all questions of the working classes of economic consideration or the really faithful representation of a class should be left in abeyance.'[42]

In an astonishing declaration, future Secretary of the Communist Party of Ireland (CPI), Walter Carpenter, stated that he 'did not believe that the working classes of Ireland were educated enough to justify the Executive in running candidates.'[43] A line of delegates were then produced to support the position of the National Executive. John Cronin, representing Limerick Trades Council, was among those delegates.

One dissenting voice was Thomas Murphy of the Irish Commercial Workers Union (ICWU). Murphy argued that

'Acting on the manifesto issued by the Executive, Dublin Trades Council held two special conferences and decided to fight four seats, for which candidates were selected, in the city of Dublin. They had some bitter fights, and at the last meeting of the Trades Council the recommendation of the two special Conferences was ratified. Now they found a recommendation asking them to forego their decision and to allow the political parties' wrangle for position and collar all the Parliamentary seats in Ireland. The Labour movement was the strongest movement they had in the country, and they were to sink their identity and allow the political parties to collar all the councils and representation of Ireland'.[44]

Murphy went on to outline that repeatedly in history,

'in the Repeal movement, the Tenant Right movement, in the land agitation of the eighties and the Home Rule movement they were asked by all the official political parties of the country during those agitations to come in and help them, and when they got what they were looking for the workers would be looked to afterwards'. In an insightful declaration Murphy argued that the delegates to the conference 'were now asked by their own Executive at this critical juncture to sink their views and Labour feelings and allow the political parties still to posses (sic) the field. They had Sinn Feiners, United Irish Leaguers and Carsonites, meeting regularly to decide how they could best divide the representatives of the workers when seeking an increase of wages, and the workers were to sink all their power and allow those people to collar the representation in Parliament and otherwise, and deprive them of the great advantage which they had taken in the industrial field'.[45]

Several ITGWU delegates questioned the decision of the leadership but when P.T. Daly attempted to speak, he was ruled out of order and the debate was closed. When Johnson attempted to reply to the debate he was heckled and then subsequently challenged by D.R. Campbell. Ultimately the decision to withdraw from the election was passed with ninety-six votes for the motion and twenty-three against.[46]

Following the election in December 1918 the First Dail met in the Mansion House on 21 January 1919. Three documents were read into the record of the First Dail, including the Democratic Programme. Shortly after the election Sinn Fein approached Thomas Johnson, then Treasurer of the ILPTUC, to write the first social and economic programme for the Dail. The Sinn Fein leadership realised that they had to respond to increased radicalization of the Irish working class and they consciously selected a labour representative who was noted for undermining the power of the workers movement. As Johnson was prone to do, he wrote quite a radical document that was then severely amended by Sean T. O'Kelly.[47]

Johnson's left reformist and, from a Sinn Fein perspective, radical programme provoked consternation among the Sinn Fein leadership. Michael Collins called a meeting of the IRB the night before the Dail was due to meet and ordered the suppression of the Democratic Programme. It was only after major alterations throughout the night by O'Kelly, without reference to Johnson, that the Democratic Programme was put before the Dail. The attitude of the Sinn Fein leadership was outlined fifty years later by Ernest Blythe in 1969.[48] Blythe stated that 'The Labour Party secured the adoption of it. I don't think anybody, practically speaking, bothered with it afterwards. It was regarded as some sort of hoisting of a flag. It wasn't regarded as significant.' The Democratic Programme had served its purpose, giving left cover to the Sinn Fein leadership who never had the slightest intention of implementing it.[49]

The Dominance of the ITGWU

By January 1919 Sinn Fein had approximately 4,600 members in Limerick city and county.[50] However, the RIC were now reporting that the influence of the ITGWU was growing. By February RIC County Inspector Yeats reported that the ITGWU were overshadowing the active local Sinn Fein clubs. Once the initial attacks occurred in the War of Independence the police were reporting that the membership of Sinn Fein and the Irish Volunteers were static or showing minimal increase, while the ITGWU membership was increasing rapidly.[51]

The frequency and intensity of strike activity, particularly involving the ITGWU, increased dramatically in the early months of 1919. In rural areas strikes were breaking out with increasing regularity and incidents of threats and assaults during industrial disputes began to emerge. Women workers in the Model Laundry in Limerick city went on strike in mid-January followed by a strike by fifty Lax Weir fishermen in Parteen at the beginning of February. Twenty two workers at S.B. Walsh and Sons in Kilmallock went on strike for 10 days in late February resulting in wages increases.[52]

In March, strikes occurred at the Askeaton Carbide Works, again at the Lax Weir in Parteen, among farm labourers at Gubbins's farm in Kilfrush and workers at the Meenahela Creamery in Templeglantine. During the strike at Gubbins' farm, police were used to carry out the work of the striking labourers, while at Meenahela the *Voice of Labour* reported that union members were assaulted, and threats were made that they would be shot. Towards the end of the month, strikes were also taking place by ITGWU members at T.A. Walsh's in Kilmallock, on the lands of Sir Gilbert Greenall at Mount Coote and at Clouncagh Co-operative Creamery near Newcastle West. A strike at Drombana Creamery resulted in the re-instatement of sacked workers. Greenall brought in strikebreakers from Warrington during the strike.[53] During the course of the strike at Clouncagh, the manager of the creamery attacked strike leaders with a coal shovel but backed off when the union activists intimated that they were carrying guns.[54] Some days later a standoff occurred when a march by strikers was met by a body of farmer's sons armed with metal piping.[55]

Along with the strike activity by members of the ITGWU, disputes also occurred among the Limerick asylum workers, drapers assistants at McBirney's and among coachbuilders in the city in the two months prior to the Limerick Soviet. Numerous strike threats which ended in agreements for wage increases also occurred in the early months of 1919.[56]

Alongside the increased intensity of strike activity, the Trades Council engaged in an ongoing debate about political representation and labour politics. Divisions occurred on the Council, primarily between delegates from the ITGWU and delegates from of the craft unions. ITGWU delegate, John Byrne, proposed a labour programme in early 1918 and attempted to get the LUTLC to discuss it repeatedly over the following months.[57] When the craft unions eventually agreed to debate the programme they made every effort to stymie any progress towards setting up a mass Labour Party in the city, fearing that the ITGWU and, in particular, the Marxist elements within the ITGWU would push the Labour Party to the left. When the efforts to get the Trades Council to actively promote the establishment of a Labour Party failed, Byrne informed the council that the ITGWU activists intended to call a meeting to form a Labour Party to operate outside of the Trades Council structures. His reference to some council members seeing 'red' was a swipe at the craft union delegates who objected to the socialist content of the proposal.[58]

This conflict over a political programme and political organisation was a constant feature at Trades Council meetings[59] ultimately spilling over into the ILPTUC Special Congress in November 1918 that ultimately saw the withdrawal of the Labour Party from the 1918 general election. Limerick Trades Council delegates, John Cronin and James Casey, withdrew an amendment that would prevent the establishment of a Labour Party separate from the Trades Council.[60] The reason for the withdrawal became clear later when delegates from the LUTLC indicated that Tom Johnson, in a private discussion, told Cronin and Casey that ILPTUC would not allow a Labour group to be formed outside of any trades council structures.[61] The issue of a Labour Party was to surface again in the run up to the Local Elections in January 1920. The ITGWU again attempted to get the LUTLC to adopt a Labour programme but to no avail. Instead individual unions nominated their own candidates. When the issue was discussed at a LUTLC meeting, John Cronin said that 'Sinn Féin was ready to help on all matters'. Sean Dowling pointed out that republicans would not accept the ILPTUC's election programme to which Cronin replied that Labour's programme was 'ideal' but 'not workable under the present state'.[62]

On political issues the conservative layers repeatedly held back the labour movement from action. In July 1919, Dowling asked the Trades Council to endorse an upcoming meeting entitled 'Hands Off Russia', Cronin and others objected. The Council decided against supporting the meeting claiming there was 'a lack of sufficient notice'.[63] Despite the efforts of the ITGWU activists, the conservative elements on the Trades Council had succeeded in preventing the establishment of a radical Labour Party in Limerick and an opportunity to build a mass political formation to represent the interests of the working class and compete with Sinn Fein for the leadership of the local independence movement was lost.

Attacks on Socialism

Opposition to the growing radicalism in Limerick was also manifest in the response of the Catholic hierarchy and republicans. Shortly after the establishment of the ITGWU in Limerick, Rev. Fr. Devane called for the establishment of a 'Catholic Social League', arguing that the leaders of the Irish Labour Party should base their programme on 'sane Catholic social principles' and not on the 'irreligious Social Democrats of the continent'.[64] The Catholic hierarchy were to regularly lecture both at mass and outside the church against the evils of socialism, sometimes with the tacit support of the more conservative elements of the LUTLC. Three weeks before the Limerick 'Soviet', elements of the crafts unions and the local catholic hierarchy held a meeting to discuss 'Labour's right to decent wages'. The ITGWU were not invited to send a speaker.[65] A few days later Rev. Fr. Murphy gave the Lenten lecture in the Augustinian Church on the 'Legitimacy of Private Profit' again attacking socialism.[66]

Republican speakers and publications regularly dismissed the suggestion that socialism was an option in Ireland. At a Sinn Féin election meeting in Rathkeale in December 1918 speakers attacked socialism saying that it was a distraction to the national struggle and that socialism did not appeal to Irish people.[67] At the height of the Limerick 'Soviet' the nationalist *New Ireland* carried an article questioning:

> 'Can any sane man really advocate the handing over of say, Limerick or Cork to the local Trades Council? A Soviet, as I understand it, is a Council of the local workers, exercising political and economic power...Anyone who knows anything of the inner state of Irish Labour must realise how uneducated and narrow-minded and incompetent the workers are as yet'.[68]

However, the radicalism generated by the ITGWU had already sunk deep roots among the Limerick working class. The struggle of ITGWU delegates to politicise the Trades Council was impacting on class consciousness. In many respects the condemnation from the Catholic hierarchy and Sinn Fein had emboldened large numbers of workers in Limerick. When the Limerick Soviet burst onto the scene of history it was a demonstration of the developing radical and left outlook of the Limerick working class and allowed the workers of Limerick to show the strength of a united workers movement when it took power into its own hands.

---

[1] *Limerick Leader,* 22 October 1917, 29 October 1917, 10 December 1917, 12 September 1917, 10 October 1917, 12 October 1917, 14 November 1917, 31 December 1917, December 1917, 31 December 1917, & 2 January 1918. Voice of Labour, 12 January 1918.

[2] *Limerick Leader,* 12 October 1917

[3] *Limerick Leader,* 2 January 1918.

[4] Crean, *The Labour Movement in Kerry and Limerick,* p. 123.

[5] *Limerick Leader,* 21 January 1918.

[6] Crean, *The Labour Movement in Kerry and Limerick,* p. 123.

[7] *Limerick Leader,* 8 February 1918.

[8] Crean, *The Labour Movement in Kerry and Limerick,* p. 123.

[9] *Voice of Labour,* 13 April 1918.

[10] *The Bottom Dog,* 8 June 1918.

[11] *Voice of Labour,* 24 August 1918.

[12] Thomas Toomey & Harry Greensmyth, *An Antique and Storied Land, A History of the*

Parish of Donoughmore, Knockea, Roxborough, Co. Limerick and Its Environs, (Limerick, 1991), p.194

[13] *Voice of Labour*, 6 April 1918.

[14] *The Bottom Dog*, 6 April 1918.

[15] *Voice of Labour*, 9 March 1918.

[16] *Voice of Labour*, 9 February 1918.

[17] *Voice of Labour*, 9 February 1918.

[18] *Voice of Labour*, 9 March 1918.

[19] *Voice of Labour*, 6 July 1918.

[20] *Voice of Labour*, 6 April 1918.

[21] *Voice of Labour*, 6 April 1918

[22] *Limerick Leader*, 12 August 1918 & *Munster News*, 17 August 1918.

[23] *Limerick Leader*, 26 August 1918.

[24] *Limerick Leader*, 18 October 1918. O'Callaghan's Tannery was owned by Michael O'Callaghan, future Sinn Fein Mayor of Limerick. O'Callaghan was murdered by the British Military in March 1921.

[25] *Limerick Leader*, 29 May 1918, *The Bottom Dog*, 3 November 1917, *The Workers Dreadnought*, (Reproduced in) 'Women Workers in Monster Houses', in David Lee & Debbie Jacobs (eds), *Made in Limerick, History of Industries, Trade and Commerce, Volume 1*, (Limerick, 2003), p. 39

[26] *Limerick Leader*, 21 June 1918.

[27] *Limerick Leader*, 14 June 1918, 8 July 1918, 26 July 1918, 29 July 1918. *Voice of Labour*, 24 August 1918, 21 December 1918.

[28] *Voice of Labour*, 5 October 1918.

[29] *Limerick Leader*, 18 October 1918

[30] *Limerick Leader*, 16 August 1918.

[31] ITGWU *Annual Report* 1918

[32] *Limerick Leader*, 24 April 1918.

[33] Dillon, J. (1918) Military Services Bill, *House of Commons Debate*, 15 April 1918 (vol. 105 cc24-7), p.24.

[34] *Limerick Leader*, 5 May 1918

[35] Irish Labour Party and Trade Union Congress, *Report to the Twenty-Fourth Annual Meeting*, 1918, p. 64-65

[36] ILPTUC, *Report to the Twenty-Fourth Annual Meeting*, 1918, p. 95-99

[37] Ibid., p. 103

[38] Ibid., p. 104

[39] Ibid., p. 104

[40] Ibid., p. 105

[41] Ibid., p. 106

[42] Ibid., p. 107-108

[43] Ibid., p. 108

[44] Ibid.,, p. 112-113

[45] Ibid.,, p. 113

[46] Ibid.,, 1918, p. 113

[47] Sean T. O'Kelly subsequently fought on the anti-Treaty side in the civil war before serving as a Fianna Fail minister and later President.

[48] Ernest Blythe was a Sinn Fein TD who later became Minister for Finance in the Cumman na

Gaedheal government in the 1920s.

[49] For more information see: Niamh Puirseil, 'The Democratic Programme and the roots of the Republic', talk delivered at *Law, Revolution and Sovereignty: Reflections on the Legal Legacy of the 1916 Rising & Declaration of Independence Conference*, (9 April 2016)

[50] Cahill, *Forgotten Revolution*, p. 42

[51] Ibid., p. 43

[52] *Limerick Leader,* 31 January 1919, 21 February 1919. *Voice of Labour,* 8 February 1919, 1 March 1919 & *Munster News,* 19 February 1919.

[53] *Voice of Labour,* 15 March 1919, 23 March 1919, 19 April 1919. *Limerick Leader,* 26 March 1919, & *Munster News,* 12 April 1919.

[54] *Voice of Labour,* 19 April 1919.

[55] *Voice of Labour*, 26 April 1919.

[56] *Munster News,* 22 February 1919, 19 March 1919, 21 March 1919.

[57] *Limerick Leader*, 11 September 1918.

[58] *Limerick Leader*, 25 September 1918.

[59] *Limerick Leader*, 7 July 1919.

[60] Irish Labour Party and Trade Union Congress, *Special Conference Report,* 1918

[61] *Limerick Leader,* 18 November 1918

[62] Limerick United Trade and Labour Council, *Minutes,* 31 December 1919

[63] *Limerick Leader,* 7 July 1919.

[64] *Limerick Leader,* 15 October 1917.

[65] *Limerick Leader,* 24 March 1919.

[66] *Limerick Leader,* 28 March 1919.

[67] *Limerick Leader,* 4 December 1918.

[68] *New Ireland,* 19 April 1919.

GENERAL STRIKE IN LIMERICK

'Labour will swamp Sinn Fein'
— Constance Markevicz warning the Sinn Fein leadership during
the Limerick Soviet

The Limerick Soviet cannot be viewed in isolation from national and international events. In the immediate period before the Soviet, national newspapers were full of articles about the Russian Civil War, the Bavarian Soviet, the Hungarian Soviet and numerous other uprisings by workers during March and April 1919.[1] The impact of the Russian Revolution was front and centre in the commentary of international developments. As was demonstrated during the Mayday protest in Limerick in 1918, the Russian Revolution had raised the class consciousness of the Limerick working class.

Similarly, Irish papers were also filled with articles about strike action throughout the country.[2] Only days before the Limerick Soviet, three striking labourers were shot and wounded by farmers in Co. Down and four labourers were arrested after a confrontation with farmers in Listowel.[3] Reports on ongoing and newly emerging strike action were a daily occurrence throughout the Limerick Soviet.

The Catalyst for a General Strike in Limerick

The catalyst for the Limerick Soviet was the decision by the British military authorities to proclaim Limerick city a special military area in response to the defiant display by the Limerick masses in attending the funeral for IRA activist Robert Byrne.

Robert Byrne came to notice of the British authorities as early as 1916 for his republican activities. Just before Christmas 1918, he was appointed Adjutant of the Second Battalion, Limerick Brigade of the IRA.[4] It was this act, more than anything else, that likely led to his dismissal from his job in January 1919. The excuse used by the employers was his attendance at the funeral of a Limerick Volunteer named John Daly.

A week later Byrne was arrested, charged with the possession of a revolver and ammunition and after a court-martial sentenced to twelve months hard labour. As was the norm with political prisoners at the time Byrne went on hunger-strike shortly after his incarceration. Force-feeding of prisoners on hunger-strike was deeply unpopular and local medical professionals were under enormous pressure not to facilitate the force-feeding of prisoners in Limerick Prison. The ending of force-feeding in Limerick coincided with Byrne beginning his hunger-strike. His condition deteriorated rapidly and within three weeks he was in the prison infirmary.

On 12 March 1919 Byrne was removed to the City Infirmary on Shelbourne Road. Seizing the opportunity, the local IRA decided on a rescue attempt. On Sunday 6 April the IRA launched their rescue attempt which did not go according to plan. During the rescue attempt several shots were fired, killing one policeman and wounding another and fatally wounding Robert Byrne. To demonstrate the shambolic nature of the rescue, the transport intended to spirit Byrne away from the hospital went to the wrong exit. As they attempted to make their escape, Byrne and the two IRA volunteers who were accompanying him, were forced to stop and board a pony and trap driven by a local man, John Ryan, who took them to his cottage in Knocklisheen. Byrne died later that evening from his wounds.

The funeral of Robert Byrne was the subject of a military order designed to prevent a show of defiance to the British military authorities. Sinn Fein and the IRA were intent on using the funeral to promote the nationalist cause and Sinn Fein mayor, Alphonsus O'Mara and the Catholic Bishop, Michael Hallinan, both played prominent roles in the funeral. Large numbers had attended the removal of Byrne's body from Meelick to the City Infirmary and the military commanders were intent on preventing a repeat performance at his funeral.[5] If anything, the attitude of the authorities ensured a large and lively funeral. Up to 15,000 people attended the funeral procession to Mount St. Lawrence Cemetery in what was a blatant demonstration that the military authorities were not going to dictate to the masses what they could and could not do.

Strike Action Outside Limerick

The day before Byrne's funeral, Sean Dowling assisted striking farm labourers in north Kerry in securing a pay increase and a reduction in the working week following a strike.[6] There was also an outbreak of strikes by farm labourers in the North West. A mass meeting of farm labourers took place in Derry and demanded a pay increase of £2 per week. Farmers declared a lock-out and carried out work under the protection of armed 'volunteers' with rifles and revolvers and the police guarded local creameries. Milk was processed but eggs and butter were not. Distillery workers engaged in solidarity action, refusing to handle grain from strike-bound farms and urban workers in Letterkenny joined the picket line.[7]

The following day four striking labourers were shot by a farmer near Letterkenny. The labourers were attempting to prevent scabs working on a strikebound farm. The Farmers' Union threatened to kill the striking workers to prevent a 'reign of terror' by the labourers and condemned the 'inactivity of the police' in not breaking the strike. Labourers blockaded roads to prevent milk and butter being delivered to Derry. In Letterkenny pickets prevented carts from collecting coal from the railway station. When the scabs refused to turn around, the pickets unhitched the horses from the carts, went off with the horses and left the carts sitting in the middle of the road. Workers at the local asylum were told by flying pickets that the patients were not to be allowed to be used to collect farmyard manure. At the large farm of General Stewart, the labourers unhitched the horses from the ploughs and carts and left the scabs with no means of doing their work. Pickets were also placed on local grocers and bakers to prevent the use of delivery vans. The farmers met in the Guildhall in Derry but the meeting was adjourned in uproar as the farmers couldn't agree what to do.[8]

At the start of the Soviet, Sinn Fein were holding a convention in Dublin. The convention debated the situation in Ulster with delegates noting the upsurge in industrial unrest and strikes. Several delegates argued that unionism in the North was capitalistic and the labour movement wanted to smash capitalism. Proposals were put to the convention to exploit what the delegates saw as the prospect of democratic labour uniting 'behind the Sinn Fein movement' by sending Protestant members of Sinn Fein to Ulster. Demonstrating his bourgeois credentials, the entire discussion was castigated by Arthur Griffith and he led the charge against the proposal.[9] The debate demonstrated the class tensions that existed within Sinn Fein. Working class delegates were expressing their innate class solidarity, while Griffith and the other representatives of capitalism in Sinn Fein were determined not to involve Sinn Fein in any activity that could threaten the rule of capital.

The General Strike Begins

It is repeatedly implied in the literature on the Limerick Soviet that the strike developed as a result of the death of Robert Byrne. However, it was the reaction of the British military authorities to the large numbers who attended the funeral that provoked the Limerick Soviet, a spontaneous response to the actions of the British in imposing martial law. Carrying through on their threat to impose restrictions on movement, the British military cordoned off the city and restricted access to the holders of permits to be issued by the military.

The imposition of martial law provoked an almost immediate reaction from the city's workers. The initial strike action began among 600 workers, with women workers taking a leading role, in the Cleeve's owned Condensed Milk factory in Landsdowne on the north side of the River Shannon.[10] It was from there that the strike action spread, and the Trades Council was forced to act.

The momentum created by the decision to strike in Cleeve's was to force the hand of even the most conservative elements within the Trades Council. Once a decision had been made to call a localised general strike it was the labour movement who were in pole position of opposition to martial law.

In the aftermath of the general strike against conscription in April 1918 and the decision by the British Government to drop their plans, British Prime Minister Lloyd George suggested that conscription might be introduced on a local or regional basis in Ireland. In response a group of industrial organisers in the ITGWU, including Sean Dowling, met and drew up plans for local or regional general strikes and the establishment of workers committees. The existence of these plans was alluded to at the 1918 Annual Meeting of the ILPTUC.[11] The blueprint for the Limerick Soviet already existed as the Trades Council delegates sat down on Sunday, 13 April 1919, to discuss their response to the imposition of martial law and the strike in the Condensed Milk factory.

The decision to call a general strike was not unanimous or even guaranteed. The conflict between the ITGWU and the craft unions was demonstrated at a meeting of the LUTLC on 11 April, right on the cusp of the Limerick Soviet. John Cronin proposed that the meeting adjourn after reading the minutes and discussing 'a matter of special importance'. as a mark of respect following the death of Robert Byrne. However, Sean Dowling was intent on forcing action from the Trades Council. The ongoing simmering tensions on the Trades Council bust open as Dowling demanded that the Council scrap its entire rule book and re-write the rules of the Trades Council. Clearly frustrated with the refusal of the craft union leaders to act in the interests of the workers of the city, he was intent on bringing the issue to a head.

When John Cronin stated that the executive of the Trades Council would consider if any changes were needed and make recommendations accordingly, Dowling accused Cronin and the other leaders of attempting to veto any changes on the Trades Council. In a further attempt to wrench control from Cronin and the others, Dowling proposed that the Trades Council should meet in the Town Hall. In the intense situation that existed in the city in the aftermath of the death of Robert Byrne, Dowling was effectively calling on the Trades Council to take over the Town Hall. Ignoring Dowling, Cronin proceeded to open a discussion on 'the matter of special importance', a mundane issue affecting the Tailors Society, the fulfilling of a contract to supply uniforms to workers in the city's asylum. Dowling and the ITGWU delegates abandoned the meeting.[12]

It is reasonable to suggest that the conservative leadership of the Trades Council would have outlined every obstacle they could think of to undermine the demand for a general strike but a combination of the determination of Sean Dowling, the other ITGWU delegates (and others like the ICWU) and the large demonstration outside the Trades Council's meeting room forced their hand. It took almost twelve hours for the Trades Council to make its decision but once the decision was made to call a general strike it was met with overwhelming support by the Limerick working class. On Monday morning 15,000 workers in Limerick were on strike, the city was at a virtual standstill and the Trades Council had transformed itself into the Strike Committee. Thousands of workers paraded through the streets, with the city a hive of activity and workers discussing the strike. The *Evening Herald* described the strike as 'a fierce struggle between organised labour and the government'.[13]

The Role of the IRA

In discussing the decision to call a general strike and the formation of a strike committee *Cahill* argued that Sinn Fein were influencing events, claiming that 'The speedy and efficient way in which the Trades' Council meeting was organised would seem to underline an element of Sinn Fein influence and support.'[14] There is little evidence to support this assertion, indeed the evidence actually suggests the contrary. In reality it was ITGWU delegates who drove the decision to call a general strike at the Trades Council meeting.

A member of the IRA was co-opted onto the strike committee. Michael Brennan was head of the East Clare Brigade of the IRA. In his witness statement to the Bureau of Military History, Brennan outlined that the IRA in the mid-west were in disarray. He pointed out that in early 1919 that many areas had no organised Volunteer units and he had difficulty contacting other Volunteers. In Limerick the local IRA were split down the middle. Brennan outlined how it was necessary to form a second separate unit of the IRA (the Second Battalion) in Limerick because of the incompetence of and lack of action by the First Battalion. There was open hostility between the two IRA Battalions in the city and Brennan was constantly acting as a mediator and a go-between for the two Limerick units. Brennan only mentions his membership of the Strike Committee in passing and clearly had little influence or impact on it.[15] The likely reason for co-opting Brennan onto the Strike Committee was to ensure that the two hostile IRA Battalions in Limerick did not disrupt the work of the Strike Committee in the city. The ITGWU delegates would have been well aware of the state of the IRA in the city. The headquarters of the Limerick IRA was housed in the ITGWU offices in John's Square.

One other factor that must be considered in relation to nationalist influence on the Soviet is the outlook of Trades Council Chairman, John Cronin. Cronin had repeatedly attempted to undermine any move towards the establishment of a Labour Party in Limerick. During a row about a 'labour' programme at a Trades Council meeting, Cronin declared that while a 'labour' programme was ideal, the Sinn Fein programme was more practical at addressing the needs of workers in the city. Cronin's approach was undoubtedly influenced by a combination of his previous support for the Irish Parliamentary Party and the fact that his son, Jeremiah Cronin, was part of the Mid-Limerick Brigade of the IRA. John Cronin, as well as Trades Council treasurer James Casey, were later to sit as judges in Republican Dail Courts.[16]

As the strike began the conservative leaders were swept along by the wave of radicalism engulfing the city. Both Sinn Fein and the Catholic hierarchy were faced with a huge dilemma, whether to condemn the Soviet or outline tacit support. Condemning the Soviet would have immediately cut both off from the mass of the working class in the city and have a profound impact across the rest of the country. The strategy adopted by both, very likely by agreement between both, was to condemn the British military for imposing the cordon around the city, calling for a British withdrawal from the city, but avoiding openly declaring support for the Soviet. The Chamber of Commerce were also faced with a dilemma, condemn the Soviet would likely provoke the anger and hostility of workers, further disrupting their enterprises. Similar to Sinn Fein and the Catholic hierarchy, the Chamber criticised the actions of the military and called on the British government to resolve the problem. In the meantime, all three wings of the nationalist movement bided their time waiting for an opportunity to undermine and ultimately defeat the Soviet.

Initially the ILPTUC leadership were also swept along with the events in Limerick. Cathal O'Shannon of the ITGWU, speaking at a meeting of the Socialist Party of Ireland in Dublin, called for 'Soviets for Ireland'.[17] However, the leadership of the ILPTUC and in particular head of the ITGWU William O'Brien and leader of the Labour Party Thomas Johnson, were to be willing allies in the efforts of the nationalist leadership to bring the strike to an end.

After the decision to call a general strike was made a group of print workers in Cornmarket Row worked throughout the night to print posters proclaiming the strike. The posters contained the following notice:

> *Limerick United Trades and Labour Council*
> *Proclamation*
> *The workers of Limerick, assembled in Council, hereby declare cessation of all work from 5 am on Monday April 14, 1919, as a protest against the decision of the British Government in compelling them to procure permits in order to earn their bread.*
> *By order of the Strike Committee*
> *Mechanics' Institute.*
> *Any information with reference to the above can be had from the Strike Committee."*

By early morning on Monday 14 April 1919, the city was plastered with posters proclaiming the general strike. *Cahill* asserted that the working class in Limerick were taken by surprise at the decision to call a general strike.[18] Again the evidence would dispute this. Martial law had been notified since before the funeral of Robert Byrne. The Cleeve's workers had already declared their strike action. The city was a hive of activity, debate and discussion about the impending imposition of martial law and hundreds of workers demonstrated outside the Trades Council meeting on the Sunday. To suggest that the bulk of the population were unaware of what was being discussed is not credible.

To show how rapidly events moved on during this period, the reaction to the inquest into Robert Byrne's death, which started on the morning of Tuesday 15 April, was muted. The *Evening Herald* reported that the inquest 'elicited little interest locally'.[19] The focus of the entire city, even the Sinn Feiners, was now on the general strike and how it would develop rather than the fall-out from the death of Robert Byrne. If a general strike had not been underway Sinn Fein would have used the inquest for propaganda purposes but now that the general strike dominated the political landscape of the city, the inquest became a footnote in the history of the Soviet.

The Strike Committee Organises

A full military mobilisation took place overnight erecting barbed wire as a cordon around the city. The bridges over the Shannon were a mass of barbed wire and soldiers with fixed bayonets were stationed on either end. Armoured vehicles and troops in full readiness moved throughout the city. Journalists noted the discipline shown by the mass of workers thronging the streets and parades took place throughout the day.[20]

The Strike Committee systematically began organising to ensure the necessities needed by the population were catered for and waste was minimised. Water, gas and electricity supplies were maintain although street lighting was switched off to conserve resources. In order to avoid the loss of perishable commodities the Strike Committee instructed workers to process remaining supplies at the city's bacon factories and tanneries. Restaurants and hotels were instructed to close in order to conserve supplies. In a crucial decision all the pubs in the city were shut and Limerick became a dry city for the duration of the Soviet.

The Strike Committee also organised teams of flying pickets, identified by a red badge, who were responsible for the maintenance of law and order and ensuring the instructions of the Strike Committee were implemented. Remarkably, there was not one single instance of disruption or anti-social behaviour recorded for the duration of the Soviet. Over the entire period not one case was brought before the city's petty-sessions court.

Most commentary on the work of the Strike Committee credits Trades Council Chairman, John Cronin, Council treasurer, James Casey and James Carr for their role in the Soviet. Undoubtedly, after their initial resistance, it is clear that all three did actively participate in the work of the Strike Committee. One figure who has been systematically ignored in writings on the Soviet is ITGWU industrial organiser and Marxist, Sean Dowling. On writings specifically on the Soviet a mention of the role of Dowling is absent. *Cahill* and *Kemmy* fail to refer to Dowling at all, Queally mentions Dowling in passing and *O'Connor Lysaght* mentions Dowling once and only in the context of the fall-out following the ending of the Soviet rather than his role during the general strike.[21]

Writing many years later English Marxist, Jack Hedley, a close collaborator of Sean Dowling in Limerick, described Dowling as the 'philosophical begetter' of the Soviet.[22] *Cahill* acknowledged what he describes as the crucial role of the ITGWU in the Soviet and what is clear is that the role played by the ITGWU was driven by Sean Dowling.

The British Military

Almost immediately the impact of martial law and the subsequent general strike was starting to bite. The police and military authorities were clearly caught by surprise at not just the calling of the general strike but the scale of the organised resistance to the decision to impose martial law. Within thirty minutes of the strike proclamation, local police chiefs were contacting Dublin asking for an extra 300 police to be dispatched to Limerick. Detective Inspector Craig commented 'the situation looks very serious'. In response Deputy Inspector-General W. M. Davies replied that it was not possible to deploy extra police to Limerick because "there are so many strikes going on elsewhere". After further assessment the Brigadier-General Joseph Byrne, the Inspector-General of the Royal Irish Constabulary (RIC) agreed to send fifty policemen to Limerick and instructed "Say to GHQ that as this is no ordinary strike it is presumed instruction will be tonight sent for military to help police."

The military authorities were shocked at the response of the workers in Limerick. Martial law was not unusual in Ireland during the War of Independence. The week before the Limerick Soviet martial law had been withdrawn in Westport. For the British military the strike was totally unexpected. Apart from troops manning the cordon thrown up around the city, the military and police were confined to barracks as the military commanders decided how to approach the strike.[23]

The Press Censor began the propaganda onslaught on the strike, stating: 'The public of Limerick are informed that although Limerick has been proclaimed a military area this in no way prohibits the inhabitants getting their supplies in the ordinary way. If owning to the wanton action of ill-disposed persons the inhabitants suffer through lack of necessities of life, the Government are in no way responsible and cannot do anything to ameliorate the consequences of such wanton action'.[24]

Will the Strike Spread?

Two important developments occurred at the beginning of the strike. Firstly, the ILPTUC declared Mayday a 'general holiday', effectively calling a general strike for Mayday. William O'Brien was promoting his 'International League of Peoples' as a counter to the establishment of the Comintern. O'Brien was planning to use Mayday as the launch for his 'League'. [25] The second development was that the railway workers immediately indicated their intent to come out on strike in support of the strike in Limerick. The members of the National Union of Railwaymen (NUR) informed their union headquarters in London of their intent to take strike action after their obligatory 48-hour strike notice expired.[26]

Tuesday 15 April started with reports of strikes breaking out in many workplaces in Thurles. Initially, the employers planned a lock-out, but then the realisation dawned that a strike in Thurles could lead to the spreading of the Soviet from Limerick. Within hours the employers were scrambling to offer pay increases to end the strike action, including one employer offering an increase of 50% to get their employees back to work.[27]

Dock workers from around the country belonging to the ITGWU were meeting in Dublin to discuss countrywide action for a pay increase.[28] Like with the railway workers, the prospect of a countrywide strike of dock workers occurring at the same time as the Soviet would have raised the prospect of the strikes merging into one wider action. The railway workers striking would have paralysed the main transport sector in the country, while a dock workers strike would have paralysed much of the trade with Britain and other countries. Crippling the entire transport infrastructure would have led to direct conflict with British imperialism and capitalism.

In Dublin goods were being refused by the railway company when it became clear that ITGWU members would refuse to handle them in Limerick. Railway passengers were refused tickets to Limerick unless they could produce a military permit to enter the city.

In Limerick, members of the ASE working in the Locomotive Works at Limerick station joined the general strike.[29] At the same time the railway workers were debating how to conduct their strike in support of the Soviet. A meeting took place of railway workers in Limerick and delegates were sent to meet with railway workers around the country.[30]

Discussion now took place about the nature of the general strike in Limerick in comparison to the Belfast engineering strike which had taken place two months earlier. From the perspective of the establishment the strike in Limerick was described as 'more dramatic' as it had caused a complete shutdown of industry in the city and posed a more comprehensive threat to the interests of capital.[31] In an effort to undermine the general strike the national newspapers constantly proclaimed that Limerick was on the verge of starvation because of a shortage of food.[32]

The Strike Committee allowed, even encouraged, journalists to conduct interviews with members of the committee about the strike. John Cronin was quoted as stating

> "The military authorities have seen fit to place Limerick under martial law. In doing that, they have fixed their boundaries inside the city, which makes it necessary for workers to pass in and out to their work. We, as organised workers, refuse to ask them for permits to earn our daily bread, and this strike is a protest against their action. What we want is to have this ban removed so that the workers may have free access to their work in and out of their native city. It is our intention to carry on the strike until this ban is removed. This strike is likely to become more serious."

With the Permission of the Strike Committee

Shops posted notices stating that they were open with the permission of the Strike Committee. Prices were strictly enforced with notices posted outlining the prices fixed by the sub-committee responsible and flying pickets wearing red badges enforced the price controls and ensured order in the queues for foodstuffs. Small shop-keepers in working class districts shut up shop and joined the strike.[33] One sector of society did suffer from food shortages, the military. Unable to secure any supplies locally, Dublin Castle were forced to supply the military in Limerick with foodstuffs from other locations.[34]

The first intervention from the British military took place on Tuesday. Brigadier-General Griffin arrived in Limerick and held a private meeting with the Chamber of Commerce.[35] Given the reaction of the workers in Limerick to the declaration of martial law, the British military faced a decision, use repression to suppress the general strike to reinforce martial law, or find a way of undermining the strike. The Chamber of Commerce were also intent on bringing the strike to an end. No public pronouncement was made, but that was only a matter of timing.

A Strike on the Railways

The *Evening Herald* noted the efficiency of the work of the Strike Committee. Coal yards were opened on Wednesday from 10am-5pm, although it was noted that coal supplies in the city were already at a low level. Farmers were supplying milk to Strike Committee food depots that had been established on the northside of the city outside the military cordon, the milk was then distributed as needed. The Strike sub-committee determined the price paid to farmers and the price which it was to be sold for. The *Evening Herald* was being sold in the city, but at a premium price with the extra payment going to the strike fund. Unskilled workers were charged three pence, while others were obliged to pay six pence.[36]

A delegation from the leadership of the NUR arrived in Dublin from London and immediately went into discussions with the leadership of the ILPTUC.[37] The sole purpose of the visit from this delegation was to undermine any attempt by the railway workers to come out on strike in support of the Soviet. Part of the reason why the NUR leadership made such strident efforts to undermine strike action by railway workers in Ireland was the indication that members of the NUR in Britain were intent in engaging in solidarity action in support of the Limerick Soviet. A TUC reported noted strong sympathy among railwaymen in support of strike action.[38] From the perspective of the conservative leadership of the railway workers, such action posed an enormous risk and could see the leadership lose control of their membership.

William O'Brien, on behalf of the National Executive of the ILPTUC, instructed the Soviet Committee to defer any attempt to call the railway workers out on strike in support of Limerick. O'Brien held out the carrot that the reason for this instruction was because 'national action' would be taken.[39] This was to be the first of numerous occasions that O'Brien and others in the national leadership were to imply that a nationwide general strike would be called in support of the Soviet. While the members of the NUR were now under instruction not to engage in strike action, another group of railway workers in Limerick station walked off the job when the boilermakers joined the strike.[40]

The threat of a strike on the railway posed a serious problem for all the concerned parties. Limerick was an important centre of operation for both the GS&WR and the W&LR and any strike in Limerick would directly impact the railway network across the southern part of the country. It is clear that railway workers with both rail companies were ready to engage in solidarity action with Limerick. A solidarity strike on the railways would have put enormous pressure on the leadership of the ILPTUC to declare a nationwide general strike. In order to undermine the potential for wildcat action on the railways, the bureaucracy based in Dublin argued that strike action on the railway network would only be successful if it was nationwide in character and that such a move should await approval from the NUR executive in London. The argument was that engaging in strike action would directly affect the working class of Limerick rather than the British military.[41] The issue was about to come to ahead as the strike notice issued by the railway workers was due to expire on Thursday 17 April.

The ILPTUC Scramble for Control

As the ILPTUC scrambled to regain control of the situation, Labour Party leader, Thomas Johnson, arrived in Limerick on Wednesday. At the same time the National Executive of the ILPTUC met in Dublin.[42] Wednesday morning also saw the first attempt by the British military to attempt to diffuse the crisis. After meeting with the Chamber of Commerce, Brigadier-General Griffin proposed that entry permits would be issued by the local employers, while no permit would be required to leave the city. Griffin outlined the proposal in a letter sent to the Strike Committee, Thomas Johnson, and notably, Sean Dowling, demonstrating that the British military recognised his importance in the context of the Soviet.[43]

The previous division between the conservative layer and the radical and socialist elements on the Trades Council did not disappear during the Soviet. When John Cronin was asked about the proposal for the employers to issue permits, he stated ''we have not turned down the offer. It will be further discussed but we are awaiting information that may be more advantage to us before we take a decision'. Instead of outright rejection of the proposal, Cronin was hedging his bets on the expectation of a proposal from the National Executive of the ILPTUC on national action.[44]

The leadership of the ILPTUC were now engaging in delaying tactics. Reports emerged that the National Executive of the ILPTUC met late into the evening, but that no statement would be issued until Friday morning. The *Cork Examiner* noted that the Strike Committee waited until late into the night for word from Dublin, but none was forthcoming.[45] The *Freeman's Journal* reported that the ILPTUC had decided on 'a definite course of action', a refrain that was to be all too common over the following days.[46] It was never outlined what this 'definite course of action' entailed.

On Wednesday morning the owners of six of the coal yards in the city refused to comply with instructions from the Strike Committee to open their yards. Shortly before noon police were deployed to guard the coal yards.[47] The primary necessity for coal was to fire the ovens in the city's bakeries. While the refusal by the coal merchants could have led to a confrontation, the reality is that coal supplies in the yards were already very low and smaller coal yards were under the control of the Strike Committee.[48] The Strike Committee did warn the coal merchants not to supply any coal to the British military but decided against any direct confrontation.[49] It has been suggested that the failure to act to get control of the coal yards was a sign of weakness on behalf of the Strike Committee. It may be that this decision was made by the conservative layers in an effort to avoid confrontation, or it may have simply been the case that the Strike Committee did not consider control of the coal yards as crucial to their work.

The *Freeman's Journal* noted that there was a plentiful supply of bread from the city's bakeries and that food supplies were being sent from Cork and other centres around with country, with British trade unions also promising support. As had been the case since the start of the general strike, thousands of workers demonstrated through the city with constant discussion and debate taking place on the situation that existed in the city.[50]

Ensuring Food Supplies

Thursday dawned with reports of a new wave of strikes around the country. The farm labourers in Donegal were joined by strikes among dock labourers in Derry, members of the NUR in Derry, women members of the ITGWU in shops in Boyle, Co. Roscommon, building workers in Dublin, council workers in Dublin, hotel workers in Dublin,[51] as well as women workers in the drapery houses in Clonmel.[52]

In Limerick the Strike Committee issued a proclamation instructing city shops to open, adding 'and we hereby warn said owners and managers that any attempt at profiteering will be sternly suppressed and that no deliveries by hired messengers, by hand, or by car, will be allowed'. The proclamation goes on to outline that flying pickets would monitor shops and queues for food supplies. Posters of the proclamation were printed by local print workers and distributed throughout the city.[53]

Following on from the meeting of the ILPTUC, on Friday morning Thomas Johnson announced, 'the full strength of the labour movement in Ireland, backed by the general public, will be exerted on behalf of the men and women of Limerick and would ensure a striking victory'. [54] Johnson was in Limerick with a specific purpose – make vague promises to the Strike Committee and the working class of the city, while at the same time work to delay any calls for solidarity and all the while wearing down the strike leaders to the point where they abandoned the strike.[55]

While Johnson was doing his best to manipulate expectations in Limerick, a delegation of NUR members from Limerick were meeting the National Executive of the ILPTUC and members of the NUR delegation from London. Once again, J.H. Thomas and William O'Brien diverted efforts for solidarity action by promising 'a definite course of action', coupled with the reconvening of the National Executive in Limerick the following Monday. It was further reported that William O'Brien and Thomas Foran would immediately make their way to Limerick.[56]

The Strike Committee was still debating whether to accept the offer of General Griffin to allow the employers issue permits. Major disagreements existed on the Strike Committee. John Cronin was attempting to avoid rejecting the offer on the basis that they wait for the arrival of O'Brien and Foran.[57] Meanwhile Sean Dowling and the other ITGWU organisers were demanding a meeting between the ITGWU and the Strike Committee to address the crisis.[58]

Cronin was forced to declare to the media that the ITGWU were not running the strike and in an effort to reinforce his weak position he announced that delegates from the Strike Committee who had visited other centres had reported back that railway workers 'were ready to act immediately the call was made'.[59]

While this disagreement was taking place, the work of the Strike Committee continued at pace with ITGWU members being the driving force behind the implementation of the decisions. Proclamations were issued setting the price of a variety of basic food products as well as coal. Vehicles moved through the city carrying posters stating: 'By permission of the Strike Committee'. Thousands of workers continued to stage protests through the city and the strike remained total.[60]

At the same time the farm labourers strike in Donegal had expanded into Fermanagh and in Co. Down farm labourers had renewed their strike action. In Donegal flying pickets were preventing the supply of milk to Derry and preventing the delivery of grain and coal to farmers in Donegal. A new branch of the Labourers Union in Manorcunningham recruited over one hundred labourers. In Clonleigh three hundred workers joined the labourers strike. Mass meetings of striking workers were held on a regular basis to plan and conduct the strike.[61] In Fermanagh more than 3,000 members of the ITGWU had engaged in strike action. Workers at the Tyrone Asylum were threatening strike action and the Asylum Committee demanded that the military be used to scab on the strike.[62] A large-scale strike of farm labourers was underway in Loughrea Co. Galway. Sinn Fein members of Loughrea District Council and Mountbellew District Council condemned the strike action and ridiculed the demands of the labourers for improved wages.[63]

Delay After Delay – The Strike Continues

On Saturday 19 April, six days into the general strike in Limerick, Thomas Johnson continued to obfuscate, issuing a communication to the Strike Committee:

> 'I have to inform you that the National Executive are giving earnest attention to the situation in Limerick. They are determined to give you and your-fellow workers in the city all possible support in your fight against aggressive militarism. They realise that while it is Limerick today, tomorrow it could be Cork, Waterford, Dublin, Derry or Belfast. You are making your protest in the most effective manner, and your fellow workers throughout the country are ready to join in the protest. All freedom-loving people are with you and the backing is assured.

> The National Executive have decided to come from Dublin to meet you in consultation and to perfect arrangements to carry on the fight. It is no longer a local struggle; it is a national one, and our reports from other centres prove that all Ireland is ready to give you active assistance.

The National Executive wish to congratulate you and the workers of Limerick on the splendid manner in which you have upheld the banner of liberty and the rights of people. The new siege of Limerick may demand the same dogged resolution and self-sacrifice as when Sarsfield led the fight. You will show that the men and women of 1919 are no less valiant than those of 1690'.[64]

On Saturday night a public meeting was held in the City Hall. The meeting was chaired by the Sinn Fein mayor, Alphonsus O'Mara. O'Mara was the son of a former Home Rule MP and part of the family ownership in the bacon industry.[65] At the meeting O'Mara attempted to open up the possibility of removing control of the strike from the Strike Committee, talking about wanting to bring 'all parties together' so that 'good work might be accomplished'. He proposed that the intervention of someone of 'standing' like the Mayor of Dublin (independent nationalist Laurence O'Neill) might lead to a resolution.[66]

Sinn Fein TD, Michael Colivet, also attempted to promote the idea of bringing in an outside mediator. However, after seeing the opposition to the proposal at the meeting, Colivet changed tack, called for support for the Strike Committee and suggested that shop owners should release food for the populace. In response John Cronin told the meeting that the Strike Committee knew which establishments were hoarding supplies.

Cronin went on to state that in the next day or two the seat of the Labour Parliament (i.e. the ILPTUC National Executive) will relocate to Limerick from Dublin. He continued that the National Executive were expected to take control of the whole strike arrangements.[67] Cronin continued by stating that the ILPTUC delegates will have the power to call an immediate strike throughout the country. Thomas Johnson addressed the meeting on behalf of the ILPTUC, but studiously avoided making any similar commitments. However, Johnson did state that the ILPTUC visitors would now not arrive until Tuesday, indicating a further delay. The ILPTUC were later to claim that they could not secure transport for Monday, but, in reality, it was more of the delaying tactics that the ILPTUC leadership had been engaged in since the beginning of the week.

The meeting was also addressed by Sean Dowling for the ITGWU and D.H. O'Donnell of the ICWU.[68] At the meeting rumours began to circulate the members of the Chambers of Commerce were going to attempt to break the strike by reopening their premises. Goodbody of the Chamber stated that he was at the meeting to keep a watching brief and report back to the daily Chamber of Commerce meeting.[69]

By Sunday the establishment were scrambling for a solution. The local magistrates called on the military authorities to extend the proclaimed area outside the main urban area in order that permits would not be needed for travel to and from work. The proposal was dismissed by the British military. At the same time shopkeepers complained that the price controls imposed by the Strike Committee were not giving them sufficient profit. Not surprisingly, their pleas fell on deaf ears. The master bakers claimed that the flour stocks were running low and Bannatyne's flour mills was placed under military control.[70] The military takeover of Bannatyne's was clearly designed to put pressure on the Strike Committee. In response the Strike Committee issued instructions to unload seven tons of Canadian grain at the docks.[71] Where necessary the Strike Committee issued requisition orders for food supplies. Police records noted that milk was being requisitioned from the Cleeve's plant. It is worth nothing that the police reported that the ITGWU, rather than the Strike Committee, were the ones issuing the requisition orders.[72]

The local clergy also attempted to influence the situation. At Sunday mass the priests called on people to stop engaging in the regular protests and not to 'hang around street corners' (discussing politics).[73] At the same time the rising industrial unrest was impacting on the consciousness of some members of the Protestant clergy. Clergymen at St. Matthias's Vestry in Killiney in Dublin were demanding a 'living wage' for the clergy and clergy in Killaloe and Ennis were also taking 'action' in support of a living wage.[74]

The control being exercised by the Strike Committee was demonstrated by *the Freeman's Journal*. The Strike Committee 'have organised a splendid system of food distribution. Measures have been taken against profiteering and hoarding and a regular system of permits is in operation'. There was a glut of milk supplies in the city. In one incident a provision store was attached to a pub. When some customers attempted to get served alcohol a flying picket ordered the premises shut down.[75] The *Cork Examiner* stated 'perfect order is being maintained'.[76] The *Independent* had to admit that the Strike Committee were, in fact, ensuring an adequate supply of food, commenting: 'It is certainly a remarkable tribute to the skill and organisation of the Strike Committee that while there has been a general suspension of all branches of industry in the city now for seven days, there has been no scarcity of food'.[77] The *Irish Times* stated: '.... though it is daily diminishing, it should not be thought there is immediate danger of serious distress...the people there are, therefore, well supplied with milk, and they also have fair supplies of other necessaries'.[78]

The *Cork Examiner* commented that the

> 'establishment of food depots directly under Strike Committee control in the poorer districts has had a major impact on the situation faced by people in these districts. Food and milk supplies have improved all round and the price controls implemented have met with widespread support. Food supplies are being distributed free to those in

need. The Strike Committee is also providing money to those who need help purchasing products not available in food depots'.

The same paper also noted 'the effective running of public services which are directly under the control of the Strike Committee'. The *Examiner* stated that 'objections have been raised to the Strike Committee issuing permits' but commented that this again has been met with widespread approval, adding that 'those who grumble are not supporting the strike action anyway'.[79]

The two organisers of the food depots are Charles Johnson of the ICWU and A. Reddan of the ITGWU, both employees at Cleeeves. The food depot in Thomondgate was under the superintendence of Mr. A Roche assisted by Fr. Moloney. Farmers were being paid 10d a gallon for milk and the milk is being sold at 3d per quart through the food depots. On Tuesday 22 April, three tons of potatoes were delivered from Newmarket-on-Fergus.[80] Food supplies were smuggled into the city at night by the Thomondgate fishermen rowing supplies across the river using boats with muffled oars. Funeral hearses were also used to transport food supplies past the military cordon.[81]

As the strike continued the British military authorities were having increasing difficulty imposing the cordon around the city. The Drapers Assistants Association reported that the 'military are very friendly' to the people in Limerick.[82] Reports later emerged that soldiers and civilians were swimming together in the River Shannon.[83] At one stage the military authorities were forced to withdraw a Scottish regiment because they were fraternising with the local population and allowing people to pass through the cordon without any permits.[84] The Strike Committee took a class position on the British troops manning the cordon. The 'Workers Bulletin - Issued by the Limerick Proletariat' declared "The English press is doing its level best to dub it a Sinn Fein one, in the hopes that the English worker will be fooled. However, this is a worker's strike and is no more Sinn Fein than any other strike against tyranny and oppression". The article continued "Tommy is not our enemy and we wish him to understand that he is merely a tool of an Imperialistic, Capitalistic Government".[85]

As the second week of the strike started the Strike Committee gave permission for the 'picture palaces' to open, but the receipts from the admission tickets were to go to the strike fund.[86] Another leading figure of the ILPTUC, Cathal O'Shannon, attended the British Socialist Party Conference and told delegates that 'if necessary a general strike will be called'.[87] All the focus was on the attitude of the national leadership of the ILPTUC. Thomas Johnson repeatedly pitched the line of 'wait and see' until the ILPTUC Executive members arrived.[88]

The Strike Committee issued the following proclamation -

'Whereas we declared a cessation of work on 14th April as a protest against the military ban on the city and whereas certain relaxations have since been permitted, now, by virtue of the powers conferred on us by the workers of Limerick, we hereby order that no work shall be carried out on Monday 21st inst., with the following exceptions (1) Distribution of milk, (2) supply of bread from bakeries, (3) Chemist shops same hours as Sunday – by order of the Strike Committee'.[89]

The frustration of members of the Chamber of Commerce came to a head on Monday. Rumours circulated that, at their daily meeting, several business owners intended to defy the Strike Committee and reopen their businesses on Tuesday. Their attempted act of defiance did not last long. The Strike Committee made it clear that flying pickets would ensure compliance with proclamations from the Strike Committee and the Chamber of Commerce decided that discretion was the better part of valour.[90]

Treasury Notes

The beginning of the second week of the strike also saw a major innovation planned by the Strike Committee. In order to address a shortage of money circulating in the city the Strike Committee decided to issue treasury notes in order to facilitate the buying and selling of goods. Detailed planning went into the idea. Workers from the finance departments of major firms in the city, including accountants, were drafted onto a sub-committee to assist.[91] The Finance Commission was to be in control of the distribution of the treasury notes. The notes were printed in denominations of 1s, 2s, 5s and 10s and printed on black, green, red and blue paper. The value was to be underwritten by the current stock of supplies, along with donations to the strike fund from outside Limerick and the volume of notes to be distributed was to be based on the volume of supplies and money available. At a later stage the treasury notes were guaranteed by ILPTUC.[92]

Distribution of the treasury notes was dependent on the acceptance by both the working class in the city and, more particularly, the local shopkeepers. A list was drawn up of merchants and shopkeepers who were willing to provide credit to the Strike Committee based on the treasury notes, and the Strike Committee decided on which shops would be approved.[93] The entire process evolved in a very matter of fact fashion.

It is not clear if the treasury notes were ever used during the general strike. The *Cork Examiner* reported that on Wednesday evening the treasury notes had not been issued, but preparations were nearly complete and 'circulation will begin in the next few days'.[94] With the strike ending two days later there was limited time to put the plan into effect. Soviet treasurer, James Casey, writing some years later claimed that when the notes were ultimately redeemed, a small surplus remained in a fund that had been subscribed to by sympathisers in all parts of Ireland.[95] Again it is not clear whether Casey was talking in the context of the notes being issued or that the costs of food distribution was covered completely from donations to the strike fund.

What is clear, irrespective of whether the treasury notes were issued or not, is that the process of organising such a mechanism demonstrated the effectiveness of the work of the Strike Committee. The plan to issue treasury notes also gained an echo at the Independent Labour Party Conference in Huddersfield. An Edinburgh councillor named Cradford suggested that he would 'like to see the working class of Great Britain follow the example of the Limerick Soviet in offering a paper currency of their own'.[96]

Crowds Attending that Hurling Match

One event that gained a lot of national and international attention was the hurling match which took place in Caherdavin on Monday, 20 April. After the hurling match in the region of a thousand people attempted to regain entry to the city. At approximately 7pm a large crowd confronted the British troops at Sarsfield Bridge. The crowd had been able to pass through the cordon on the outward journey because the military had already relaxed the restrictions. Permits were only required for entry into the city area. Troops with fixed bayonets emerged from the Shannon Rowing Club to confront the crowd and a tank was made ready on the opposite side of the bridge. More police and troops were deployed from the city area and the *Cork Examiner* reported that thousands gathered in support of those attempting to re-enter the city.

The crowd remained until after midnight with large numbers on both sides of the bridge. Local residents provided food and clothing for the protesters. Stewards from the Strike Committee maintained order on the demonstration and acted to avoid any unnecessary confrontation with the military. By midnight many of the protesters were lying on the pavement with British troops standing on guard over them.[97]

Overnight those prohibited from re-entering the city were housed in Thomondgate.[98] Many of the protesters entered the city during the night after the Thomondgate fishermen brought them by boat across the river. The following morning the British soldiers allowed women to pass unhindered through the cordon.[99] The remaining three hundred protesters made their way to Longpavement and boarded a train bound for Limerick station. In an effort to prevent the protesters breaking the cordon the police locked the doors of the train, but the protesters managed to exit through the side of the train away from the platform and made their way through a side exit of the station to the cheers from an assembled crowd and the fumbling attempt of an isolated policeman to stop them.[100]

The National Media

Not surprisingly the national media were openly hostile to the Limerick Soviet. Repeatedly claiming that the city's working class were facing disaster, with food shortages imminent. It was only very reluctantly after a week that the national media were forced to acknowledge that the Strike Committee 'have organised a splendid system of food distribution. Measures have been taken against profiteering and hoarding and a regular system of permits is in operation'[101] and 'the effective running of public services which are directly under the control of the Strike Committee'.[102] But this begrudging acknowledgement was the exception rather than the rule.

In firing a salvo against the role of the ITGWU in Limerick, the *Evening Herald* stated that

> 'The ITGWU is fermenting strikes in different centres in the hope of producing an industrial deadlock throughout Ireland. Political grievances are a secondary consideration with the labour wing whose chief aims are indistinguishable from similar movements in other countries. The trouble in Limerick has given them the chance they were looking for, but if it had not occurred they would undoubtedly found some other occasion for their purpose'.[103]

The Strike Committee were very effective in their use of propaganda. Proclamations were regularly posted throughout the city. Print workers produced a daily 'Workers Bulletin'. Strike Committee members made themselves available for interview by the media and public statements from the Strike Committee were issued regularly.

The Arrival of the National Executive of the ILPTUC

A joint meeting of the Strike Committee and the representatives of the National Executive of the ILPTUC took place on Wednesday. Along with Johnson, there were six members of the National Executive in Limerick, Thomas Farren, Vice Chariman of the ILPTUC, Ms. Rose Timmon of the Irish National Teachers Organisation, J.F. O'Farrell of the Railway Clerks, TC Daly of the National Union of Railwaymen, M. Egan of the Coachmakers Union in Cork and MJ O'Lehane, head of the Drapers Assistants Union.[104] DH O'Donnell head of the ICWU was also in Limerick but, at the time he was not a member of the National Executive. It was noted that William O'Brien, despite his promises, did not travel to Limerick, despite claims that he had bought his train ticket – and secured a travel permit from the British military.[105] O'Brien didn't travel in order to ensure he would have clean hands on whatever happened in Limerick.

While hundreds of protesters rallied outside the meeting, after several hours Farren told the media that the joint meeting was adjourned and would reconvene in the afternoon and issue a statement afterwards. The reconvened meeting continued in session late into the evening, after which a further statement was issued that stated 'important decisions were being made and the meeting would reconvene the following morning'.[106] Despite the fact that the media were commenting that a 'prolonged crisis is expected',[107] it is clear that the bureaucratic leaders of the ILPTUC were now intent on bringing the general strike in Limerick to an end. Large crowds were protesting throughout the city late into the night demonstrating their willingness to continue the struggle.

The meeting between the Strike Committee and the National Executive members resumed on Thursday morning and continued throughout the day. At a meeting of Cork Trades Council, one of the more left-wing representatives, L.J. Duffy of the Drapers Assistants, announced that 'in the next 24 hours a 'turn' will take place that will 'upset the calculations of many in the trade union movement and the military authorities'. He was backed in his comments by John Good of the NUR. The message of 'national action' perpetrated by Johnson and the leaders of the ILPTUC was still gaining traction among activists around the country.[108]

While the Strike Committee and the National Executive were meeting, discussions were also taking place between Sinn Fein mayor, Alphonsus O'Mara and Brigadier-General Griffin.[109] A series of meetings involving O'Mara, Griffin and Catholic Bishop, Dennis Hallinan, took place throughout the day as all three were attempting to undermine the strike and work with the members of the National Executive to bring it to an end. As a compromise, O'Mara and Hallinan agreed with Griffin that workers in possession of permits would be allowed to pass unhindered through the cordon without any checks. O'Mara and Hallinan proclaimed that continuation of the strike would lead to 'a very grave hardship for the workers and the city generally' and pressurised John Cronin to call off the strike.[110]

William O'Brien

William O'Brien was trying to manage the crisis in Limerick through his role as Chairman of the ILPTUC. As an individual who had played a role in the workers struggle during the 1913 Lockout and administered a recovery in ITGWU membership after the Easter Rising, O'Brien was also readily supporting Sinn Fein from its emergence as the developing nationalist force in 1917. During the first electoral victory for Sinn Fein in the Roscommon North by-election of February 1917, O'Brien actively participated in the election campaign. During the Conscription Crisis in April 1918, O'Brien supported a cross-class alliance of labour, Sinn Fein, the IPP and the Catholic Church in opposition to conscription, rather than pursue an independent class-based, labour movement campaign. Similarly, in December 1918, O'Brien was instrumental in the Labour Party deciding not to contest the post-war general election allowing Sinn Fein free-rein to claim the role as representatives of the Irish working class (or at least those workers from a Catholic background).

This attitude of William O'Brien was also to impact on his approach to the Limerick Soviet. Not alone was O'Brien using his position within the ILPTUC to control the response to the Soviet and prevent any nationwide action in support of it, during the Soviet he was actively working with Sinn Fein to undermine the general strike in Limerick. Over three days William O'Brien met with the leadership of Sinn Fein to discuss the Limerick Soviet and what they would like to see happen.[111] Most likely O'Brien met with Eamonn DeValera, they were to develop a personal friendship over the following decades. Certainly, Sinn Fein would have been opposed to any escalation of the general strike in Limerick. William O'Brien was only too happy to oblige.

At the same time he was meeting O'Brien, DeValera was downplaying the influence of socialist ideas in Ireland. In a newspaper interview DeValera claimed that there was no support for a 'workers republic' in Ireland. He continued stating that 'Sinn Fein in conjunction with Irish Labour will evolve a social programme of its own based on even-handed justice and Christian cooperation'. Eoin MacNeill went further, condemning any association with Bolshevism and saying that Sinn Fein 'will not commit for any special programme of reform or against any'.[112]

The General Strike is Called Off

Several thousand workers staged a protest outside the Mechanics Institute in Lower Glentworth Street as the Strike Committee and the National Executive members met inside. The 'national action' promised by the National Executive was not a nationwide general strike, but a proposal for the workers to evacuate the city and 'leave it as an empty shell'. The national leadership had to been seen to be making some sort of proposal, but the suggestion that workers to abandon the city was preposterous and was never going to happen. One this proposal was put on the table and rejected, the remainder of the time was spent trying to brow-beat the Strike Committee into abandoning the general strike in Limerick.

As the meeting concluded late in the evening John Cronin appeared at a window to address them. Cronin then read out what had been agreed with the National Executive members and concluded by stating 'the struggle would go on and the flag would be kept flying'.[113] Labour Councillor, R.P. O'Connor, read out the text of the proclamation to be posted around the city.[114] It was then the turn of Thomas Johnson to speak to the assembled workers. Johnson said he

> 'believed it (the general strike) was a fight taken up by the workers of Limerick on behalf of the people of Ireland as a whole, and it was the duty of Ireland to continue it. The working class everywhere were

interested in a fight such as that against the tyranny of a military autocracy. After very careful consideration they had decided that those workers who were not under the necessity of applying for permits to go to and from their daily work should resume their work and that those who had taken up the fight against this subjugation should continue to do so, confident that their fellow countrymen would back them up and keep them provided with funds equally as well as though they were working.'

Johnson then attempted to sugar-coat the call for a return to work by stating that he 'would do his best to provide the funds and called on people to support them. They would call a representative gathering of all the trade unions throughout Ireland, and they would have to decide how the fight should be continued'. He then went on to place the role of the trade union movement as an auxiliary to the nationalist movement by stating that 'They believed that it was only by the trades unions or the Labour Party that it would be taken up as the fight against conscription by all sections of the people who claimed to be nationalists, who claimed to be Irishmen and who claimed to be democrats.'

Johnson declared 'If Ireland is going to let down the workers of Limerick then Ireland should be ashamed of herself, and may no longer call herself a fighter for freedom' and stated that he was convinced that 'Ireland would not let the workers of Limerick down'.[115]

The report of the mood among the workers on the protest outside the Mechanics Institute was telling. The *Irish Independent* reported that the crowd was 'quiet' as it dispersed.[116] It was clear that opposition to abandoning the strike action existed and this opposition was to harden in the following hours. The Strike Committee posted proclamation notices around the city calling for a return to work. Rank-and-file members of the ITGWU went through the city ripping down the proclamation notices.[117]

The national media reported a mood of anger among sections of workers in Limerick with rumours that workers would 'supplant the Strike Committee'. A mass meeting of residents in Thomondgate was held on Friday night in support of workers still affected by the military restrictions. The residents blockaded Thomond Bridge on Saturday morning preventing people with a permit from crossing for a short time. The crowd dispersed after the arrival of the police.[118]

However, given the abandonment of the strike by the ILPTUC leadership, such a prospect was unlikely to gain traction. As the realisation that the general strike was ending, anger was now being directed at the nature of the return to work proposed by the Strike Committee. As soon as the Strike Committee called off the strike, the National Executive members, their objective achieved, left the city to avoid becoming a target for the anger of workers. Thomas Johnson remained until Sunday to ensure there was no backsliding on the decision to abandon the strike.

A Return to Work

The British military were providing large numbers of permit booklets to the employers in the mistaken belief that the workers, abandoned by the ILPTUC leaders, would accept the military diktats to produce permits. That was never going to be the case. However, the Strike Committee did come under severe criticism for its approach. Workers who couldn't return to work out of a need for permits were now reliant on support from the national trade union movement for strike pay and the ILPTUC had not been the most active in raising funds for the strike fund. The ILPTUC itself made a miserly donation of £50 during the strike. A total of £1,500 had been donated to the strike fund and more was to be raised the following weekend.

Local unions met with the Strike Committee to discuss the return to work. Approximately half the workers in the city resumed work under instructions from the Strike Committee.[119] Van drivers who had resumed work refused permits from their employers and wouldn't deliver goods outside the proclaimed area. Cases of need were dealt with by a sub-committee from strike funds. Local trade union branches around the country embarked on a fund-raising campaign for the Limerick Strike Committee. All 600 women workers in the Limerick Clothing Factory marched back to work together on Friday morning. The 690 mostly women workers at the Condensed Milk Company were to do likewise on Monday.[120]

On the night of Monday, 28 April the Trades Council held a meeting to discuss participating in the general strike on Mayday. There was a large demonstration of workers, including a large number of railway workers, through the city that ended up outside the meeting demanding participation in the nationwide Mayday protests. The conservative leadership of the Trades Council decided against calling the workers out on Mayday. In response the 800 railway workers in the city declared they would strike anyway.[121]

It didn't take long for the attacks on the Strike Committee to begin. At Sunday mass in St. Michael's Parish Church Fr. Dwane stated that 'neither His Lordship the Bishop, Most Reverend Dr. Michael Hallinan, nor the clergy were consulted before the strike was started and that they were totally opposed to its continuance'. Dwane continued stating that he hoped that 'the honest working men of Limerick would in future duly consider any action they were about to take and be guided only by leaders whom they could rely on and not be fooled or deceived by anyone whatsoever'.[122]

The national media then launched their propaganda campaign attacking the left and socialist activists, stating 'the people and indeed every section of the community, save the extremists, are greatly elated that the strike is over and that the peace and good order that prevailed all through the continuance has remained undisturbed to the end'.[123] The British Chief Secretary, Ian McPherson, stated that 'Happily the crisis which might have developed if its authors had their way, is now over' and he 'was glad to say that the wiser and more experienced leaders of labour had been among the first to condemn such a reckless, arbitrary and reprehensible manipulation of industrial means for political ends'.[124] The scale of the sell-out by the leadership of the ILPTUC (and the British Trade Union Congress) was amply demonstrated when they received praise from the head of the British Imperialist presence in Ireland.

By the time the strike ended the workers of Limerick had demonstrated the strength of the working class to manage their own affairs. Despite tensions between the radical and conservative wings of the Trades Council and a constant debate over tactics, there was no breaking of ranks. The Limerick Soviet was to prove to be a crucial juncture in the development of class consciousness and the radicalisation of the workers movement in Ireland. The blueprint for strike action and occupations was snow clear and the process of establishing workers committees, making decisions and implementing those decisions was amply demonstrated. Many of the tactics used on Limerick were to be replicated during the workplace soviets over 1920-1922 and in strikes and land seizures that were commonplace during the revolutionary period in Ireland.

---

[1] *Freeman's Journal*, 10 April 1919. This issue of the paper carried articles on the Battle for Odessa, the Bavarian Soviet, Bolshevism in Italy, a Bolshevik uprising in Serbia, Russian Bolsheviks being deported from England and Bolsheviks in Sweden.

[2] *Freeman's Journal*, 11 April 1919. This issue carried reports of strikes in Donegal, Loughrea, the Curragh Camp and a separate dispute at the Curragh racecourse, Carlow, Kilkenny and two separate strikes in Kerry.

[3] *Kerry News*, 9 April 1919.

[4] Cahill, *Forgotten Revolution*, p. 45

[5] *Freeman's Journal*, 10 April 1919.

[6] *Kerry News*, 11 April 1919

[7] *Freeman's Journal*, 11 April 1919, *Derry Journal*, 11 April 1919

[8] *Donegal News*, 12 April 1919

[9] *Derry Journal*, 11 April 1919, *Donegal News*, 12 April 1919.

[10] *Evening Herald*, 14 April 1919.

[11] Irish Labour Party and Trade Union Congress, *Report to the Twenty-Fourth Annual Meeting*, 1918, p. 12

[12] Limerick United Trade and Labour Council, *Minutes*, 11 April 1919.

[13] *Evening Herald*, 14 April 1919.

[14] Cahill, p. 64

[15] Lieut.-General Michael Brennan, *Statement by Witness, Bureau of Military History 1913-1921*, Document No. W.S. 1,068, File No. S.337. [Available at: http://www.bureauofmilitaryhistory.ie/reels/bmh/BMH.WS1068.pdf] (Accessed on: 25 January, 2018)

[16] Volunteer Jeremiah Cronin, *Statement by Witness, Bureau of Military History 1913-1921*,

Document No. W.S. 1,432, File No. S.2748. [Available at:
http://www.bureauofmilitaryhistory.ie/reels/bmh/BMH.WS1432.pdf] (Accessed on: 25
January, 2018)

[17] *Freeman's Journal,* 14 April 1919.

[18] Cahill, p. 64

[19] *Evening Herald,* 15 April 1919.

[20] *Evening Herald,* 15 April 1919

[21] O'Connor Lysaght, *The Story of the Limerick Soviet,* p. 24

[22] Greaves, *The Irish Transport and General Workers Union*, p. 236

[23] *Freeman's Journal,* 15 April 1919

[24] *Freeman's Journal,* 15 April 1919

[25] *Cork Examiner,* 15 April 1919. The Comintern, also know as the Third International, was an international organisation of Marxist parties. The first congress of the Comintern was held in Moscow in early March 1919.

[26] *Cork Examiner,* 15 April 1919

[27] *Cork Examiner,* 16 April 1919

[28] *Cork Examiner,* 16 April 1919

[29] *Freeman's Journal,* 16 April 1919

[30] ILPTUC, *Report to the Twenty-Fifth Annual Meeting,* 1919, p. 77

[31] *Cork Examiner,* 16 April 1919.

[32] *Cork Examiner,* 16 April 1919.

[33] *Cork Examiner,* 16 April 1919.

[34] *Freeman's Journal,* 16 April 1919

[35] *Cork Examiner,* 16 April 1919.

[36] *Evening Herald,* 16 April 1919

[37] *Cork Examiner,* 17 April 1919

[38] Conor Kostick, *Revolution in Ireland: Popular Militancy 1917 to 1923* (London, 1996), p. 77

[39] *Cork Examiner,* 17 April 1919

[40] *Cork Examiner,* 17 April 1919

[41] *Irish Independent,* 16 April 1919

[42] *Evening Herald,* 17 April 1919

[43] *Evening Herald,* 17 April 1919, *Cork Examiner,* 18 April 1919

[44] *Cork Examiner,* 18 April 1919

[45] *Cork Examiner,* 18 April 1919

[46] *Freeman's Journal,* 18 April 1919

[47] *Evening Herald,* 17 April 1919

[48] *Cork Examiner,* 18 April 1919

[49] Cahill, *Forgotten Revolution,* p. 75

[50] *Freeman's Journal,* 17 April 1919.

[51] *Freeman's Journal,* 18 April 1919

[52] *Cork Examiner,* 18 April 1919

[53] *Freeman's Journal,* 18 April 1919

[54] *Cork Examiner,* 19 April 1919

[55] Kostick, , p. 77

[56] *Cork Examiner,* 19 April 1919

[57] *Cork Examiner,* 19 April 1919

[58] *Skibbereen Eagle,* 19 April 1919
[59] *Cork Examiner,* 19 April 1919
[60] *Cork Examiner,* 19 April 1919
[61] *Connaught Tribune,* 19 April 1919
[62] *Fermanagh Herald,* 19 April 1919
[63] *Connaught Tribune,* 19 April 1919
[64] *Sunday Independent,* 20 April 1919
[65] Eugene J. Foley, 'Donnellys of Cork Street', *Dublin Historical Record,* Vol. 51, No. 1, (Spring, 1998), pp. 74-80
[66] *Freeman's Journal,* 21 April 1919
[67] *Sunday Independent,* 20 April 1919
[68] *Cork Examiner,* 21 April 1919
[69] *Sunday Independent,* 20 April 1919
[70] *Cork Examiner,* 21 April 1919
[71] Cahill, p. 73
[72] Ibid., p. 73
[73] *Freeman's Journal,* 21 April 1919
[74] *Irish Independent,* 21 April 1919
[75] *Freeman's Journal,* 21 April 1919
[76] *Cork Examiner,* 21 April 1919
[77] *Irish Independent,* 21 April 1919
[78] *Irish Times,* 21 April 1919
[79] *Cork Examiner,* 22 April 1919
[80] *Freeman's Journal,* 23 April 1919
[81] Cahill, p. 74
[82] *Cork Examiner,* 22 April 1919
[83] *Freeman's Journal,* 23 April 1919
[84] Russell, *What's the matter with Ireland?* p. 131
[85] *Workers Bulletin,* 21 April 1919
[86] *Cork Examiner,* 21 April 1919
[87] *Cork Examiner,* 22 April 1919
[88] *Cork Examiner,* 22 April 1919
[89] *Cork Examiner,* 22 April 1919
[90] *Evening Herald,* 22 April 1919
[91] Cahill, *Forgotten Revolution,* p. 75
[92] *Cork Examiner,* 22 April 1919
[93] Cahill, , p. 75
[94] *Cork Examiner,* 24 April 1919
[95] James Casey, 'A Limerick Challenge to British Tyranny', in Ruan O'Donnell, (ed.) *Limerick's Fighting Story: Told by the Men Who Made It,* (Dublin, 2009), p. 98
[96] *Irish Independent,* 23 April 1919
[97] *Cork Examiner,* 24 April 1919
[98] *Evening Herald,* 22 April 1919
[99] *Freeman's Journal,* 23 April 1919
[100] *Freeman's Journal,* 23 April 1919
[101] *Freeman's Journal,* 21 April 1919
[102] *Cork Examiner,* 22 April 1919

[103] *Evening Herald,* 22 April 1919

[104] *Cork Examiner,* 24 April 1919

[105] ILPTUC, *Report to the Twenty-Fifth Annual Meeting,* 1919, p. 83

[106] *Cork Examiner,* 24 April 1919

[107] *Cork Examiner,* 24 April 1919

[108] *Cork Examiner,* 25 April 1919

[109] *Cork Examiner,* 25 April 1919

[110] *Cork Examiner,* 25 April 1919

[111] Kostick, *Revolution in Ireland,* p. 78

[112] *Freeman's Journal,* 25 April 1919

[113] *Freeman's Journal,* 25 April 1919

[114] *Irish Independent,* 25 April 1919

[115] *Cork Examiner,* 25 April 1919

[116] *Irish Independent,* 25 April 1919

[117] *Cork Examiner,* 26 April 1919

[118] *Cork Examiner,* 28 April 1919

[119] *Cork Examiner,* 26 April 1919

[120] *Cork Examiner,* 28 April 1919

[121] *Cork Examiner,* 29 April 1919

[122] *Cork Examiner,* 28 April 1919

[123] *Cork Examiner,* 29 April 1919

[124] *Cork Examiner,* 30 April 1919

AFTER THE SOVIET

'A political leader who desires to be useful to the revolutionary
proletariat must be able to distinguish concrete cases of
compromises that are inexcusable and those that are an expression
of opportunism and treachery.'
—Vladimir Lenin[1]

Jim Kemmy argued that the workers of Limerick had grown in political consciousness under the leadership of the LUTLC[2]. But it can be seen from what has already been outlined that the majority of the leadership of the LUTLC played a conservative role in the months and years before the 'Soviet'. It was the impact of the ITGWU and others that led to the radicalisation of the Limerick working class and the development of a class consciousness among the workers, not alone in Limerick city and county, but throughout the entire country.

Republican criticism of the strike committee followed the 'Soviet'. In a scurrilous attack a republican newspaper, The *Republic*, declared that the leaders had 'bowed the knee in shameful submission to the army of occupation'[3]. This is despite the fact that the Sinn Fein Mayor, Alphonsus O'Mara, was instrumental in working with Bishop Hallinan to get the Strike Committee to call off the strike. The strong criticism from Republicans may have had more to do with the lack of influence that they had within the Limerick working class at the time. Following the ending of the Soviet Sinn Fein representatives also attacked socialist ideas and denigrated the working class, claiming:

> 'The Ideal (of a soviet) is a foreign importation...there are very grave religious and ethical problems in the sudden seizure of all political and economic control by a section of the community. Besides these workers are at present quite unfit to carry on the business of the country...'[4]

As outlined in the introduction the more conscious spokespersons for capital made a much more sober assessment of the Soviet outlining the power and impact working class action.[5] As with the conscription crisis, the Limerick Soviet posed the challenge to the leadership of the ILPTUC, were they willing to take the leadership of the struggle for self-determination and promote it on a class basis by developing a conscious class movement, not just for independence from Britain, but taking the levers of power into the hands of the working class.

The Limerick Soviet once against demonstrated that the leadership of the ILPTUC were unwilling to play a role in placing the labour movement at the head of the struggle for political, social and economic emancipation. Given that the general strike in Limerick was seen as a direct confrontation to the authority of British Imperialism, expanding the Limerick strike into a general strike across the entire island would have also meant confronting Imperialism on a national basis. It would also have forced the leadership of the ILPTUC to place the labour movement at the head of the liberation struggle and to have fought that struggle on a class, rather and a nationalist, basis. This was the primary reason why the national leadership effectively sabotaged the Soviet and its potential.

Furthermore, the Limerick Soviet was a key juncture in the development of the class struggle in Ireland. It raised the political consciousness of workers and demonstrated an element of workers control not previously seen in the country. The class struggle that developed in the post- Limerick Soviet period flowed from the developments that took place in Limerick. It acted as an exemplar for future workplace soviets and significantly enhanced the profile of the radical left-wing industrial organisers within the ITGWU. The Soviet also demonstrated a significant degree of independence of the rank-and-file of the trade union movement. As the class struggle developed the conflict saw the ranks of the trade unions, particularly the ITGWU, operating in defiance of the leadership and often working outside the official structures of the unions. Over time this was to become more and more evident.

The Leadership Defend Their Actions

The outlook of the leadership of the ILPTUC was amply demonstrated by the debate on the Limerick Soviet at the ILPTUC Annual Meeting held in Drogheda at the beginning of August 1919. The Annual Report contained a section on the 'Limerick Strike' detailing the approach of the ILPTUC leadership. The first statement exposing the attitude of the leadership was the claim that the ILPTUC never had any intention of taking control of the strike, or extending the action.[6] Less than three pages were devoted to outlining the events in Limerick, despite it being the most significant labour event of the year (the Belfast engineering strike accounted for six sentences in the entire 169 page report).

When the debate on the Soviet began at the Annual Meeting, William O'Brien launched a stinging attack on those he claimed were making 'certain statements' about the role of the ILPTUC leadership during the Soviet. It was left to D.H. O'Donnell of the ICWU to question the role of the ILPTUC leadership. O'Donnell questioned the repeated delays in the actions of the ILPTUC leadership, stating that some people were arguing that the proposal to evacuate Limerick 'was made by the Executive to break up the strike'.[7]

After his intervention, O'Donnell faced a wave of attacks from supporters of the leadership for daring to question their role during the Soviet. David Douglas from Belfast argued that both the Belfast and Limerick strikes should never have happened and both strikes were 'abortive' because the strike leaders didn't prepare properly. Several other delegates repeated this refrain and argued that without money the strikes could not have succeeded. It was left to Tom MacPartlan of the Amalgamated Society of Carpenters in Dublin to tell delegates 'to get out of their head that a little subscription here or there would win strikes'.[8]

O'Brien went on another rampage accusing O'Donnell of repeating 'lying and slanderous charges' and that 'a persistent campaign of lying and innuendo was going on against the Executive'. O'Brien then went on to produce a litany of excuses to explain the delays in the actions of the Executive.[9] He was followed by Thomas Farren, soon to be President of the ILPTUC, who repeated the excuses and came to O'Brien's defence.[10] O'Donnell responded to the accusations by repeating his claim that the delay in the Executive going to Limerick 'allowed certain undercurrents to work to sap and undermine the movement in Limerick'.[11]

Ultimately the debate circulated around two crucial issues, firstly whether the National Executive of the ILPTUC had a right to call a nationwide general strike and secondly, if such a general strike was called, what would be the consequences. Several delegates claimed that the Executive had no authority to call a general strike.[12] Delegates from the NUR defended the railway workers against claims that they sabotaged the Soviet by not striking in support of Limerick workers. They repeatedly stated that the railway workers were ready to act as soon as instructed to do so by the National Executive of the ILPTUC.[13]

The consequences of calling a nationwide general strike was a key factor in the defence of the National Executive. Thomas Farren, the vice-chairman of the ILPTUC, outlined that he told the Limerick Strike Committee that the National Executive had no power to call a nationwide general strike. He stated that the question of calling a national conference of the ILPTUC to decide on a general strike was discussed, but the National Executive members stated that if such a conference decided to call a general strike, it would be of limited duration because 'under the existing state of affairs they were not prepared for the Revolution'.[14] D.H. O'Donnell argued that a

Special Congress should have been held before the National Executive decamped to Limerick.[15]

The reality is that the argument that the National Executive did not have the power to call a general strike was used as an excuse for the failure to act in support of the Limerick Soviet. The hypocrisy of the leadership was demonstrated the following April when a two-day general strike was called to force the British authorities to release hunger-striking prisoners from jail. No excuses were made on that occasion about the National Executive not having the authority to call strike action.

As he had done during the special conference in 1918 to withdraw from the general election of that year, Walter Carpenter of the International Tailors and later the CPI, defended the National Executive stating that he

> 'knew what a General Strike meant – that it has got to be backed up by guns, that it meant a Revolution; and until they were prepared for Revolution there was no use in calling a General Strike. Unless they were prepared to use guns and hoist the Red Flag from one end of the country to the other there was no use in condemning the National Executive... the workers were not class conscious enough, not educated enough and not ready for a General Strike'.

Carpenter went on to state 'when the day came that they were class conscious and educated they would not want leaders – they would go out themselves'.[16]

The comments from Carpenter demonstrate a complete lack of understanding about the process of revolution and the nature of revolutionary movements. In particular, he failed to recognise the key role of a revolutionary party in the process of revolution, failings that he was to carry into his time as a member of the CPI.

Thomas Johnson's intervention in the debate demonstrated all his skills at obfuscation. He claimed that an attack on the National Executive was an attack on the workers of Limerick. Johnson then argued 'They could never win a strike by downing tools against the British Army' and followed this by stating that 'there was always the possibility in Ireland that aggressive action on this side might prompt aggressive action on the other side of the Channel'. He further argued that 'their knowledge of England and Scotland did not lead them to think that any action in Ireland would have brought a responsive movement in those countries'.[17]

These comments were made despite the fact that support for the Soviet was promised by the Independent Labour Party in Britain, which had a membership in the region of 50,000,[18] the British Socialist Party, which at the time had a membership of over 6,000,[19] and the Scottish Trades Union Congress.[20] On top of that the London leadership of the NUR were terrified that a strike by railway workers in Ireland would lead to an outbreak of sympathy strikes by rail workers in Britain.

Johnson's objective was to present a defeatist outlook to justify refusing to call a general strike.

In his following remarks Johnson stated that 'A general strike could have been legitimately called on twelve occasions within the last two years. But it was not a question of justification. It was a question of strategy. Were they to take the enemy's time or were they to take their own?'[21] For Johnson, the strategy was how to avoid calling a general strike. If the calling of a general strike was legitimate then it should have been called, as it had been during the conscription crisis. The leadership of the ILPTUC were intent on avoiding such action precisely because it had no control over what would happen in the event of such strike action.

Johnson then went on to outline the argument against calling a general strike in support of the Limerick Soviet, claiming that 'They knew that if the railwaymen came out the soldiers would have taken on the railways next day. They knew if the soldiers were put on the railways, the railways would have been blown up. They knew that would have meant armed revolt.' He then went on to pose the question 'Did they as Trades Unionists suggest that it was for their Executive to say such action should be taken at a particular time, knowing, assured as they were, that it would have resulted in armed revolt in Ireland.' Johnson was attempting to use the fear of the consequences of an armed revolt to block a general strike, at a time when Ireland was already in armed revolt. In reality, if a general strike was called with the potential for the transport network to be paralysed, it is likely that some combination of the British military, the business elites, Sinn Fein and the Catholic hierarchy would have cobbled together some cessation of martial law in Limerick to diffuse the situation.

However, Johnson went further, demonstrating again his ability to promise the earth with the objective of delivering nothing. Johnson in a stunning declaration stated that he believed

> 'it was quite possible that it would be by the action of the Labour movement in Ireland that insurrection would some day be developed. There might be occasion to decide on a down tools policy which would have the effect of calling out the armed forces of the Crown. But Limerick was not the occasion.'[22]

The reality for Johnson and the rest of the bureaucratic leadership of the ILPTUC is that there would never be an occasion for an 'insurrection' and they would do everything in their power to undermine the potential for it.

Thomas Johnson gave an insight to the actual approach of the leadership of the ILPTUC towards the Limerick Soviet. After more than a week of delaying tactics, the ILPTUC leadership went to Limerick 'with a definite proposition' – to evacuate the city and leave it as an 'empty shell in the hands of the military'. In effect Johnson and the ILPTUC leaders were calling on the Limerick working class to abandon their struggle, a struggle that had the potential to evolve into a nationwide general strike supported by the mass of the working class and spreading through solidarity action with workers in Britain.

The argument was that evacuating the city would have been a good propaganda stunt and, again inciting fear, 'would not have cost a single life'. Johnson was ignoring the fact that, during the Soviet, striking workers had been shot in Co. Down and Co. Donegal as farmers and the police attempted to suppress strike action. Strikes became increasingly violent in the period after the Soviet as farmers attempted to resist pay demands by carrying out attacks on striking workers and workplace occupations were regularly threatened by the IRA during 1920-1922.

It is an open question as to how British Imperialism would have reacted to a nationwide general strike in support of the Limerick Soviet. Could the British military have attempted to violently suppress the general strike? That was a possibility. The British army had been deployed in Glasgow during the '40-hours' strike. More than 10,000 British soldiers were sent to Glasgow in order to break the strike. Despite this there was no direct confrontation between the troops and the striking workers.[23] Attempting to use military repression against a general strike in Ireland would have led to a huge backlash from the mass of the population and also opened up the possibility of widespread strike action in Britain in opposition to the oppression of a general strike. At the height of the war in 1918 the British government had made major concessions when the ILPTUC organised a general strike against conscription and were to do so again in April 1920 during the two-day general strike in support of hunger-striking prisoners.

A more likely possibility was that the British military would have made considerable concessions in order to dissipate the anger towards the imposition of martial law, sufficient concessions that would have quickly brought the strike action to an end while allowing for some saving of face by the British authorities. Certainly, while martial law was initially imposed with the intent of implementing it to the fullest extent, the emergence of a general strike in Limerick immediately led to the British commanders in Limerick offering concessions, the lax imposition of the permit restrictions and by the second week of the strike many workers were passing through the cordons unhindered.

In his final comments to the ILPTUC meeting Johnson downplayed the importance of the Limerick Soviet, stating 'Let them remember what the strike was. It was a protest... against a military tyranny. They did not expect to beat the British Army. They intended to protest and their protest was effective; and they did the wise thing in the end. Rather than have one going back to-day and another to-morrow they called the strike off.'[24]

One important issue that has never been addressed in any of the literature on the Limerick Soviet is why the ILPTUC leadership were intent on bringing the general strike in Limerick to an end as soon as possible. It is clear that the British military authorities were considering making further concessions during the second week of the Soviet. They were facing difficulties enforcing the cordon around the city, with the troops unwilling to act against people breaking the cordon. There were three shooting incidents at different times during strike, but these were random, isolated incidents that didn't result in any consequences. When there was an organised effort to break the cordon, as with the protesters at the train station after the hurling match, there was no attempt to prevent progress. Despite this, the ILPTUC leadership were determined to undermine the strike rather than bring it to a successful conclusion.

William O'Brien and the rest of the trade union bureaucracy faced another difficult problem. At the beginning of the general strike in Limerick, O'Brien had already called for a 'labour holiday' on Mayday, effectively calling a general strike for Mayday 1919. The problem for O'Brien was that if the general strike was continuing in Limerick up to Mayday, then it was inevitable that the Mayday strike and protests would have become a general strike in support of Limerick. In such an eventuality it is possible that the Mayday general strike could have evolved into an extended general strike to force a climb down by the British authorities. Such a development would have meant that the leadership of the ILPTUC would have lost control of the situation and local activists would have been leading the struggle in support of the Limerick Soviet. Such a scenario would have been catastrophic for the ILPTUC leaders, and particularly William O'Brien. Bringing the strike in Limerick to an end before Mayday became a crucial aspect for the leadership of the ILPTUC.

Sean Dowling and the Revolutionary Socialist Party

In the aftermath of the Limerick Soviet, Sean Dowling, along with the other Marxist activists, threw himself into organising industrial struggle. He also recognised the necessity for building a new political formation to represent the revolutionary tradition of James Connolly. Dowling saw the Socialist Party of Ireland as an openly reformist party, dominated by the bureaucratic leadership of the ILPTUC. Two weeks after the ending of the Limerick Soviet he was in Belfast at the founding meeting of the Revolutionary Socialist Party (RSP).[25]

While Sean Dowling was regarded as the main theoretician of this new socialist grouping he remained a syndicalist in outlook. Dowling does not appear to have understood the need to build a revolutionary party to attract the most class conscious workers and to develop a revolutionary cadre capable of drawing on the historical lessons of class struggle. A party capable of analysing fast moving developments and able to adapt to changing circumstances in order to advance the cause of socialism. It is unfortunate that there does not appear to be any political writings by Dowling in existence that could have given an insight to his approach.

The RSP initially attracted a layer of Marxists and trade unionists. The party claimed the affiliation of seven full-time industrial organisers, out of a total of twenty-one industrial organisers, in the ITGWU.[26] It also appears to have attracted the support of a layer of workers in Belfast, particularly among Protestant workers in East Belfast. The party maintained a certain level of support in the city with newspapers reporting meetings with an attendance of 500 in East Belfast. The Belfast Pogrom in July 1920 seems to have resulted in the death knell for the RSP. The labour hall in East Belfast where it held its meetings was one of the first building burned by loyalist thugs and there is no reference in relation to the party after this time.[27] While the RSP saw the grouping together of Marxist elements, it did not operate as a revolutionary party in the same way as the Bolsheviks. There seems to have been little effort to educate activists in the methods of Marxism and to build a revolutionary cadre.

The Revolutionary Party

In 1871 the masses of Paris rose up and formed the Paris Commune. The Commune governed Paris for just over two months before it was brutally suppressed by the French army. In his writings on the Paris Commune, Karl Marx described the Commune as the prototype for a revolutionary government of the masses.[28] This prototype later developed into Workers, Soldiers and Peasants Soviets during the revolutionary period in Russia. The Soviets by their nature are a demonstration of the working class exercising power.[29] In Ireland the Trades Councils offered the potential infrastructure for building workers soviets. The Limerick Soviet was a form of dual power being exercised in the city while the British exercised military power in the country. It demonstrated the ability of the working class to exercise political power and posed a challenge to the leadership of the labour movement to recognise its potential and the potential of the labour movement to evolve into a revolutionary movement and exercise political power in Ireland.

The Paris Commune emerged unexpectedly, taking French revolutionaries by surprise.[30] On the eve of the Commune Marx advised the communards of the need to organise in a revolutionary party.[31] The failure to do so contributed to the crushing of the Paris Commune. In contrast, the Bolsheviks in Russia consciously organised into a revolutionary party, a party learning from the events of history, capable of analysing developments and preparing to intervene in these events. In particular, the Bolsheviks used the period between the February and October Revolutions in Russia to win support on the Workers and Soldiers Councils (the Soviets) in Petrograd, Moscow and other industrial centres.[32]

These Soviets operated in an environment of dual power where the workers movement exercised political power at the same time as Kerensky's liberal, pro-capitalist, Provisional Government. The nature of this dual power was demonstrated in September 1917 when the Tsarist Army Commander, General Kornilov, attempted to overthrow the Provisional government by a military coup-d'état. Knowing that they were incapable of defeating the coup attempt, the Provisional Government appealed to the Soviets to defend the revolution. The liberal government needed the assistance of the revolutionary workers movement to save them from military intervention. The Petrograd Soviet demanded that leading Bolsheviks, like Leon Trotsky, were released from prison to assist in organising the defeat of the coup. Railway workers inhibited the transportation of troops and equipment. The Soviets infiltrated Kornilov's army and propagandised among the rank-and-file soldiers to desert and join the revolution and the Kerensky government armed the workers of Petrograd under the leadership of the Petrograd Soviet to defend the city from Kornilov's army.

Leon Trotsky later explained the political necessity for a revolutionary workers party as the workers movement in Europe faced the brutal face of fascism in the early 1930s. He stated:

'The interests of the class cannot be formulated otherwise than in the shape of a program; the program cannot be defended otherwise than by creating the party. The class, taken by itself, is only material for exploitation. The proletariat assumes an independent role only at that moment when from a social class in itself it becomes a political class for itself. This cannot take place otherwise than through the medium of a party. The party is that historical organ by means of which the class becomes class conscious.'[33]

One of the factors in the success of the Russian Revolution only weeks later, was the approach of the Bolsheviks, as a revolutionary workers party, to propagandise among the working class for the workers movement to act on an independent class basis. Writing at the time of the coup attempt, Lenin outlined that 'The Kornilov revolt is a most unexpected (unexpected at such a moment and in such a form) and downright unbelievably sharp turn in events. Like every sharp turn, it calls for a revision and change of tactics'. The 'change of tactics' that Lenin argued for was a change in the criticisms of Kerensky, to accuse him of '*weakness* and *vacillation*', and demand a more active, truly revolutionary war against Kornilov.[34] During the Kornilov coup attempt Lenin sharply criticised elements within the Bolsheviks who wanted to give full support to Kerensky's Provisional Government and demanded that the Bolsheviks advocate for an independent class approach within the workers movement. This had the impact of raising the class consciousness of workers and winning the more conscious layers to the Bolshevik party.

The approach of Lenin and the Bolsheviks can be seen in contrast to the approach of William O'Brien and the other 'leaders' of the ILPTUC. Instead of forging an independent class approach and demonstrating the role and intent of the nationalist leaders of Sinn Fein, William O'Brien repeatedly used the ILPTUC as an auxiliary to the nationalist movement supporting the nationalist leadership, even when their objective was in direct conflict with the interests of the Irish working class.

The Marxist current that existed in Ireland during the revolutionary period was committed to a syndicalist approach. In other countries the syndicalists were won over to the Communist International. In Ireland neither the Revolutionary Socialist Party, nor the later emerging Communist Party of Ireland, were able to break with syndicalism and win the best activists to a revolutionary workers party using the method of Marxism.[35] If Sean Dowling, Jack Hedley and the other Marxist activists had understood the necessity to build a revolutionary party to intervene in unfolding events, the potential existed for this party to grow rapidly and play a decisive role in the unfolding revolutionary period.

These deficiencies should not detract from the role Sean Dowling was playing in the workers movement. We shall see that in the three years following the Limerick Soviet Dowling played a crucial role in all the major working class struggles in Ireland. His legacy as a Marxist and trade union activist needs to be recognised and socialists should become advocates in highlighting his achievements and those of the workers he represented.

Mayday 1919

The leadership of the Trades Council lapsed back into their usual conservative approach after the end of the Limerick Soviet. It is clear that there was a significant element of demoralisation, particularly among the more conservative layers. In an effort to bolster the confidence of the craft delegates on Limerick Trades Council, the leadership of the ILPTUC offered John Cronin the position of Vice- Chairman of the ILPTUC. However, Cronin was so impacted in the aftermath of the Soviet that he turned down the offer and even refused to attend the Annual Meeting of the ILPTUC in August.[36]

The Mayday general strike of 1919 once again demonstrated the strength of the labour movement in Ireland. With the exception of Limerick practically the entire country was once again shut down. While the scale of the shutdown was impressive it was not as complete as for the conscription crisis. This is hardly a surprise. The ILPTUC were seen to have abandoned the general strike in Limerick and the vague call for an 'International League of Peoples' was hardly a lightning rod for the working masses.

In Dublin there were no trams, no sailings, no theatres, no cinemas, no electric power, no taxis, no newspapers, no restaurants or licenced premises open and no trains except on the Great Northern Railway line. 'Nearly all business houses and industrial firms... were closed'. The ICWU defied British threats to sack any worker in the civil service who took part in the strike. A confrontation occurred at the army pay office where more than 100 striking clerks were picketing. The Army claimed that because a strike hadn't actually been called by the ILPTUC then the picketing was illegal, and the strikers would be arrested if they didn't disperse. The ICWU threatened to shut down the civil service if any of its members were arrested or sacked.[37] The demonstration in Dublin was haphazard. The ILPTUC hadn't organised a march and tens of thousands of workers milled around the streets of the city, with the ILPTUC leadership noticeable by their absence. O'Brien wanted a holiday, the working class wanted to demonstrate their power and organisation.

The Mayday protest in Derry was banned and the city placed under martial law after the Apprentice Boys claimed that a proposed workers demonstration along the City Walls would be 'provocative'. The City Walls were occupied by the army and the Trades Council caved in and called off the demonstration. The Ulster Unionist Labour Association was used in an attempt to divide workers along sectarian lines.[38] Despite the cancellation of the demonstration many workers in Derry walked off the job and held a mass meeting. Rumours that 'loyalist rowdies' were being drafted into the city to attack the meeting proved unfounded.[39]

In Drogheda the RIC outlawed the carrying of red flags and threatened to arrest the leaders of the Trades Council if any red flags appeared on the Mayday protest. In panic the Trades Council called off the protest. However, the ITGWU branch in the town ignored the decision of the Trades Council leaders and called on all workers to join them in a mass protest through the town. Thousands joined the demonstration led by local bands behind large red banners. The streets of Drogheda were a sea of red and the head of the ITGWU in the town told workers that they 'would not allow a policeman to tell them the colour of their flag. The workers later dispersed but only after a rousing rendition of the 'Red Flag'.[40]

In Dundalk thousands of workers paraded through the streets carrying red flags. All bar 40 of the 600 workers employed at the railway works walked off and took part in the demonstration.[41]

The turnout in Cashel was smaller than elsewhere. The town was under martial law and Sinn Fein used the demonstration to protest against the British military. When the RIC approached the organisers they were informed that the demonstration would be forcibly dispersed as it did not have the required permit. By the time a detachment of armed soldiers arrived the protesters had left.

In Cork 20,000 workers participated in a Mayday demonstration. As in Limerick the conservative nature of the craft union leaders of the Trades council was demonstrated. A local priest was invited to address the crowd. In Cobh a leading member of Sinn Fein, Professor Rahilly[42] addressed the workers demonstration. Large protests were also held in Bandon, Skibbereen and Fermoy. In Skibbereen, a large demonstration marched behind a red banner emblazoned with 'Workers of the World Unite'. Not surprisingly, the nationalist *Skibbereen Eagle* launched an attack on the 'disastrous' general strike in Limerick, claiming that workers should not get involved in political issues if they want to grow the trade union movement.[43]

Further large protests were held in Waterford, Ennis and Glin, Co. Limerick. Thurles was convulsed with a very bitter strike where the carters in the town were engaged in strikebreaking. After a confrontation between strikers and scabs on the Friday evening, the police exacted revenge by baton charging the Mayday march the following day. In response the ITGWU called all its members out on strike.[44] Open hostility towards the Mayday strike was displayed by nationalists and by the British authorities.

In Nenagh a 'Vast Parade by Workers in North Tipperary' took place. Flying pickets were stationed in various parts of the town to ensure compliance with the general strike. There was no need for the pickets as the entire town was shut down for Mayday. When ITGWU members from Newport arrived behind a flag bearer carrying a red flag the police attempted, but failed, to confiscate it. The workers formed a cordon around the flag to prevent its removal and the police withdrew rather than engage in a confrontation. The ITGWU and the NUR dominated the demonstration.[45]

The *Irish Independent* noted that the workers demonstration in Enniskillen saw 'Sinn Feiners, Orangemen and Hibernians working together in the interests of Labour'. The nationalist *Fermanagh Herald* completely ignored the Mayday strike, instead focussing on promoting Sinn Fein initiatives in the area. Although not participating in the Mayday strike, workers in Belfast did take to the streets on Sunday 3 May. The *Belfast Newsletter* described how "a little band of disgruntled Red Socialists" led 100,000 workers through the streets of Belfast.[46]

The protest in Belfast was a demonstration that a class-based approach could break down sectarian barriers and bring together Catholic and Protestant workers. Similar protests took place in other parts of the North.

In Co. Meath Mayday protests, led by a red flag, took place in Navan, Dunshaughlin, Drumree, Skryne, Crossakiel, Trim and Kells. In Moyvane, Co. Kerry, 200 striking farm labourers staged a Mayday march through the village only to be confronted by a large group of farmers armed with 'pikes and other weapons'. A full-scale riot was only averted when the local priest persuaded the farmers to withdraw. Negotiations then took place and the farmers conceded a pay increase to the labourers.[47]

While the Mayday general strike could have, once again, placed the labour movement at the head of the ongoing struggle in Ireland, O'Brien and the ILPTUC leadership were intent on keeping it a low key affair and tinging it with nationalism as a result of the focus of motions from the leadership emphasising the issue of self-determination while failing to address any class-issues. The leadership still feared the potential for the Mayday protests to spiral out of control in the immediate aftermath of the Limerick Soviet.

Limerick After the Soviet

Several commentaries on the Limerick Soviet have suggested that in the aftermath of the Limerick 'Soviet' the militancy of the workers became dissipated[48] and that locally employers regained their previous authority and the workers fell back into passivity[49]. This was not the case and the strike wave that existed before the Soviet continued and even intensified over the rest of the year.

Conflict did occur within the trade union movement both locally and nationally as a result of the fall-out from the 'Soviet'. Within the LUTLC the antagonism between the delegates of the old-style craft unions and the ITGWU came to the surface. John Cronin opposed the ITGWU's desire to criticise the National Executive and refused to attend Congress[50]. Nationally divisions also existed within the ITGWU. It was expected that the debate on the Limerick 'Soviet' would be the pivotal battleground between the two factions at Congress, the leadership around William O'Brien and the supporters of James Larkin organised around P.T. Daly. Ultimately Daly backed out of the fight and his influence continued to wane in the trade union movement. Daly attempted to organise an open-air meeting in Limerick to judge the mood in the city in June, but the meeting was banned because Daly hadn't applied for a permit.[51].

During June 1919, Sean Dowling was joined in Limerick by another ITGWU organiser and Marxist, Jack McGrath. Shortly afterwards English Marxist Jack Hedley arrived in Limerick to assist with the work of the ITGWU. Between them Dowling, McGrath and Hedley were to be intimately involved in the industrial struggles and workplace occupations in Limerick city and county over the next three years.

Industrial Conflict Becomes the Norm

Within two weeks of the end of the Limerick 'Soviet' the workers in the Cleeves creameries in County Limerick and Tipperary were on strike[52]. The workers at the Cleeve's owned Knocklong creamery were out for seven weeks.[53] During the course of the strike at Knocklong reports appeared that strikers engaged in spilling the milk of farmers who had diverted supplies to other creameries[54]. Before the end of May coachmakers in Limerick city were on strike,[55] as were drapers assistants at O'Mahonys of William Street.[56] In June ITGWU members at Clouncagh Creamery were out again[57] and another dispute arose on Limerick docks.[58] During the strike at

Clouncagh, the creamery manager attempted to carry out work normally done by the strikers by collecting coal from Newcastle West railway station only to be surrounded by flying pickets, his horse unharnessed and his trap thrown off a bridge into the River Deel.[59] Compensation was claimed for the destruction of the carts of four farmers drawing coal to the creamery during the strike.[60] June also saw a strike by over three hundred building workers, ignoring pleas from the Sinn Fein Mayor O'Meara to postpone the strike,[61] and ITGWU members struck at O'Callaghan's Tannery. July was to see further unrest in the city with strikes by tailors and in the furniture trade,[62] amongst ITGWU members at the Model Laundry, Spaights timber yard and a lock out of ITGWU members at McMahons.[63]

Industrial unrest, particularly involving the ITGWU, was to continue for the rest of the year. In August farm labourers at Feenagh went on strike,[64] followed at the beginning of September by one hundred and fifty labourers on the Dunraven Estate in Adare. A large force of police were drafted in during the dispute when the water supply to the village was cut off.[65] In October a strike occurred at the farmyard of Mr. C.F. Drew in Drewscourt over the employment of non-union labour.[66] That month also saw the beginning of a long and bitter strike by law clerks employed by the city solicitors, a strike that was actively supported by the ITGWU.[67] A new local workers paper the *Watchdog of Labour* took up the cause of the striking clerks[68] and during the course of the strike the law clerks published their own newspaper *The Red Flag.*[69] The LUTLC denounced the solicitors[70] and following the refusal of the solicitors to go to arbitration the Trades Council passed a resolution to collect a voluntary levy from all affiliated unions and societies.[71] Four weeks into the strike a legal bureau was set up in the ITGWU offices manned by the striking law clerks and providing free legal advice to the public.[72] At the end of October porters, packers and carmen, members of the ITGWU, employed at Hassetts, P.D. Bourke, Spaights, J.P. Evans and Newsoms all went on strike.[73] The strike lasted for five weeks.[74] Farm labourers staged a one-day strike at Bulgaden in search of a harvest bonus.[75]

At the beginning of November ITGWU members working in the saddlery trade went on strike demanding 1s 8d per hour for a forty seven hour week and following the intervention of Fr. Kelly their demands were conceded.[76] On 8 November seven hundred road workers from all over the county demonstrated in Limerick city marching from an adjourned County Council meeting to Bank Place where they were joined by the striking law clerks and hardware workers.[77] Strikes broke out in the city drapery stores two weeks later.[78] Farm labourers were again out on strike at Bulgaden with the press reporting that blows were freely exchanged with farmers during the strike.[79] Farmers who didn't pay the harvest bonus had their milk refused by the creamery workers at Bruff.[80] The ITGWU branch secretary in Newcastle West was re-instated following a strike at O'Shaughnessy's Sawmills after an attempt by the employer to sack him.[81] Shortly afterwards twenty-four members of the ITGWU went on strike at the Abbey Tannery in Athlunkard.[82]

Not alone did industrial disputes continue after the Limerick Soviet but the scale and tempo intensified. The number of disputes that involved violence or active sabotage was also increasing. The situation in Limerick was being replicated in other parts of the country.

The Catholic Hierarchy felt the need to combat the impact of the ideas of socialism by initiating a series of lectures, given by Rev. Murphy in the Augustinian Church, attacking socialism with the local press describing the lectures as a 'Searching Analysis of a Dangerous Theory'.[83] The lectures were transcribed in their entirety in the *Limerick Leader*.

Strike on the Docks

The beginning of December 1919 saw the most bitter strike yet to hit the city with a further dispute breaking out on the docks. Four hundred dock labourers went on strike demanding an increase of 4s per day for casual workers and 10s per week for constant men. Two cargo vessels full of coal and a third with grain were not discharged and arrangements had been made to ensure they would not be discharged elsewhere if diverted to another port. Messrs. Wallace Brothers conceded the demand immediately and were allowed to continue working. Pickets were also sent to the railway station to prevent the delivery of any coal by rail.[84]

It is clear from the tone of the commentary at the start of the dock strike that business and political interests in the city were worried about the likely impact of this dispute. A meeting of the Limerick Harbour Board discussed the strike on 15 December indicating that 'at present there was no prospect of a settlement' and that the strike 'was inflicting a big hardship on the city and the men'.[85] On the same day Ballantyne's flour mills issued a week's notice to its workers as a result of being unable to discharge its grain cargoes at the docks.[86] The police and military were drafted onto the docks to carry out guard duty and on 17 December tragedy struck when two sailors onboard Ballantyne's grain ship were drowned while 'running the lines' in preparation for the ship leaving the port.[87] Arrangements were made by agreement with the strikers that the city gasworks would continue to be supplied with coal and five hundred and thirty flour mills workers were laid off as a result of the strike.[88] By Christmas Eve the *Limerick Leader* estimated that over one thousand workers had been laid off because of developments on the docks.[89] The potential existed for this strike to have an enormous impact on the city and as the year closed this dispute was also to have an important impact on the Limerick labour movement.

As the dock strike continued into January, a meeting of Limerick Corporation took place. Mr. P. O'Flynn blamed the scarcity of coal 'mainly due to the Shylocks of the coal ring in the city'.[90] The LUTLC had been making efforts to arbitrate in the dispute but to no avail. The dockers facilitated the delivery of coal to the Condensed Milk Company in order to prevent further lay-offs[91] but Cleeve's did close down the Caramel factory laying off one hundred and seventy workers.[92] The divisions on the LUTLC surfaced at a meeting on 2 January when John Cronin and James Carr complained that the ITGWU were ignoring them in relation to the strike.[93]

The dock strike finally led to the successful establishment of the Limerick Conciliation Board which received the enthusiastic backing of the craft unions LUTLC. At a conference to launch the Conciliation Board, John Cronin, in seconding the motion establishing the Board, stated

> 'the old plan of trying to settle disputes in trade led to misunderstandings and confusion. There was a lot of nonsense introduced into labour disputes which should never have been and it gives me great pleasure to see the principle of conciliation in order to obviate labour disputes'.

His comments were met with applause from the business owners attending.[94]

Following the intervention by the Conciliation Board both the employers and the ITGWU accepted a four-point plan to end the dispute. The plan was accepted by a majority of the workers at a general meeting but then the employers backed off and rejected the settlement plan[95]. The response of the ITGWU was to escalate the strike. Carters at Messrs Wallis and the Limerick Carting Company were called out. The ITGWU informed merchants that they would have to apply for a permit from the Union if they wanted to move goods from the Railway Station. It was indicated that gas workers would be the next to be brought out in solidarity.[96] The Conciliation Board, having such difficulty in achieving a settlement, indicated they intended dropping the case only for Bishop Hallinan, recognising that a failure in this dispute would spell the death knell of the Board, pleaded with them not to do so.[97]

New Sinn Fein Mayor Michael O'Callaghan intervened and with other Corporation members met with the merchants and strikers.[98] The strike ended on 4 February following the intervention of a representative of the Bishop with terms that casual labourers would receive 13s 6d per day. Other matters were to be considered by the Conciliation Board.[99] The *Watchword of Labour* claimed the settlement as a victory for the workers[100] and the strike laid the basis for further pay increases for the dock workers the following June.[101] However, the conservative leadership now had their desired outcome, a conciliation board that could be used to undermine strike action and an accommodation with the nationalist leadership in the city.

The ITGWU and County Limerick

In the aftermath of the dock strike a period of industrial peace existed in the city. Much of the focus for the ITGWU shifted to the continued organisation of workers in the county. There were enormous difficulties in recruiting farm labourers into trade unions, including the seasonal nature of the work, the living-in system, the problem of dealing with strike-breakers and the large number of 'assisting relatives' in agriculture.[102] Surmounting these difficulties helped to copper-fasten trade unionism in 1918 & 1919.[103] It was also significant that few ITGWU organisers were tested bureaucrats. They mostly rose from the ranks of the union and their instincts lay with the membership rather than the bureaucracy.[104] This facilitated the tactics employed in the running battles between the union and employers in rural areas right throughout the period up to Independence.

At the end of 1919 the ITGWU had thirty-eight branches in County Limerick,[105] largely or exclusively comprised of farm labourers.[106] In response farmers began organising themselves as part of the Farmers Association. At a meeting of the Limerick Farmers Association on 2 January 1920, Farmers Association organiser Mr. M.J. Curtin advocated the 'formation of vigilance committees in every branch to see that nothing would militate against the farmers interests and the protection of property'. The *Watchword of Labour* reported that towards the end of January armed farmers were operating as scouting parties around Newcastle West and Abbeyfeale.[107] The meeting also discussed the training of farmer's sons in the general work of creameries in order to facilitate scabbing during industrial disputes.[108] A further meeting was held a week later that discussed the advisability of recruiting farm labourers from Connaught in order to undermine the ITGWU in rural areas.[109] A meeting of the Ballyneety branch of the ITGWU condemned this action claiming that 'there was plenty of surplus labour to be had in Limerick if they only pay them a living wage'.[110] Farm labourers in Ballybricken were in dispute with farmers in the area and subsequently the police raided the houses of striking workers.[111] Threats were made to close the Greybridge co-operative creamery in Grange as a result of the refusal of workers to accept milk from farmers refusing to pay bonuses.[112] The threat was met by the ITGWU refusing to handle the creameries products and the closure threat was withdrawn.[113]

The ITGWU also became the focal point for social activities in the county. Hurling tournaments and dances were organised, sometimes to raise funds for workers on strike but often as social occasions[114]. However, the work of the ITGWU primarily concerned the livelihood of their members and as the year progressed disagreements between workers and employers gathered pace.

Local Elections 1920

The 1920 local elections were the last elections to take place on an all-Ireland basis. In January 1920 elections took place to 126 separate urban councils, with rural district councils being elected in June 1920. Unlike in 1918 when Sinn Fein were given a free run by the ILPTUC, these local elections were now fought across all parts of the country. Only nine local councils had uncontested elections.

Sinn Fein were expected to sweep the elections in a manner similar to the general election fourteen months previously. The result in January 1920 sent shockwaves through the nationalist leadership. When the votes were counted Sinn Fein secured 27% of the vote, the same percentage as the Unionists, with the Labour Party securing 18%. After all the seats were allocated following the urban and rural elections the breakdown of seats was as follows:

Party	Seats
Sinn Fein	550
Labour Party	394
Unionists	355
Other Nationalists	238
Independents	161
Municipal Reform Party	108
Total	1806

Sinn Fein secured just over 30% of the seats, while Labour secured almost 22% of the available seats. In Belfast Labour secured 13 seats winning approximately 20% of the vote. Many of the elected candidates were strike leaders during the engineering strike the previous year. As during the general election in 1918, the Unionists used the banner of 'Labour Unionist' in several areas to undermine support for Labour candidates. In Dublin Labour won 14 seats out of 80, but failed to stand candidates in several areas and stood an insufficient number in others. In electoral area no.10 the sole Labour candidate was William O'Brien who comfortably exceeded the quota on the first count but had no running-mate to take advantage.

Of the elected Labour councillors, 137 were members of the ITGWU. After disagreements on the Dublin Trades Council, the ITGWU and two other unions ran separate candidates. In total nine candidates ran under the banner of 'Workers Republicans' with an emphasis on the notion of supporting a workers republic. How far their intent was depicted by their banner is debateable, but clearly, they were reflecting a mood among the Dublin working class. Eight of the nine candidates were elected.[115] In Cork the ITGWU stood on a joint list with Sinn Fein.[116] In Limerick Labour ran a very low-key election campaign. Six councillors were elected out of a total of 40 seats. All the Labour councillors were members of the craft unions. In contrast to other areas the ITGWU in Limerick city appears to have ignored the election completely. It is possible that the ongoing disputes between the ITGWU and the craft unions on the Trades Council contributed to this, coupled with the instructions from Thomas Johnson that all labour candidates must be agreed through the Trades Council.

The Sinn Fein leadership carried out an internal investigation into their poor performance in the local elections. The report, written by Michael Collins contains a noteworthy comment about the local election result in Belfast. Collins commented that the labour vote in Belfast was 'not Carsonite, but clearly internationalist'.[117] This posed a major threat to Sinn Fein as it clearly implied that there was a growing class consciousness among the Protestant working class.

In terms of strikes 1920 saw a highpoint of strike activity in the country. A total of 233 strikes were recorded, many of them prolonged and involving tens of thousands of workers.[118]

---

[1] V. I. Lenin, *Left-Wing Communism: An Infantile Disorder,* (New York, 1940), p. 22

[2] Jim Kemmy, 'Introduction', in Liam Cahill, *Forgotten Revolution – Limerick Soviet 1919, A Threat to British Power in Ireland,* (Dublin, 1990), p.7.

[3] O'Callaghan, *Revolutionary Limerick,* p. 122

[4] *New Ireland,* 3 May 1919.

[5] See the introduction for quotes from the London *Times,* Constance Markievicz and the report to the US Secretary of State.

[6] Irish Labour Party and Trade Union Congress, *Report of the Twenty-Fifth Annual Meeting,* 1919, p. 57

[7] ILPTUC, *Report of the Twenty-Fifth Annual Meeting,* 1919, p. 73

[8] Ibid., p. 75

[9] ILPTUC, *Report of the Twenty-Fifth Annual Meeting,* 1919, p. 76-77

[10] Ibid., p. 77-78

[11] Ibid., p. 81

[12] Ibid., p. 75 & 79

[13] Ibid., p. 77 & 79

[14] Ibid., p. 81

[15] Ibid., p. 81

[16] Ibid., p. 80

[17] Ibid., p. 81

[18] *Evening Herald,* 22 April 1919

[19] *Evening Herald,* 21 April 1919. The British Socialist Party subsequently became the largest element of the newly founded Communist Party of Great Britain.

[20] *Evening Herald,* 24 April 1919

[21] ILPTUC, *Report of the Twenty-Fifth Annual Meeting,* 1919, p. 81

[22] Ibid., p. 81 & 82

[23] The 40-hours strike began in Glasgow on 29 January 1919, organised by the Clydeside Workers Committee. The striking workers were demanding a reduction in the working week from 54 hours to 40 hours in order to create employment for demobilised soldiers. The Belfast Engineering strike was also linked to the Glasgow Strike. After police attacked a workers protest in George's Square on 31 January, large numbers of troops were deployed to Glasgow. The 40-hours strike was called off ten days later without any direct confrontation with the army.

[24] ILPTUC, *Report of the Twenty-Fifth Annual Meeting,* 1919, p. 82

[25] Kostick, *Revolution in Ireland*, p. 67.

[26] Greaves, *The Irish Transport and General Workers Union*, p. 236

[27] *Belfast Weekly Telegraph*, 5 July 1920

[28] Karl Marx, *Civil War in France*, (New York, 2005), p. 105

[29] The nature and operation of the Soviets was described by John Reed in an article entitled 'Soviets in Action' in *The Liberator* from October 1918. The article can be found here: [https://www.marxists.org/archive/reed/1918/soviets.htm]

[30] Leon Trotsky, *Terrorism and Communism, A Reply to Karl Kautsky*, (New York, 1922), p. 70

[31] Ibid., p. 73

[32] Ibid.

[33] Leon Trotsky, *What Next? Vital Questions for the German Proletariat*, [https://www.marxists.org/archive/trotsky/germany/1932-ger/index.htm]

[34] V. I. Lenin, 'To the Central Committee of the R.D.S.L.P.', First published in *Pravda* No. 250, November 7, 1920, *Lenin Collected Works*, Volume 25, (Moscow, 1977), pp. 289-293.

[35] Tom Crean, 'The Socialist Challenge in Ireland', in Cillian Gillespie (ed.), *Ireland's Lost Revolution 1916-1923*, (London, 2016), p. 171

[36] Cahill, *Forgotten Revolution*, p. 141

[37] *Irish Independent*, 2 May 1919

[38] *Derry Journal*, 2 May 1919

[39] *Irish Independent*, 2 May 1919

[40] *Irish Independent*, 2 May 1919

[41] *Irish Independent*, 2 May 1919

[42] Rahilly was the writer who claimed prior to the Limerick Soviet that workers were too ignorant to take over and run a city.

[43] *Skibbereen Eagle*, 3 May 1919.

[44] *Nenagh News*, 3 May 1919

[45] *Nenagh Guardian*, 3 May 1919

[46] Austen Morgan, *Labour and Partition: The Belfast Working Class 1905 - 23*, (London, 1991), p. 248

[47] *Cork Examiner*, 2 May 1919

[48] Kemmy, 'Introduction', p. 9.

[49] Kostick, p.81.

[50] Cahill, p. 141.

[51] *Limerick Leader*, 18 June 1919.

[52] *Voice of Labour*, 17 May 1919.

[53] D.R. O'Connor Lysaght, 'The Munster Soviet Creameries', in *Saothalann Staire Eireann*, No.1, (Dublin, 1981), p.41.

[54] Emmet O' Connor, 'Active Sabotage in Industrial Conflict 1917-1923', *Irish Economic and Social History*, Vol. XII, (1985), p. 59

[55] *Munster News*, 21 May 1919.

[56] *Munster News*, 31 May 1919.

[57] *Limerick Leader*, 6 June 1919.

[58] *Munster News*, 16 June 1919.

[59] *Limerick Leader*, 6 June 1919.

[60] *Munster News*, 30 August 1919.

[61] *Limerick Leader*, 21 June 1919, & *Munster News*, 23 June 1919.

[62] *Munster News*, 2 July 1919.

[63] *Limerick Leader*, 16 July 1919, & *Voice of Labour*, 26 July 1919.

[64] *Munster News*, 16 August 1919.

[65] *Limerick Leader*, 3 September 1919, *Munster News*, 3 September 1919, & *Voice of Labour*, 29 September 1919.

[66] *Munster News*, 8 October 1919.

[67] *Limerick Leader*, 17 October 1919.

[68] *Watchdog of Labour*, 11, 13, 15 & 18 November 1919.

[69] *The Red Flag*, 20 & 27 November 1919.

[70] *LUTLC Minutes*, 28 October 1919.

[71] *LUTLC Minutes*, 31 October 1919.

[72] *Limerick Leader*, 17 November 1919.

[73] *Limerick Leader*, 29 October 1919.

[74] *Limerick Leader*, 3 December 1919.

[75] *Munster News*, 18 October 1919.

[76] *Limerick Leader*, 7 November 1919.

[77] *Watchdog of Labour*, 11 November 1919.

[78] *Limerick Leader*, 21 November 1919 & *Watchdog of Labour*, 22 November 1919.

[79] *Limerick Leader*, 13 November 1919, & Dan Bradley, *Farm Labourers Irish Struggle 1900-1976*, (Belfast, 1988), p.45.

[80] *Watchword of Labour*, 13 December 1919.

[81] *Watchword of Labour*, 22 November 1919.

[82] *Munster News*, 3 December 1919.

[83] *Limerick Leader*, 5 December 1919.

[84] *Limerick Leader*, 8 December 1919.

[85] *Limerick Leader*, 15 December 1919.

[86] *Limerick Leader*, 15 December 1919.

[87] *Limerick Leader*, 17 December 1919.

[88] *Limerick Leader*, 19 December 1919.

[89] *Limerick Leader*, 24 December 1919.

[90] *Limerick Leader*, 12 January 1920.

[91] *Watchword of Labour*, 31 January 1920.

[92] *Limerick Leader*, 19 January 1920.

[93] *LUTLC Minutes*, 2 January 1920.

[94] *Limerick Leader*, 5 January 1920.

[95] *Watchword of Labour*, 31 January 1920.

[96] *Limerick Leader*, 23 January 1920.

[97] *Limerick Leader*, 2 February 1920.

[98] *Limerick Leader*, 2 February 1920.

[99] *Limerick Leader*, 4 February 1920.

[100] *Watchword of Labour*, 14 February 1920.

[101] Crean, *The Labour Movement in Kerry and Limerick 1914-1921*, p. 228.

[102] Emmet O'Connor, *Syndicalism in Ireland*, (Cork, 1988), p. 34.

[103] O'Connor, *A Labour History of Ireland*, p. 98.

[104] Ibid., p. 100.

[105] *ITGWU Annual Report* 1919.

[106] Tom Crean, 'From Petrograd to Bruree', in David Fitzpatrick (ed.), *Revolution? Ireland 1917-1923*, (Dublin, 1990), p. 148

[107] *Watchword of Labour*, 31 January 1920.

[108] *Limerick Leader*, 2 January 1920.

[109] *Limerick Leader*, 9 January 1920.

[110] *Limerick Leader*, 16 February 1920.

[111] *Limerick Leader*, 2 February 1920.

[112] *Limerick Leader*, 20 February 1920.

[113] *Watchword of Labour*, 24 January 1920.

[114] *Limerick Leader*, 12 March 1920.

[115] Greaves, *The Irish Transport and General Workers Union*, p. 258

[116] Ibid., p. 259

[117] *Dail Eireann Secretariat Files 1919-1922*, DE 2/81, 'Local Government Elections 1920, Analysis for Propaganda Purposes', Document 81A & 81B.

[118] David Fitzpatrick, 'Strikes in Ireland, 1914-1921', *Saothar*, (Volume 6, 1980), p. 38

A GRAVE DANGER
THREATENING THE
FOUNDATIONS OF
THE REPUBLIC

*'On the second day of the strike we held a public meeting in the
Market Square and publicly proclaimed the establishment of a
Provisional Soviet Government, policed the town to keep order and
ration out our food supplies...'.*
—Report from Bagnelstown, Co. Carlow during the general strike.
April 1920[1]

Land Agitation was to develop to a significant degree particularly during 1920 and centered in the West of Ireland.[2] Sinn Fein had organised some cattle drives in 1918 for propaganda purposes but the seizures of 1920 were on a much larger and more comprehensive scale.[3] *Campbell* argued that the social conflict of the period, including the land seizures, threatened to fragment the nationalist movement, a fragmentation that would occur along class lines. During 1920 hundreds of landed estates and large farms were seized by landless labourers and holders of small uneconomic holdings. These small farmers were primarily the tenant farmers who didn't benefit from the previous Land Acts. By April 1920 the land seizures were proving very effective. Larger landowners were avoiding taking 'eleven-month lettings', allowing the small farmers and the labourers to rent land they wouldn't have previously been able to acquire.[4] On top of that the ITGWU regularly accused farmers of ignoring or hoodwinking Department of Agriculture inspectors and profiteering by hiking up the price of foodstuffs.[5]

The Dail Ministry for Home Affairs described developments as 'a grave danger threatening the foundations of the Republic'.[6] They went on to say:

1920 was no ordinary outbreak...an immense rise in the value of land and farm products threw into more vivid relief than ever before the high profits of ranchers, and the hopeless outlook of the landless men and uneconomic holders...All this was a grave menace to the Republic. The mind of the people was being diverted from the struggle for freedom by a class war, and there was every likelihood that this class war might be carried into the ranks of the republican army itself which was drawn in the main from the agricultural population and was largely officered by farmer's sons...The republican police had been established just in time to grapple with the growing disorder and withstood the strain upon its own discipline.[7]

The nationalist leadership had two potential approaches to the crisis. Firstly, they could use the IRA to suppress the land agitation. This posed an enormous risk for the nationalist movement. Those involved in the land seizures were the section of the population where Sinn Fein drew much of its support. This was compounded by the fact that the agitation was on such a scale that it is debatable whether the IRA would have had the resources to suppress the conflict, coupled with the fact that it could, as the leadership were worried, have torn the IRA apart along class lines.

The second option was to use the Sinn Fein arbitration courts, using these courts to rule against the seizures and then use the IRA to impose the court decisions. To complement this approach Sinn Fein organised a series of Land Conferences to promote Sinn Fein's agriculture policy. Again, the primary intention of these conferences was to bring the 'land movement' under Sinn Fein control. Further to this Sinn Fein decided that anyone involved in the seizure of land would be automatically excluded from any future distribution of land. The third Sinn Fein Land Conference ruled that any seizures of land could only be instigated on the orders of Austin Stack, the Dail Minster for Justice.[8] In Kerry the four Sinn Fein TDs issued a manifesto to their constituents in the county. In this manifesto they warned that 'the forces of the Republic will be used to protect the citizens against the adaption of high-handed methods'. Michael Collins threatened the members of the IRA in Kerry that if they broke ranks and supported the land agitation they would be subjected to court-martial.[9]

Arthur Griffith warned that he 'took the gravest view of the Western outbreak and said that if it was not immediately dealt with, it could well wreck the entire national movement'. Griffith sent Kevin O'Sheil, a solicitor from Omagh, Co. Tyrone, to deal with the much more serious situation in Connacht. After arriving in the province O'Sheil reported that there was no popular demand to replace the local British run courts and only for the seriousness of the situation from a nationalist perspective the leaders of Sinn Fein would not have attempted to impose the Dail courts.[10] In O'Sheil's first decision as a judge in the Dail court during a hearing in Ballinarobe, he found in favour of returning the occupied land to the landowner. When the leaders of the occupation publicly declared that they would not abide by the decision O'Sheil reported the situation to Cathal Brugha, Dail Minster for Defence.[11] A few days later the leaders of the occupation were kidnapped by the IRA and imprisoned on an island in Lough Corrib for several weeks.[12]

While the suppression of the land seizure in Ballinrobe was a success for the IRA, Roscommon was to prove much more difficult. O'Sheil was to declare that there was an 'agrarian avalanche' in Roscommon that was 'almost impossible to cope with'. According to O'Sheil the workers and the small farmers exhibited an 'aggressive Bolshie spirit'.[13] Similar reports came from Galway where the Sinn Fein controlled *Galway Express* denounced 'Bolshevism in Kinvara' because any land agitation beyond the nationalist movement's control was intolerable.[14] O'Sheil outlined that the earliest supporters of the Dail land courts were not the small farmers of the west, but the landowners who were the victims of the new agitation:

> 'Eastbound trains brought to Dublin terrified landowners who came looking to the Dail for protection, many of whom urged it to set up, immediately, independent land courts to check the outbreak. It was . . . a strange anomaly that amongst the first persons to advocate the setting up of a Dail judiciary were, not the Sinn Feiners - who, at that time, were dubious of its effectiveness - but harassed landowners, mainly strong unionists and opposed to the Dail, in principle'.

O'Sheil, like other judges in the Dail Courts, was noted for regularly finding in favour of landlords and large landowners in his judgements at the court.[15]

To finally diffuse the agitation Sinn Fein purchased grazing land and then distributed it to small farmers. The proposal to establish an Agricultural Loan Bank came before the Dail as early as August 1919, with those small farmers and labourers wishing to purchase the land obliged to fund a twenty-five percent deposit. By June 1920 the bank was finally established, with the Dail funding six branches in different parts of the west of Ireland assisting local co-operative societies to purchase land from large landowners and by the end of the year the bank had advanced over £180,000 to small farmers to purchase 6,882 acres.[16] Some landowners claimed that Sinn Fein paid more for the land than was being offered by the Congested Districts Board coupled with the fact that Sinn Fein paid in cash.[17]

Running in conjunction with the land seizures were strikes by farm labourers. Employers were becoming alarmed at the implications of the class nature of the struggle and were becoming particularly annoyed at the failure of both the British authorities and the IRA to suppress 'law-breaking' and 'violence' during strikes.[18] The Irish Farmers Association advocated the establishment of a body, the Farmers Freedom Force, intended to provide a 'permanent organised body in each branch...capable of meeting force by force...in the interests of the country and of the farmer'. The F.F.F. was effectively a quasi-fascist force whose objective was to smash strikes by farm labourers. The Farmers' Association argued that in response to agricultural labour strikes the 'F.F.F. should take action as may be required'. The farmers' organisations made clear their priority in political terms, 'the F.F.F. is required as a national bulwark against Labour, Socialism and Bolshevism, irrespective of whatever political developments may take place in the country'.[19]

Fear that the suppression of the land seizures could fracture the local IRA units was also prominent in the minds of the nationalist leadership. In one incident in Mayo where the local community objected to the judgement of a Dail Court IRA Volunteers were drafted in from Clare and Donegal to enforce the court's decision. The IRA took twenty-four local men hostage in order to break the resistance of the local community.[20] Peadar O'Donnell later recounted:

> 'During the fever of the Tan days it took all the influence of the Republican Government and the use of Republican forces to hold the land struggle in check. It was a period when the middle-class leadership exerted itself frantically to keep the movement "clean". Even the ranchers themselves helped in this work.'[21]

The Sinn Fein leadership were serving the class forces they represented. When it came to a choice of protecting the interests of the property-owning class or the mass of the population it was an easy decision for the representatives of nationalism to protect bourgeois interests. Demonstrating the class interests of the leadership of Sinn Fein, McNamara commented that:

> 'the courts were to become the most remarkable achievement of the revolutionary movement in (Galway) and the widespread acceptance of their rulings in 1920 attested to their seminal role in gaining Sinn Fein the allegiance of property owners...Far from being Bolshevik – as their most ardent opponents claimed – the courts allowed Sinn Fein to be seen as the only legitimate safeguard against a potential plebeian revolution'.[22]

Even from a historian viewing the revolutionary period from a nationalist perspective, the intent of Sinn Fein was clear, protect the interests of property from the potential of a workers' revolution. *Greaves* was to comment that the primary reason Sinn Fein were capable of suppressing the land seizure movement in the counties on the west coast was that union organisation was weaker in this region that in the rest of the country. As we shall see, while the nationalist leadership attempted to use the same methods of repression against with workers movement in the rest of the country, here they faced a much better organised labour movement who were capable of resisting the intimidation and repression that the IRA attempted to impose.[23] In Limerick the presence of Marxists like Sean Dowling, Jack McGrath and Jack Hedley were to prove instrumental in organising workers as they fought to defend their class interests.

General Strike 1920

The highpoint of intensity of workers struggle occurred in April 1920. Increased British repression had led to more than one hundred prisoners being detained in Mountjoy prison. On 5 April 1920 thirty-six of the prisoners went on hunger strike. They were joined by another thirty prisoners the following day[24] with the number rising to roughly one hundred. The nationalist narrative is that these prisoners were republican activists and the general strike was a nationalist strike to force the release of republican prisoners. However, the evidence demonstrates that the nationalist narrative does not fit with the historical evidence.

The beginning of 1920 had seen a significant increase in repression by the British authorities on the labour movement. On a weekly basis the *Watchword of Labour* was confiscated by Dublin Castle with the editor of the paper on the run evading arrest. More than a dozen officials and organisers of the ITGWU had been arrested and deported to Britain. ITGWU offices had been raided and Liberty Hall had been repeatedly raided and searched during the first months of the year. The RIC were breaking up union meetings around the country at gunpoint.[25]

Among those arrested was ITGWU leader William O'Brien. After being detained in Mountjoy, O'Brien was transferred to Wormwood Scrubs prison in London. He joined in a hunger strike organised with republican prisoners on 18 March, but his condition quickly deteriorated, and he was moved to a nursing home to convalesce.[26] While O'Brien was on hunger-strike a British Parliamentary by-election was called in Stockport. Stockport had a significant Irish-born population and a mass meeting of Irish workers in Stockport decided to nominate O'Brien as a candidate. In the by-election O'Brien was listed as standing as a Irish Workers Republican candidate receiving 2,336 votes, approximately three percent of the vote.[27]

On 11 April Cathal O'Shannon was arrested while attending an international Labour meeting in London. He was deported back to Ireland, charged in Kells with making a seditious speech and was imprisoned in Mountjoy as the general strike was taking place.[28]

Among those trade union activists who were on hunger-strike in Mountjoy was an ITGWU organiser from Meath and RSP member Jack Hedley who had been arrested on a picket line in Belfast. In all, the *Watchword of Labour* claimed that a majority of the hunger-strikers were trade unionists. As news of the hunger strike in Mountjoy spread spontaneous demonstrations began, growing with each passing day until more than 40,000 protested outside Mountjoy.[29]

Throughout the week pressure was rising on the leadership of the trade union movement. With O'Brien in prison the leadership of the ILPTUC didn't have a direct link to the Sinn Fein leadership. Decisions on what to do were left to Thomas Johnson and Thomas MacPartlin. In response to the huge protest outside Mountjoy a meeting of the Dublin based members of the ILPTUC leadership was called. In the expectation that a general strike would be called Johnson had actually written the 'manifesto' for a one-day general strike the night before the meeting took place.[30] The meeting was held at 10.30am on Monday morning and the decision to call the strike taken very soon afterwards.[31] The manifesto of the leadership of the ILPTUC was for a one day strike calling for the release of 'Our fellow-workers now in Mountjoy, Wormwood Scrubs and other prisons'.[32]

The speed at which the general strike was called in this situation was in stark contrast to the response to the Limerick Soviet. Gone were all the different excuses about why a general strike couldn't be called. The manifesto written by Johnson even stated: 'There is no time to gather your delegates into conference'.[33] In April 1920 the leadership were unable to resist the pressure from the masses in Dublin. With William O'Brien still in prison the leadership were missing the key figure capable of acting to restrain the movement. Whether O'Brien would have wanted to or been able to prevent the strike is an open question, but his absence certainly meant that the remaining leading members of the ILPTUC Executive were more susceptible to pressure from the masses.

It wasn't only the ILPTUC leadership that demonstrated an about face. NUR leader, J.H. Thomas, had sabotaged the potential of a nationwide rail strike in support of the Limerick Soviet because the strike was political. However, in this case, he praised the strike action, claiming that it was 'a strike for principle'.[34]

Workers Take Control

With the exception of Belfast the general strike was complete. It wasn't just the scale of the strike that was impressive, it was the level of control over the strike exercised by local elements of the labour movement. Examples from throughout the country demonstrate the complete nature of control by workers. One striking example of the mood among workers was a demonstration in what was then Bagnelstown, Co. Carlow. A report from the demonstration declared:

> 'On the second day of the strike we held a public meeting in the Market Square and publicly proclaimed the establishment of a Provisional Soviet Government, policed the town to keep order and ration out our food supplies...'.[35]

In Kilkenny the entire city was shut down with the exception of government buildings. Despite constant rain crowds thronged the streets. A large demonstration took place with the 'Labour contingent' dominating the protest. The attempt to restrain the demands was demonstrated when a local priest addressed the protest. Fr. Matthew declared that the prisoners 'did not want release but to be treated... as political prisoners' and that the strike was to be a 'solemn protest', finishing by making an appeal for calm. A torch-light demonstration of workers in Thomastown heard an appeal from the local priest for 'Sinn Fein and the Labour Party to compromise'.[36]

A strike committee was formed in Cavan and met late into the night on the first day of the strike making arrangements for the following day. Flying pickets were sent out early the following morning. In one incident people were refused the possibility of posting letters. All transport into and through the town was stopped and required to apply for a permit from the strike committee. Bakers and butchers were allowed to open under permit to ensure food supplies. Later in the morning flying pickets obliged the local judge to adjourn court hearings.[37]

In Galway, food supplies were allowed into the city, but farmers selling at the market were compelled to comply with price orders from flying pickets. There was a complete shutdown of electricity and gas supplies which directly impacted on the city hospital. A delegated from the ICWU pleaded with the strike committee to exempt the hospital from the measures but the strike committee voted to continue to enforce the shutdown. Several public houses attempted to open but were immediately shut by pickets. A prisoner from Co. Cavan who was released from Galway jail had to apply for a permit from the strike committee to travel home. Coal was rationed at the city's coal yards with the supplies being confined to households. In what seems to have been a conscious decision around the country, news of the release of the prisoners was supplied to a local priest. This appears to have been designed to control how the information was made public, coming from the supporters of nationalism rather than the strike committee. When the information was released in Galway by Fr. Foley, the strike committee refused to call off the strike until they had received confirmation from the ILPTUC.[38] In Tuam the strike committee was organised by the ITGWU and the Drapers Association. The cinema and the billiards club were among the premises shut by the pickets.[39]

Similar action took place in Castlebar, Ballina, Claremorris, Swinford, Charlestown, Ballinrobe, Westport, Balla, and Ballyhaunis. The Connaught Telegraph declared that 'the British government was brought to its knees by the united forces of Irish Labour'.[40]

Derry Trades Council met on Tuesday night and called for a general strike in the city on Wednesday. The call was responded to by dock workers and carters and a large number of corporation employees.[41] In response to the strike call the Ulster

Unionist Labour Association called on Protestant workers to ignore the strike and for Protestant owned businesses to remain open.[42] During the strike action in Derry a major confrontation occurred with the army when they attempted to transport a Sinn Fein prisoner from the railway station. The crowd on the streets attempted to prevent the troops carrying out their action. The confrontation resulted in several people being injured by bayonets. That night unionists staged a sectarian riot in a confrontation with Sinn Fein members.[43]

The general strike was imposed in Carrick-on-Shannon by flying pickets.[44] In Longford the ITGWU ran the strike and shut down the town[45] On Wednesday the strike committee in Navan ordered the opening of a number of shops for three hours to provide 'essential foodstuffs' and then sent pickets to the shops to ensure they closed at the appointed time. In Kells the strike committee took over the Town Hall and ran the strike from that location. After driving a train from Dublin which supplied newspapers from the capital, the train driver was ordered not to drive the train for the remainder of the strike. On Wednesday morning flying pickets ordered clerical staff out of Kells railway station as well as controlling the opening of several shops for a short period. Trim was completely shut down, however, in Athboy a few shops attempted to break the strike until a large force of flying pickets forced their closure. The ITGWU enforced the general strike in Dunboyne, with the same situation in Nobber. The only town where there does not appear to have been a complete shutdown in Co. Meath appears to have been Oldcastle where picketing was 'not carried out so thoroughly as in Kells'.[46]

The strike in Sligo was under the control of the ITGWU with the parades led by the union's fife and drum band. A mass meeting involving thousands took place in the square outside the Town Hall. Sligo was one of the few areas in the country where the clergy played little role in the protests.[47] More than 200 former world war one soldiers joined the demonstration in the town.[48] The class nature of the general strike cut across the hostility normally demonstrated by the nationalist movement towards ex-soldiers.

Workers in Nenagh, Co. Tipperary, did not received any communication from Dublin in relation to the general strike. On seeing a copy of a Dublin evening newspaper Monday evening, the ITGWU called a mass meeting of workers in the town. A strike committee was established with three delegates from each trade union in the area. Under the supervision of pickets, grocers, butchers and bakeries opened from 4pm-6pm on Wednesday evening. After a demonstration on Tuesday evening, the police baton charged a smaller number of people who were still hanging around the streets.[49]

In Clonmel flying pickets ensured compliance with the strike call. A bulletin board outside the Trades Council office kept people informed of proclamations from 'the new local authority'. In Cashel the strike committee comprised of members of the ITGWU 'who carried out their programme very effectively'. In Carrick-on-Suir pickets from the ITGWU shut down local public houses. In one pub they found two policemen and unceremoniously threw them out onto the street. In rural districts around Thurles, pickets forced farmers with carts going to local creameries to turn back. Youth from Thurles participated in this action. *The Nationalist* noted that farmers expressed relief when the strike was called off on Wednesday night. There was a major protest in Emly in Wednesday and striking workers led by the ITGWU marched through the town in formation.[50]

A mass meeting in Tullamore organised the strike in the town. Even here the clergy were forced to acknowledge the dominance of the workers movement. Fr. Burbage stated:

> 'that there was no class within the four corners of our land who thinks so little of themselves, and who are ready to make such sacrifices for their country as the working men of Ireland ... when the banner of Liberty is flying free in our cities and towns it will be resting on the solid foundation composed of men of that class'.[51]

While acknowledging the role of the working class in freeing the prisoners in Mountjoy and Wormwood Scrubs, these comments are also condescending in tone and reflect the longstanding approach of the defenders of capitalist property that 'labour must wait'. The demonstration in Tullamore was led by the ITGWU and workers brass and pipe bands. Importantly, as in other towns, ex-soldiers, played an active role in the demonstrations.[52]

In Maryborough (now Portlaoise) the flying pickets ejected patrons from public houses who refused to follow the strike committee's instructions to shut their doors. Meanwhile, in Carlow flying pickets ordered players off the golf course.[53]

A refrain that became common during the general strike was that of members of the Catholic Hierarchy. Repeatedly the workers were counselled to exercise prudence, caution and prayer.[54] The greatest fear of the Catholic hierarchy was that the workers would act independently on a class basis. At the same time as the clergy was urging workers to exercise caution in the general strike, they were attacking the Irish National Teachers Organisation for supporting the MacPherson Bill which intended to introduce compulsory non-denominational state education. The clergy claimed that the union was willing to 'sell its birthright for a pottage – to sacrifice the interests of religion and patriotism to the lure of wages'. Newspapers supporting Sinn Fein, which in other columns were praising workers for forcing the release of prisoners were condemning teachers for having unionists as friends.[55]

In Belfast, dock workers who were members of the ITGWU staged strike action over both days.[56] On Wednesday transport workers in Belfast joined the strike. Postal workers in Banbridge and Portadown joined the strike the same day.[57] Eight hundred workers demonstrated through Drogheda on Wednesday evening.[58]

More than 5,000 marched through Tralee in pouring rain, with women workers playing a prominent role, and it was noteworthy again that ex-soldiers participated in the demonstration. Children walked out of school to join the demonstration with their parents. At a second demonstration on Wednesday night one of the speakers to rousing cheers stated that the general strike demonstrated 'the power of labour when united'.[59] The strike committee in Tralee comprised of one delegate from each trade union which issued instructions to be carried out by workers. While the strike committee was meeting on Tuesday the police raided the Trades Council offices and searched each member of the strike committee. Subsequently, police fired on a lorry travelling through the town leading to a confrontation between the police and the 'Red Guards'. The police agreed to withdraw from the town after the strike committee stated that they would ensure order in the town. Pickets immediately set off to shut the public houses.[60] At the same time than 1,000 workers marched through Killarney.[61]

During a torchlight demonstration in Miltown Malbay on Wednesday evening to celebrate the release of the prisoners, police and the military opened fire on the demonstrators killing three men and wounding seven others.[62]

The weekend following the general strike hundreds of workers attended a public meeting in Tralee addressed by Hanna Sheehy-Skeffington.[63] Sheehy-Skeffington stated at the meeting that 'Labour had smashed conscription', calling on workers to stand by the 'principles of solidarity' as espoused by James Connolly and stating that the 'hope of labour the world over was the death of Imperialism'. She called on women to join the trade union movement and, expressing surprise that there were no women on Tralee Trades Council. She urged the trade unions to actively involve women in trade unions, arguing that equality for women was part of the struggle for 'freedom for labour'. She concluded her comments by stating that there was a 'rising tide' of labour that could not 'be kept back' no more than it could be kept back in any country in the world.[64]

The most striking example of workers control during the strike came in Waterford. As a demonstration on Wednesday night passed through the streets of Waterford red flags hung from windows along the streets. Luke Larkin, President of the Workers Council, declared 'The manifestation of Labour's power makes epoch in the history of the working class in Ireland'. Women workers and girl workers took a prominent role in the demonstrations. Groups of flying pickets, many armed with sticks ensured the strike was implemented. When the Waterford Board of Guardians met, they were confronted by a contingent of flying pickets backed up by a large crowd who marched to the meeting rooms. The Board members were forced to adjourn the meeting. Workers who were regarded as doing essential work for the

Guardians were allowed to continue at work, but only after they had secured a permit from the strike committee. The court sittings were also adjourned.[65]

The later reports on the events in Waterford make for more interesting reading. *The Guardian* reported that the Sinn Fein mayor had handed Waterford over to 'a Soviet Commissioner and three associates'. The *Daily Herald* spoke about the 'red guards' controlling Waterford, with a red flag flying over the City Hall. The red guards were reported to be under the control of three ITGWU activists. The Sinn Fein mayor was forced to recognise the impact of the strike, congratulating 'the Soviet Government of Waterford on a very effective, masterly, and successful demonstration' and that 'the Soviet Government of Waterford will have an opportunity of again demonstrating the powers which it undoubtedly possesses'.[66]

Members of the ITGWU blockaded the roads entering Monasterevan. Barbed wire entanglements were placed across the Dublin road.[67] The stable boys at the Curragh, under instructions from the ITGWU, refused to handle any horses intended for the Punchestown races. At the Curragh Camp a British General named Skinner sacked striking workers. The ITWGU then gave strike notice forcing their reinstatement.[68]

More than 60,000 workers, with 10,000 of them women workers, demonstrated through Dublin on the Tuesday of the strike. The most noticeable factor in Dublin was the lack of any kind of transport. Visitors staying in the city's hotels had to fend for themselves as hotel workers walked out to join the strike.[69] During the strike old age pensions in Dublin were paid by workers appointed by the strike committee.[70]

Sinn Fein controlled newspapers attempted to present the general strike as a joint effort by both the ILPTUC and Sinn Fein. The *Offaly Independent* declared 'General Strike – and Victory! Labour and Sinn Fein Unconquerable'.[71] At the same time that the media were praising the general strike, some newspapers were also warning about the threats to 'fixity of tenure' and 'free sale' by the landless labourers. The *Skibbereen Eagle* warned that 'no people in the world should be more careful to avoid revolution than the Irish'.[72]

Not surprisingly the strike in Cork and Limerick was completely solid. In Limerick the strike committee posted proclamations throughout the city calling for a general strike. Storm conditions existed in Limerick with high winds and driving rain which limited public demonstrations. All businesses except for the banks, the post office and government buildings shut down. Limerick was also the only place in the country where the strike committee wouldn't allow the local newspapers to be produced.[73] On the second day of the strike the bank workers and post office workers were brought out.[74]

Commenting on the general strike the British *Daily News* stated that the strike saw 'Bishops behind the Bolsheviks', forcing 'Mr. Arthur Griffith, the conservative, to march under the red flag'. The *Daily News* noted that the numbers participating in the general strike significantly exceeded the numbers of organised workers.

Organised labour provided the foundations that the mass movement was built on.[75] An estimated 340,000 workers participated in the general strike.[76]

Aftermath of the General Strike

The narrative of Irish nationalism is that the prisoners were released as a result of the determination and commitment of those on hunger strike. From the perspective of the leadership of Sinn Fein it was crucial to down play the importance of the general strike and, more importantly, to downplay the impact of the workers' councils that spontaneously sprung up throughout the country to run the strike. The importance of the dispute was not lost on the spokespeople for the capitalist class and British Imperialism.

The *Irish Times* commented that

> 'A wave of Bolshevism before which Sinn Fein itself stands appalled, menaces, with many other institutions, our whole system of land tenure'[77] and that 'A continuation of the strike which ended yesterday might have witnessed the establishment of Soviets of workmen in all parts of Ireland.'[78]

The *Manchester Guardian* was even more pronounced:

> 'The directions of affairs passed during the strike to these [workers'] councils which were formed not on a local basis but on a class basis... it is no exaggeration to trace a flavour of proletarian dictatorship about some aspects of the strike.'[79]

O'Connor asserted that the general strike uncovered the social revolutionary dynamic bubbling at the base of the movement.[80] The two days of general strike did more to undermine British Authority than months of armed struggle by the IRA. Sinn Fein politicians were side-lined by events. They did not want to be seen to oppose a popular strike against British Imperialism, but at the same time they recognised that the working classes' independent activity was an implicit challenge for the leadership of the national movement.[81] The objective of the Sinn Fein leadership was to downplay the impact of the strike and in that endeavour they had willing accomplices in the leadership of the ILPTUC.

The labour newspaper the *Watchword of Labour* lead not with a report of the general strike but by outlining a factional dispute between the supporters of O'Brien and P.T. Daly on Dublin Trades Council.[82] The report of the strike was designed to downplay both the importance and the radical nature of the strike:

> 'A word of warning is necessary. A general strike in Ireland alone won't bring freedom, won't even bring down a government. For an

industrial object a general strike in Ireland won't embarrass the British Government overmuch.'[83]

The British government were shocked by the effectiveness of the general strike with MPs noting it as a 'most remarkable feature'.[84] Of much greater concern for the British establishment was the potential for the general strike to spread to Britain creating 'a situation that many of us would deplore'. The 'Irish Office' were condemned for engaging in 'folly' that could result in the British ruling class suffering as a result of strike action on both sides of the Irish sea.[85]

British Imperialism had another problem to assess. By side-lining the nationalist leadership, the general strike had displayed the power of the working class and the ability of the labour movement to take the leadership in the struggle for self-determination. With the working class fighting for political, social and economic emancipation, the struggle could develop into a life and death class struggle with British Imperialism. Coupled with this was the potential for such a development significantly impacting on the British working class and the emergence of a strike movement in Britain that could move rapidly to the left. The growing class consciousness and the radicalisation of the Irish working class posed a major threat for both British Imperialism and the Irish nationalist leadership and the British establishment were determined to undermine it.

At the time of the general strike Sir Nevil Macready took over as commander of the British military in Ireland. Macready is quoted as saying that 'red murder stalked through the length and breadth of the land'.[86] While it was clear that Macready was regarding that the revolutionary upheaval as left-wing in character, he was clearly propagandising about the role of Sinn Fein in the situation. One of the first acts of Macready when he arrived in Ireland was to look for the release of William O'Brien and then seek a meeting with the ILPTUC leader.[87] Macready recognised that O'Brien could be a useful asset in undermining strike action in the country.

Railway workers and Dock workers

While the general strike was underway, railway and dock workers were planning industrial action to prevent the export of food stuffs from the country. Rising prices had made it increasingly difficult for the working class to buy specific food products, particularly bacon. The crisis was caused by the removal of price controls by the British government following the ending of World War One. The general strike gave these workers the confidence to engage in solidarity action to ensure continued food supplies for the Irish working class. Dock workers began discussing blocking the export of butter and bacon in March. As was the norm, the ILPTUC obfuscated and delayed. However, after the general strike they were unable to behave in the same manner and sanctioned the action.[88] The embargo had an immediate impact, resulting in the farmers and merchants agreeing to supply bacon and butter at fixed prices. The trade unions threatened to reimpose the embargo if there was any row-back from the merchants and the prices were maintained for two months.[89]

At the same time railway workers were embarking on the munitions strike. The inspiration for the strike came from the decision of London dock workers to stop the shipment of munitions to Poland for use by the White counter-revolutionary forces in Russia.[90] The boycott of the British military in Ireland began in mid-May 1920 when dock workers refused to unload a cargo of military equipment. British troops then unloaded the cargo instead. At this point the railway workers in what was then Kingstown (Dun Laoghaire) refused to transport any munitions from the cargo. The NUR Executive leadership in London was instructing 'our members to refuse to handle any material which is intended to assist Poland against the Russian people'. The NUR members in Ireland took the spirit of the resolution and implemented it in Ireland.

Townshend argued that the strike had a 'clear nationalist political orientation'. Not surprisingly he fails to make any characterisation of the 'orientation' of the strike against munitions shipments to the Russian White army but concludes that because the railwaymen were blocking transport of British military material (and then personnel) in Ireland, the strike had to be politically nationalist.[91] After a haphazard beginning the boycott of the British military was applied nationwide. The railway companies responded by sacking workers who refused to handle military materials or transport troops. Soon after the start of the boycott up to 400 railway workers were sacked.[92]

In effect the railway workers were left to their own devices, with the NUR leadership and the ILPTUC both backing off direct support for the workers. Workers were making individual decisions on whether to participate in the action with no support from the official trade union movement. William O'Brien and Thomas Foran issued directions to the dock labourers not to unload munitions ships. O'Brien recounted in his memoirs that he was much more concerned about the railway workers working for the London, Midland and Scottish Railway on the docks than he was about the dock workers. The dock workers who were members of the ITGWU were casual labourers and O'Brien felt no responsibility to help these workers, stating 'in the case of our own dockers, no payment would arise' while 'the L.M.S workers would expect to be paid – they were permanent workers, not casuals'. Almost immediately O'Brien sought a meeting with the Sinn Fein leadership and met twice with Arthur Griffith. O'Brien and Foran also met with prominent Home Ruler John Dillon.[93] The purpose of these meetings was to get access to funds raised by the cross-class alliance O'Brien had participated in during the conscription crisis. Once again O'Brien was willing to compromise with the nationalist leadership and seek an accommodation in how to run an industrial dispute.

In early June NUR leader J.H. Thomas issued instructions for railway workers involved in the boycott to return to work. The NUR Executive stated that the union did 'not want to make itself responsible for revolution on either side of the channel'.[94] The ILPTUC did set up a fund to subsidise railway workers who were suspended or sacked for refusing to transport the British military but hedged providing any further support.[95]

The railway workers refused to carry munitions and armed troops but did transport unarmed troops and normal non-munitions supplies. The military response was to board the trains and then refuse to leave. This resulted in large sections of the railway network grinding to a halt. The railway company owners were convinced that the strike would disintegrate within days, but it continued for several months. This fact showed the enormous resilience of the railway workers, despite the lack of support from the NUR and the ILPTUC as well as the threat of being dismissed.

Despite claiming otherwise, the strike was clearly impacting on the British military. Major-General Jeudwine, warned that a stoppage of the railway system would have a catastrophic effect on military communication. By the end of July, the military authorities had all but accepted that they had to find other methods of communication and transportation, with the railways no longer being used for transporting armed troops or munitions. However, the British government quickly countermanded the order on the grounds that it could be 'widely misinterpreted as a concession on the part of the government'.[96]

From July the dispute was a stalemate. Passenger services had largely ceased in many parts of the country while at the same time close to one thousand workers on the railways had been dismissed. The government put increased pressure on the railway companies to defeat the strike, threatening to withdraw state subsidies to the railways. The railways hired scabs to replace the workers dismissed for taking part in the strike.[97] As a result of the haphazard nature of the strike action it was difficult for the railway workers to combat the introduction of scabs, particularly given the lack of support from the official trade union leadership in Ireland and in Britain.

There is clear evidence that the IRA did involve themselves in the dispute. In August the following notice was reputed to have been sent to railway workers:

> GOVERNMENT OF THE IRISH REPUBLIC
> Acting under instructions, you are hereby notified that after this date you are forbidden to drive any train, or assist in any way the transport of armed forces of the British Government.
> By Order,
> MINISTRY OF WAR.

William O'Brien and the leadership of the ILPTUC condemned the notice as a forgery, it was, however, widely disseminated in the international media.[98] There are several reported incidents of IRA men kidnapping drivers scabbing on the dispute. In one incident in Co. Cavan the IRA kidnapped one driver named McGuigan and court-martialed him. He was fined £10 and ordered not to drive the British forces again. When McGuigan refused to pay the fine he was held by the IRA until the Black and Tans threatened to burn down Cavan town unless McGuigan was released. When the IRA complied with the demand the RIC rounded up large numbers of suspected IRA supporters in the town.[99] The reality was that the actions of the IRA actually undermined the ability of the railway workers to conduct their dispute.

The high-point of the munitions strike developed by mid-November. The toll of participating in the dispute was having a significant effect on the railway workers. There was particular disgruntlement among the engine drivers. While the drivers were paid a significantly higher wage than the railway porters, all those suspended or dismissed during the dispute were paid £3 per week.[100] During the second week of November railway workers met with the Republican leadership. The purpose of the meeting was to try and secure funds from the nationalist movement to keep the strike going. The request met with a cool reception.[101]

On 12 November a meeting of Sinn Fein county and borough councillors was held in Dublin. This meeting decided to organise an All-Ireland Conference along the lines of the cross-class Anti-Conscription convention that involved Sinn Fein, the Catholic hierarchy, the IPP and the ILPTUC. In effect the ILPTUC were looking for a way out of supporting the continuation of the dispute without facing the blame for abandoning it. On 14 December the National Executive of the ILPTUC issued an instruction which stated: 'we have decided to advise the Railway and Dock Workers to alter the position, and to offer in carry everything that the British Authorities are willing to risk on the trains'. With the exception of the Great Northern Railway, the workers dismissed during the dispute were reinstated.[102]

---

[1] Greaves, *The Irish Transport and General Workers Union*, p. 266

[2] E. Rumpf & A.C. Hepburn, *Nationalism and Socialism in Twentieth Century Ireland*, (Liverpool, 1977), p. 24.

[3] The IRA would drive off the cattle of the landowners in various estates. For example, East Clare IRA commander in Clare Michael Brennan carried out cattle drives in Bodyke in February 1918.

[4] Fergus Campbell & Kevin O'Shiel, 'The Last Land War? Kevin O'Shiel's Memoir of the Irish Revolution 1916-21', *Archivium Hibernicum,* Vol. 57 (2003), p. 165

[5] *Watchword of Labour,* 6 March 1920.

[6] Ministry for Home Affairs, *The Constructive Work of Dail Eireann, No.1, The National Police and Courts of Justice*, (Dublin, 1921), p. 10.

[7] Ibid., p.12.

[8] Fergus Campbell, *Land and Revolution: Nationalist Politics in the West of Ireland 1891-*

1921, (Oxford, 2005), p. 255-256

[9] Mitchell, *Revolutionary Government in Ireland*, p. 134

[10] Ibid., p. 134-135

[11] Ibid., p. 135

[12] Campbell, 'The Last Land War? p. 168

[13] Ibid., p. 171

[14] Conor McNamara, *Politics and Society in East Galway, 1914-21*, (PhD Thesis, St. Patrick's College, Drumcondra, 2008), p. 148

[15] Campbell, 'The Last Land War? p. 171

[16] Joseph T. Sheehan, *Land Purchase Policy in Ireland 1917-1923,* (MA Thesis Maynooth, 1993), p.84-85

[17] Campbell, *Land and Revolution,* p. 255-256

[18] O'Connor, *Syndicalism in Ireland,* p.59.

[19] *Watchword of Labour*, 5 June 1920.

[20] C. Desmond Greaves, *Liam Mellows and the Irish Revolution*, (London, 1971), p. 188

[21] Kostick, *Revolution in Ireland,* p. 105

[22] Conor McNamara, *War and Revolution in the West of Ireland: Galway, 1913–1922*, (Newbridge, 2018), p. 103

[23] Greaves, *Liam Mellows and the Irish Revolution*, p. 188-189

[24] Kostick, p. 120

[25] Greaves, *The Irish Transport and General Workers Union*, p. 263

[26] Ibid., p. 264

[27] Mervyn Busteed, *The Irish in Manchester C.1750-1921: Resistance, Adaptation and Identity,* (Manchester, 2016), p. 199

[28] Greaves, *The Irish Transport and General Workers Union,* p. 264-265

[29] Kostick, p. 120 & 121

[30] William O'Brien, *Forth the Banners Go*, as told to Edward MacLysaght, (Dublin 1969), p. 191.

[31] Irish Labour Party and Trade Union Congress, *Report of the Twenty-Sixth Annual Meeting,* 1920, p. 34

[32] Ibid., p. 34

[33] Ibid., p. 35

[34] *Freeman's Journal*, 15 April 1920

[35] Greaves, *The Irish Transport and General Workers Union,* p. 266

[36] *Kilkenny People*, 17 April 1920

[37] *Anglo-Celt*, 17 April 1920

[38] *Connacht Tribune*, 17 April 1920

[39] *Tuam Herald*, 17 April 1920

[40] *Connaught Telegraph*, 17 April 1920

[41] *Donegal News*, 17 April 1920

[42] *Irish Independent,* 15 April 1920

[43] *Derry Journal,* 16 April 1920

[44] *Leitrim Observer,* 17 April 1920

[45] *Longford Leader,* 17 April 1920

[46] *Meath Chronicle,* 17 April 1920

[47] *Sligo Champion,* 17 April 1920

[48] *Freeman's Journal*, 15 April 1920

49 *Nenagh Guardian,* 17 April 1920

50 *The Nationalist,* 17 April 1920

51 *Offaly Independent,* 17 April 1920

52 *Offaly Independent,* 17 April 1920

53 *Nationalist and Leinster Times,* 17 April 1920

54 *Drogheda Independent,* 17 April 1920

55 *Kerry Weekly Reporter,* 17 April 1920

56 *Donegal News,* 17 April 1920

57 *Irish Independent,* 15 April 1920

58 *Drogheda Independent,* 17 April 1920

59 *Kerry News,* 16 April 1920

60 *The Liberator,* 15 April 1920

61 *Killarney Echo and South Kerry Chronicle,* 17 April 1920

62 *Skibbereen Eagle,* 17 April 1920

63 Hanna Sheehy-Skeffington was a suffragette and one of the founders of the Irish Women Workers' Union. She was a member of Sinn Fein and opposed the Treaty, supporting the anti-Treaty side in the civil war. She later joined Fianna Fail when it was founded by DeValera in 1926.

64 *Kerry Weekly Reporter,* 17 April 1920

65 *Munster Express,* 17 April 1920

66 Emmet O'Connor, 'The Waterford Soviet: Fact or fancy?', *History Ireland,* Volume 8, Issue 1, (2000), p. 11   p. 10-12

67 *Freeman's Journal,* 15 April 1920

68 *Evening Herald,* 13 April 1920

69 *Evening Herald,* 13 April 1920

70 *Irish Times,* 15 April 1920

71 *Offaly Independent,* 17 April 1920

72 *Skibbereen Eagle,* 17 April 1920

73 *Cork Examiner,* 14 April 1920

74 *Cork Examiner,* 15 April 1920

75 *Cork Examiner,* 16 April 1920

76 *Irish Times,* 14 April 1920

77 *Irish Times,* 15 April 1920

78 Mike Milotte, *Communism in Modern Ireland: The Pursuit of the Workers' Republic Since 1916,* (Dublin, 1984), p. 31

79 *Manchester Guardian,* 20 April 1920, quoted in Emmet O'Connor, 'War and Syndicalism 1914-1923', in Donal Nevin (ed.), *Trade Union Century,* (Dublin, 1994), p. 62

80 O'Connor, 'War and Syndicalism 1914-1923', p. 62

81 Kostick, *Revolution in Ireland,* p. 127-128

82 A rival Trades Council was subsequently established by the trade union bureaucracy.

83 Quoted in Kostick, p. 128

84 Walter Smith MP, *House of Commons Debate,* 13 April 1920 (Volume 127, cc1641-6)

85 James Hogge MP, *House of Commons Debate,* 13 April 1920 (Volume 127, cc1641-6)

86 Sir Nevil Macready, *Annals Of An Active Life Volume 2,* (London, 1925), p. 445

87 O'Brien, *Forth the Banners Go,* p. 193-194

88 O'Connor, 'The Waterford Soviet: Fact or fancy?', p. 11

89 ILPTUC, *Report of the Twenty-Sixth Annual Meeting,* 1920, p. 30

[90] ILPTUC, *Report of the Twenty-Sixth Annual Meeting,* 1920, p. 41

[91] Charles Townshend, 'The Irish Railway Strike of 1920: Industrial Action and Civil Resistance in the Struggle for Independence', *Irish Historical Studies,* Vol. 22, No. 83 (March 1979), p. 265   pp. 265-282

[92] ILPTUC, *Report of the Twenty-Sixth Annual Meeting,* 1920, p. 42

[93] O'Brien, *Forth the Banners Go,* p. 196

[94] *Irish Times,* 1 June 1920

[95] ILPTUC, *Report of the Twenty-Sixth Annual Meeting,* 1920, p. 41-46 & 51-54

[96] Townshend, p. 270-271

[97] Ibid., p. 273-274

[98] ILPTUC, *Report of the Twenty-Seventh Annual Meeting,* 1921, p. 7

[99] Townshend, p. 273-274

[100] O'Brien, *Forth the Banners Go,* p. 197

[101] Townshend, p. 278

[102] ILPTUC, *Report of the Twenty-Seventh Annual Meeting,* 1921, p. 10-11

SOVIETS OF IRELAND

*'When they raised their Red flag, people laughed at them and said
they were a pack of sillies. They had proved that whatever flag they
had faith in, the workers had faith in the Red flag, and the Red flag
only'*
—*Robert Day, leader of the Cork Harbour Soviet.*
September 1921

The Knocklong 'Soviet'

A series of workplace occupations, threatened occupations and a localised general strike took place in County Limerick between 1920-1922. The first of these was the Knocklong 'Soviet', beginning on Sunday 16 May 1920 and lasting five days. The occupation of Knocklong Creamery included twelve auxiliary creameries at Ballinamona, Gormanstown, Kilteely, Elton, Knockcarron, Hospital, Knockaney, Ballingaddy, Kilbreedy, Bilboa, Lisnakilla and Ballylanders. In contrast to the Limerick 'Soviet' which was to all intents and purposes a spontaneous affair, the Knocklong 'Soviet' was a carefully planned and calculated tactic.[1] While the occupation was primarily designed to secure an increase in wages and the removal of a hated creamery manager, Riordan, there was also a political dimension to the 'Soviet'.[2] ITGWU organiser Sean Dowling was the prime mover behind the occupation and was intent on demonstrating that workers were capable of running industry on a co-operative basis. He viewed it as an educational tool for the working class.

The Knocklong Soviet began on Sunday 16 May. Jack Hedley, who was now using the pseudonym Sean O'Hagan, was installed as manager following the removal of Riordan who was ordered to 'keep off the job'. Hedley had moved to Limerick only days before, but it was clearly a calculated decision to reinforce the influence of the Marxist industrial organisers based in Limerick.

During the first evening of the occupation Riordan was found having sneaked back into the building. The *Watchword of Labour* stated that he was 'jokingly told next time he appeared he would be shot'. Also in the office with Hedley was local ITGWU secretary John O'Dwyer, an employee of the creamery. Sean Dowling and Jack McGrath were present to 'watch progress on behalf of the union'. The workers immediately painted the green entrance door red, removed the name-plate and substituted a new one with the inscription 'The Knocklong Soviet Creamery' and unfurled a banner with the slogan 'We Make Butter Not Profit'. The red flag and the tricolour were hoisted over the building. Work continued as normal in the creamery and the auxiliaries. Ninety-seven percent of farmers continued to supply the creamery and an output of two tons a day was reached. After several approaches from the owners the 'Soviet' agreed to hand back the property on the basis of a signed agreement guaranteeing the demanded wages increases and the permanent removal of the creamery manager Riordan.[3] The *Freeman's Journal* claimed that the 'Soviet' was 'A Light From Limerick That Failed' and then went on to detail the background to the dispute and how successful the workers were at operating the creamery over the five day period of the Soviet.[4]

The Koncklong 'Soviet' enormously increased the prestige of the ITGWU in the region[5] and John O'Dwyer indicated an increase in membership, including women workers, recruited as a result of the 'Soviet'.[6] The 'Soviet' also encouraged similar type occupations in other Cleeve's plants. In July women workers at the company's plant in Tipperary town occupied in pursuit of a wage claim.[7] In October discussions took place over the possible occupation of three creameries at Oola following their closure by their English owners, Alpin & Barrett.[8] Cleeves took over these creameries in November.[9] As the War of Independence intensified creameries were occasionally the targeted and burnt down by Crown Forces. In August another dispute was looming in Knocklong over threatened lay-offs.[10] It is reported that Cleeves insured the creamery against fire on 24 August and the creamery was burnt down by uniformed men two days later.[11]

The Struggle Continues

Following the strikes in May, farmers decided to invite the ITGWU onto a committee that paved the way for a settlement on a county wide basis.[12] As a result farm labourers received a significant pay increase across the county. In effect the ITGWU was able to use this arrangement to lodge wage claims on a countywide basis and then impose the settlement on all the farmers in the county. This settlement, along with the difficulties arising later in the year with army curfews that hampered union work,[13] saw a decline in disputes.

The August strike at Kilfrush near Knocklong provided an example of the approach employed by the ITGWU. Farm Labourers at Kilfrush were paid 30s for sixty hours work. Previous efforts to improve wages had been scuppered due to strike-breaking by labourers who were not members of the union. The first task for the union was to ensure all labourers were recruited to the ITGWU. Success was initially achieved by securing a 5s increase on wages. This succeeded in giving the workers confidence and at the end of May the ITGWU submitted a demand for a rate of 50s, with overtime rates to apply. After eight weeks of protracted negotiations a strike began on Friday 8 August.

The success of recruiting all the labourers ensured no strike-breaking occurred. In one incident on the day the strike started, an under-steward and an ex-army officer collected a supply of 80 gallons of petrol and a cart full of coal from Knocklong Railway Station. On the way home to Kilfrush the ex-army officer was dumped into the river, the petrol disappeared, and the coal was distributed free to locals in the area. The following morning negotiations re-opened and by Tuesday morning the men were back at work. Within a few hours one farmer, a prominent member of Sinn Fein, named Laffan[14] refused to pay the increase and all the men struck again. By Wednesday night union organiser Jack McGrath negotiated a 42s minimum rate, eight weeks arrears, timber for firewood at a nominal rate and a written guarantee of no change in wage rates before March 1921.[15]

Despite the county-wide agreement between the ITGWU and the farmers, strikes did break out in Ballyneety in September[16] and in Parteen in October.[17] Farm labourers had managed to survive the collapse in the agricultural economy in the Autumn of 1920[18] but things were to be more difficult in the months ahead. In April 1921 the Dail Cabinet was so worried that the situation between farmers and agricultural works would get out of hand that they instructed the Departments of Labour, Agriculture and Industry to confer and 'see what could be done to prevent anything like a class war developing'. It was suggested that they try and get a conference organised between farmers and labour representatives.[19]

The Impact of the War of Independence

The War of Independence with rebel attacks and state reprisals made things increasingly difficult as the year progressed. Cork bore the brunt of rebel activity and Limerick was one of the few other areas that saw significant fighting at this time.[20] However, Limerick city was the scene for a number of strikes that broke out in May and June 1920, with the ITGWU involved in strikes in the city's hotels,[21] among carters at O'Callaghan's Tannery[22] and two separate disputes involving different sets of workers at the city's sawmills.[23] During the strike of carters and yardmen at Spaights, pickets locked in a military truck with the drivers that was attempting to remove strike-bound goods. A force of one hundred soldiers had to be called in order to free them.[24] Limerick City was shot up by police on 27 April and again on 1 May but this in no way deterred the gas workers from going on strike on 8 May.[25]

Economic Decline and the Return of Industrial Conflict

With the calling of the truce in July 1921 industrial conflict returned with renewed strength. The character of the period had changed with the development of a major economic recession. Employers were attempting to take back many of the gains secured by workers over the previous four years. The economic downturn was significant. The index of agricultural prices fell from 288 in 1920 to 160 by 1924.[26] During 1921 manufacturing trade was almost halved and by December 1921 over twenty-six per cent of workers were out of work.[27] Figures from Limerick City show 1,580 applicants at the Labour Exchange on 24 October 1921.[28] Three weeks later there were 2,500 unemployed.[29] Writing in the aftermath of the truce Constance Markievicz outlined that:

> 'the unemployed are already looking to us to do something towards providing work...one has to face the fact that complaints have come to this office of men of the I.R.A. taking part in labour disputes. Evidence has also come to me that in some areas the workers are not willing to submit to the authority of their Executive and are beginning to get out of hand. What is to be feared in the near future is:- small local outbreaks growing more and more frequent and violent, the immediate result of which will be, destruction of property and much misery which will tend to disrupt the Republican cause'.[30]

For Sinn Fein the crisis of 1920 was now re-emerging in the latter half of 1921. The economic crisis and the ending of the guerrilla campaign led to a situation where, once again, the cause of labour was threatening to displace the cause of the republic in many areas of the country.[31]

Bruree Soviet Mills

In August 1921, workers at the Cleeves' plant in Bruree occupied the Flour Mill and Bakery. The dispute arose over the dismissal of three workers several months previously. In February 1921 the ITGWU demanded the re-instatement of the sacked workers and the payment of wages while they were laid off. Management refused and the dispute festered until the plant was occupied on 26 August 1921. Sean Dowling and Jack McGrath were again instrumental in organising the occupation.[32] Local ITGWU representative, Patrick Doherty, was appointed manager. The customary red flag and tricolour were hoisted over the plant and a banner proclaiming 'BRUREE WORKERS SOVIET MILLS we make BREAD not PROFITS' was hung over the entrance. The workers awarded themselves a wage increase of 7s 6d and reduced prices for consumers. The media reported that the business proceeded with clockwork precision and a continuous stream of customers called to the bakery 'all of whom seemed to appreciate the change'. Union officials claimed to have doubled the output of the bakery and that extra workers could be employed.[33] The occupation ended as a result of a conference in Liberty Hall, Dublin on 2 September where the workers' demands were met.[34] During the negotiations Constance Markiewicz threatened to use the IRA to remove the workers from the plant, only for the union to respond with the promise of a local general strike if she acted on her threat.[35] Demonstrating the control exercised by the workers, the *Limerick Leader* commented that when a reporter visited Bruree the previous Friday the 'Soviet' was found to be in full control of the village, 'both industrially and otherwise'.[36]

The Castleconnell Soviet

The threat of the use of the I.R.A. to remove occupying workers also occurred in relation to the Castleconnell 'Soviet' some months later. The dispute at the Castleconnell fisheries, owned by prominent Sinn Fein councillor, Anthony Mackey, had been ongoing for a considerable period. As far back as October 1920, under the threat of a strike, Mackey offered to submit to a Dail Court for arbitration in the dispute.[37] After failing to turn up for a hearing, Mackey claimed, deceptively, that the dispute had been settled.[38] The arbitration hearing was eventually held in May 1921 and resulted in an award in favour of the workers with payment backdated to the previous October.[39] Mackey continued to avoid paying the increases and back wages and the workers eventually went on strike on 22 October.[40] Within a week Mackey agreed to pay the workers the arbitrator's award, but the workers decided not to resume work until they actually received the money.[41] Mackey arrived at Liberty Hall a few days later saying he would pay the men on resumption of work, but was given short shrift by union officials.[42] The following week Mackey again failed to turn up to a meeting with a representative of the Department for Labour to arrange payment of the arbitration award[43] resulting in the workers occupying the Castleconnell fisheries at the end of November.[44]

On 2 December the Dail Cabinet sanctioned 'the Minister for Home Affairs to instruct police to proceed with the aid of volunteers to eject strikers from Mr. Mackey's premises. Minister for Labour was instructed to 'interview' Liberty Hall officials in the meantime with a view to having 'an organiser sent down to settle the dispute'.[45] On 12 December Mackey signed an agreement that as soon as the premises was vacated, he would re-employ all the workers without victimisation and fully adhere to the May arbitration award.[46] When the union representative went to hand back the premises the following day he discovered that Mackey intended to replace some of the men who had been on strike. The premises was eventually vacated on 22 December after Mackey agreed to a further round of arbitration which took place on 11 January 1922. The arbitrator's decision was announced on 18 January 1922 and awarded £53 0s 2d to the ten men for wages due and a further £81 5s 0d for the five-week period of the strike on the grounds that Mackey had failed to comply with the previous arbitration award. The ITGWU was ordered to pay Mackey £6 in respect of rent and taxes during the occupation and a further £20 in respect of nominal damages and the use of gear and premises during the occupation.[47] Once again the workers secured their demands and demonstrated a willingness to take radical action in support of their objectives. Despite repeated threats the nationalist leadership could not use the IRA to break strikes out of fear that such action could support a large-scale response from the workers movement.

The Dail Courts

The Dail Courts emerged in June 1920 as the Sinn Fein strategy to undermine the serious threat of class warfare being posed by the land occupations and cattle drives. The objective was not to create a parallel justice system but to create an adjudication process to control the land agitation. The local clergy provided the driving force for the establishment of the Dail Courts in local districts.[48] By September the IRA resorted to intimidation as a mechanism for enforcing the decisions of the Courts.[49]

Given the difficult circumstances arising out the conflict during the War of Independence, many branches in rural parts of Limerick fell apart in the latter half of 1920 and early 1921. The District Secretary in West Limerick described the situation as follows 'I found on my arrival here a fortnight ago, that the union was practically dead in West Limerick'.[50] The *Voice of Labour* regularly refers to 'slackers'[51] who had not paid their union dues. The ITGWU paper was often scathing in its comments on lapsed members. Referring to the situation in Killeedy 'We must give this place a shake-up on the 11th inst, and we advise some slackers to buck up. We're having no trifling'.[52] In Knockaderry 'We said in a previous report that we should make some traitors squeal here. So we did. Enough said'.[53] And in Ballylanders 'A few slaves in a local creamery had better become men, pay up and look pleasant, or the alternative dose may not taste so sweet'.[54]

Within weeks of the emergence of the Dail Courts it was claimed that the workers 'are taking strong exception to some of the decisions of these Courts'.[55] The difficulties being experienced by farm labourers was outlined in the ITGWU newspaper:

> 'dozens of farm workers in West Limerick have not had more than a fortnights work from the farmers this year...The farmers are worse landlords than the old ones whom the workers helped the farmers drive out...road stewards...are dishing out carting jobs'...to...'men with four or five cows before men who have no cows'.[56]

The process of reorganising the branches on Limerick County was a slow and arduous process. Regular mass meetings were held and over time many branches were revived. Sean Dowling was once again the driving force behind the efforts to re-organise, and regularly attempted to insert a political message into his work. In the middle of the Bruree 'Soviet' Dowling addressed a meeting of ITGWU members in Ballyneety where he said 'workers must become class conscious and in all future elections put in men of their own class'.[57]

Both nationally and locally employers were reacting to the economic recession by demanding wage reductions and job losses.[58] Trapped between the intentions of the employers and the militancy of its members, it was claimed that the ILPTUC executive, instead of organising trade union wide opposition to the onslaught, threw the onus of action back onto individual unions.[59]

The suddenness and pace of the advance in the ITGWU since 1917, had led to a largely independent rank and file.[60] As the slump progressed this independence of the rank and file was to create problems for the leadership of the union.[61] From the middle of 1921 onwards the workplace occupations that occurred were progressively taking on the role of an alternative form of struggle outside the control of the ILPTUC, rather than playing an auxiliary role in wage disputes.[62] The ability of the trade union movement in Limerick City and County to resist the onslaught of the employers finally rested on two long and very bitter disputes both involving the ITGWU.

Class Struggle to the Fore

By the end of 1921 Ireland was engulfed in a major strike wave and a rash of workplace Soviets. The economic crisis saw the employers going on a major offensive to slash jobs and wages, ably abetted by the Sinn Fein leadership. This period was marked by two significant developments, firstly the emergence of widespread strikes by farm labourers and secondly by the existence of workplace soviets throughout the country.

The strike wave by farm labourers engulfed large swathes of the country. The strike followed a well-developed pattern of disputes in the agricultural sector. The competing class forces jostled for control over transport and communications. Farmers, with the support of the IRA attempted to keep roads free in order to continue supplies to creameries. The striking labourers were determined to prevent the farmers conducting their normal business, by blockading roads, disrupting communications and damaging farming equipment. Creamery workers supported the farm labourers by refusing to process milk from farmers involved in disputes. In response farmers established 'co-operative' creameries directly under farmers control with farmers' sons providing the workforce for these creameries. There was a systematic attempt by the IRA to suppress strikes by farm labourers and support the farming class.

A major farm labourers dispute arose in Co. Limerick as a result of a demand by the ITGWU for the payment of a £4 harvest bonus submitted to the farmers in the Bulgaden area near Kilmallock. The Dail sent a written request to both parties asking for the case to be submitted to arbitration. The union agreed but the farmers failed to respond to the request.[63] It appears some workers went on strike during the first week of November 1921,[64] but by 9 November all the workers were out.[65] The farmers then claimed they never received the letter from the Dail but when the union once again suggested arbitration the farmers refused emphatically.[66] The farmers in the area had made their intention clear. A meeting of the Limerick Farmers Association offered the Bulgaden farmers the wholehearted support of the organisation in their efforts to break the strike.[67]

At this stage the dispute became increasingly confrontational. Workers at the dozen or so creameries in the locality refused to accept milk from the strike-bound farmers and, as a consequence, the farmers demanded that the Sinn Fein leadership act.[68] It is worth noting that this was the last mention of the strike in the *Voice of Labour*. It signalled a change in the approach of O'Brien and the leadership of the ITGWU and their abandonment of the farm labourers engaged in struggle.

Within days of the start of the strike Bulgaden creamery closed down and shortly afterwards a farmer's house was raided at night and a milk separator that he had purchased to process his own milk was smashed up.[69] At this stage four of the strike leaders, including Sean Dowling, were arrested by the IRA. The ITGWU called a general strike in Kilmallock and three hundred workers marched through Kilmallock behind a red flag demanding the release of the strikers.[70] The following day the workers were released, and the general strike was called off.[71] On the 26 November the Limerick Farmer's Association held a meeting in the Glentworth Hotel in Limerick and called on 'all co-operative creameries not to refuse milk from any farmer who is a member of this Union at the dictates of the ITGWU or any outside body'.[72]

Around the middle of December two more farmer's houses were raided and milk separators smashed.[73] At this time the farmers once again refused to submit the dispute to Dail arbitration.[74] Violence continued with hay being burned,[75] trees felled blocking roads, fencing dismantled and cattle driven.[76] Sometime during the second week of January a local farmer, Patrick O'Donnell, was kidnapped.[77] On the night of Friday 13 January another kidnapping took place near Mallow, this time of Major Hallinan who was a prominent employer in the Bulgaden area.[78] The following night two lorries arrived outside an ITGWU meeting in Kilmallock. Local union activist Michael Lenihan was asked to step outside where he was bundled into the back of one of the lorries and driven off.[79] Shortly afterwards those who were kidnapped were released by the competing sides.[80]

Sometime during these events a deputation from the Irish Farmer's Association met with Arthur Griffith demanding action be taken against the strikers.[81] On 21 January 1922 Donncha O'Hannigan O/C of the East Limerick Brigade IRA had declared martial law around Kilmallock.[82] Two hundred IRA men were drafted into the Bulgaden area.[83] Small parties of IRA men protected local farmers and armed volunteers patrolled the streets of Kilmallock night and day.[84] ITGWU organiser Jack McGrath threatened drastic steps against 'anyone who endeavours to charge members of the union with such occurrences'.[85] Talks were held on 23 January, under the direction of Brigadier Hannigan, and both sides agreed to submit to arbitration.[86] Local press reports indicate that between £6,000 - £7,000 worth of farm produce was destroyed, separators broken, fencing broken down and cattle driven, tress felled across roads, bridges broken,[87] fairs and markets held up, hay, straw and farm buildings burned down,[88] walls knocked and telegraph and electric light cables severed[89] during the dispute. Towards the end of February twenty cases were heard at the Arbitration Court in Kilmallock for breach of curfew during martial law and the commandant prosecuted the individuals and imposed nominal fines.[90] The defeat for the strike was complete with the Arbitration Board comprising of Dr. Murnane, Sinn Fein TD, Sean Moylan and Fr. Higgins issued a finding that the strike was subversive and that the workers had inadequate grounds for claiming the harvest bonus. They rejected the claim for payment for the period of the strike and condemned 'the wanton and cowardly destruction of property'.[91]

Farm Labourers on Strike

Throughout the country farm labourers engaged in strike action from mid-1921 onwards. The strike action and the response of the nationalist leadership and the farmers' union set the scene for widespread class conflict that often turned violent. The intense nature of the class conflict demonstrated the determination of the nationalist leadership to preserve the rule of capital.

Along with strikes among farm labourers in Limerick, the industrial action of farm labourers in Waterford was indicative of the nature of such strikes. In May 1921 labourers in Waterford embarked on a countywide strike when the Waterford Farmers Association (WFA) refused to enter negotiations. The nationalist leaders in Waterford attempted to draft thirty IRA men into the area in support of the farmers. Reflecting the class tensions within the IRA, local Volunteers objected suggesting that if there was any shooting to be done then the targets would be the farmers rather than the striking labourers. The resistance of the farmers quickly dissipated.[92] A year later strike action broke out again. The WFA had engaged in widespread agitation among farmers to try and bolster their ranks and were confident of victory.

168

The farmers attempted to sow division between urban and rural workers, declaring that if urban and rural workers were organised in a single big trade union (i.e. the ITGWU) 'the country workers will be made subservient to the town workers'. However, the class instincts of the workers supplanted any attempt by the farmers to sow division. The farmers were intent on destroying union organisation among farm labourers. 'Illegal Labour doctrines had been countered in the parishes of Rathgormack and Ballinameela... The hour of action is at hand. The time of resolutions is past'.[93] The objective of the farmers was to drive down wages and increase working hours. For the workers struggle was necessary to maintain the wages and conditions that they had already secured.

The union was well prepared for the strike. They had succeeded in organising at least ninety-seven percent of farm labourers in the county. Unemployed members in each branch were mobilised into 'flying columns' which could be deployed in the event of violence against pickets.[94]

The confidence of the farmers leaders was misplaced. Very quickly the resolve of the farmers began to crumble. On the second day farmers in many districts had signed an agreement to accept existing wage rates and conditions. Picketing was widespread and the striking workers blocked roads to prevent the movement of goods. Farmers who had signed the agreement were issued with permits that allowed them to pass through the roadblocks and ensure that their goods were not blacklisted by union members at the creameries or the railways. In Dungarvan, farmers without permits were unable to sell their produce and in one incident a farmer who had purchased a milk separator had it confiscated by flying pickets who returned it to the merchant.

In conjunction with the farm labourers strike, workers in creameries were now occupying the plants throughout Limerick, Tipperary, North cork and West Waterford, as part of the 'Munster Soviets'. Violence and threats of violence were becoming the norm. On the morning of Tuesday 23 May a farmer without a permit was attempting to transport milk to Waterford. He was confronted by flying pickets at a roadblock. The farmer produced a revolver and threatened to shoot the pickets if they refused to allow him to pass, which they acquiesced to.[95] After this incident many of the 'flying columns' of workers armed themselves when mounting roadblocks and pickets.

Regular protests were now taking place involving striking labourers and unemployed members of the ITGWU. These protests were led by workers carrying a red flag. Victory in this dispute hinged on the ability of the striking workers to impose a boycott of the farmers and prevent the movement of farm produce. Intermittent IRA interference did occur, but the IRA were largely distracted by the split in their movement and the approaching civil war. One confrontation did occur with a local IRA unit near Kilmacthomas. The IRA attempted to control traffic movements in the locality. A Labour 'flying column' from Stradbally was sent to force a withdrawal by the IRA. After discussions the IRA members withdrew, and the Labour flying column took over the roadblocks in the locality.[96]

As the number of farmers agreeing to settle increased, the ITGWU focused their campaign on putting more intense pressure of the remaining farmers to agree to the workers terms. Around Dungarvan domestic servants formed a 'Women's Battalion' and refused to work for strike-bound farmers. Sympathetic strike action increased the pressure. Ultimately, the large estate landowners in West Waterford managed to sustain their opposition to the strike, with the result that the strike action was eighty percent successful, but workers for the larger landowners were forced to give significant concessions.[97]

General Election June 1922

A general election was held in Ireland on 16 June 1922. The divided Sinn Fein leadership attempted to cobble together a 'pact' to manipulate the outcome of the election. The pact dictated that the pro- and anti-Treaty factions should nominate the number of candidates equivalent to the number of outgoing TDs on either side and that all nominated candidates would stand on a joint panel of Sinn Fein candidates. The outgoing Dail members had all been 'elected' unopposed in the uncontested election of 1921 (including the four independent Unionists representing Trinity College). However, the political landscape had altered dramatically since May 1921.

Greaves argued that the emergence of the 'pact' allowed the pro- and anti-Treaty elements to form 'a joint struggle against Labour'.[98] Once the 'pact' was agreed widespread propaganda and intimidation was used to force Labour candidates to withdraw. Candidates were accused of not having been 'in prison, nor in an ambush'.[99] Sinn Fein couldn't just target Labour alone, to do so would have clearly undermined their own organisation as workers within the ranks of Sinn Fein would opposed such actions by the leadership. Instead the Sinn Fein leaders put pressure on all non-Sinn Fein candidates to withdraw as a pretext for being able to target Labour. In Clare for example, the farmers' candidate agreed to withdraw on condition that Labour's Paddy Hogan also agreed not to contest the election. Hogan resisted right up to the deadline for nominations before caving into pressure.[100] In many areas where Labour refused to withdraw the farmers candidates insisted on standing in opposition.

Labour stood on a manifesto calling for a 'Workers Republic'. The manifesto was decided at an ILPTUC conference in February 1922. While this was a reflection in part of the pressure from the rank-and-file on the leadership, it also reflected the fact that, once again, the leadership were making promises that they had no intention of fulfilling. More importantly the leadership studiously avoided taking any position on the Treaty claiming that to do so would potentially lead to a split in the trade union movement. The National Executive urged workers to remain neutral, an astonishing assertion given that the country was hurtling towards civil war with the Treaty forming the backdrop of such a development. There was opposition to the refusal of the ILPTUC leadership to take a position on the Treaty, but it was disorganised and haphazard in its approach.[101] The lack of a revolutionary party, capable of understanding the processes at work, was crucial at this juncture. Jim Larkin opposed the Treaty but was still in America and his declarations were having little impact. The Marxist organisers of the ITGWU were wrapped up in the ongoing strikes and occupations that were underway. The ILPTUC called for a plebiscite on the Treaty. From the perspective of the leadership this would have left them off the hook in terms of having to take a clear position on whether to support or oppose the Treaty and the consequences of same. It was also clear that a proposal to hold a referendum was not going to be considered by either of the Sinn Fein factions.

The ILPTUC did organise a general strike against 'militarism' on 24 April 1922. The strike was as effective as in 1918 and 1920 but was of a different character. While the strike was billed as being against 'militarism' it was supported by pro-Treaty Sinn Fein, the Catholic hierarchy and businesses interests. The strike was seen ostensibly as being in support of the Treaty and opposing the actions of the anti-Treaty IRA. Many on the anti-Treaty side had illusions in William O'Brien and the ILPTUC leadership. They had the attitude that O'Brien would stick to Connolly's position of opposing the carnival of reaction that would result from partition. Peadar O'Donnell believed that O'Brien would be steadfast in the 'hour of crisis' because 'he was a strict taskmaster whose speeches invariably contained a firm, uncompromising stand on the national questions'.[102] His confidence was built on a foundation of sand.

The Communist Party of Ireland had been established in October 1921 following the takeover of the Socialist Party of Ireland by James Connolly's son, Roddy Connolly, and his supporters. However, the membership amounted to fewer than thirty activists and the CPI adopted a sectarian attitude towards the working class, demanding that they abandon all class demands, support anti-Treaty Sinn Fein and participate in the anti-Treaty IRA.

In total eighteen Labour candidates stood in a total of thirteen constituencies. Many of the Labour candidates were strike leaders, including Robert Day, leader of the Cork Harbour Soviet and Nicholas Phelan, leader of the farm labourers strikes in Waterford. Seventeen of the eighteen Labour candidates were elected, with the losing candidate failing to be elected by thirteen votes. Day and Phelan were elected as was Patrick Gaffney, a member of the CPI, who secured almost thirty-five percent of the vote in Carlow-Kilkenny. Labour secured more than twenty-one percent of the vote despite only standing in thirteen of the twenty-eight constituencies. The Labour vote was comparable to the vote of anti-Treaty Sinn Fein. Running extra candidates in every constituency could potentially have seen Labour become the second largest political grouping and possibly even becoming the biggest political party in the Third Dail.

Sinn Fein were accused of widespread intimidation and impersonation on election day, including the kidnapping of non-Sinn Fein election agents.[103] *Gallagher* asserted that it would be naïve to assume that Labour's vote came from people sympathetic to the party's social and economic policies, suggesting that much of the support came from former IPP voters. *Gallagher* ignores the fact that the election took place during a major strike wave and large numbers of workplace soviets, with many of the candidates directly involved in strike action. Repeatedly Labour candidates were accused of being communists and atheists, and not without validity.[104]

An Irish Workers Army

During January 1922 attempts were initiated to create a 'Workers Army' by elements within the ITGWU. William O'Brien makes no mention of this development in his memoirs, but there are documents in the National Library of Ireland that indicate the leadership of the ITGWU were involved to some degree.[105] At the time the remnants of the Irish Citizen's Army had an estimated two hundred members. It is argued that the reason for this initiative was an attempt by the leadership of the ITGWU to bring the Citizen's Army under their control, and to convert it into a pro-Treaty formation. The 'Workers Army' initiative led to the formation of a committee comprising five members of the Citizen's Army and five trade unionists. The purpose of this committee was to begin recruiting workers to the new force. Branches of the ITGWU were contacted and the response was considered as 'very encouraging'. In early April an army convention of the Workers Army was held, and a number of units established.[106] Its aims were stated as being to defend Ireland against foreign aggression, to protect strikers, to secure the rights of workers as citizens and to fight for the workers' republic.[107]

On 13 April the anti-Treaty IRA seized the Four Courts. A week later the ILPTUC's strike against militarism took place. On the day of the general strike a member of the committee to organise the Workers Army instructed members of the Citizen's Army to guard speakers at a labour public meeting. The tone of the meeting was directed against the occupation of the Four Courts by the anti-Treaty IRA and the Citizen Army activists protested to their Army Council. The incident led to the splintering of the Citizens Army. A majority of the activists, led by John Hanratty, joined forces with the anti-Treaty IRA.[108] At the same time the anti-Treaty IRA had arrested and locked-up a Citizens Army officer in Roscrea.[109] The ITGWU continued to recruit for the Workers Army and as late as the beginning of June 1922 a member of the organising committee, Michael Kelly, was stating that the committee still favoured the creation of the army. After this it looks like William O'Brien buried the initiative in the run up to the general election in June.

What potential existed for the development of a Workers Army in the first half of 1922 is an open question. Given the widespread nature of strike action and workers soviets that were facing repression from both pro-Treaty and anti-Treaty forces, along with farmers organisations, the potential for such an armed defence force for workers clearly did exist. As late as May 1922 Michael Donnelly and John Byrne, part of the organising committee, were claiming that there was 'growing demand' among trade unionists for such a force.[110] The lack of a revolutionary party contributed to the failure to develop such a Workers Army. The fact that William O'Brien was attempting to exercise control over the Citizens Army contributed to the split in the Citizens Army and inhibited the development of a wider force to defend the working class.

The failure of the newly founded CPI to forge an independent class position on the Anglo-Irish Treaty and build a revolutionary party contributed to the consequences of partition and the civil war. The leadership of the CPI gave uncritical support to the anti-Treaty forces, providing uncensored access to three-quarters of the pages of the CPI newspaper. Worse still, even where the CPI had a support base, the leadership called on communists to abandon the workplace soviets and join the anti-Treaty forces.[111]

Soviets of Ireland

The first workplace soviet to emerge was as early as January 1919 when workers, supported by patients, took over what was then known as the Monaghan Lunatic Asylum. Organised by then ITGWU organiser, Peadar O'Donnell when police descended on the town the workers barricaded themselves into the hospital. Initially the authorities offered a pay rise but excluded the female staff. The workers rejected the offer, holding out for pay parity. When the soviet ended after two weeks workers saw their working week cut from 93 hours per week to 56 hours and also received a pay rise. For the first time, married workers were allowed to go home after their shift ended instead of being forced to remain on the premises.[112]

Outside of Limerick several examples of workplace soviets emerged in 1921. Mineworkers at the Arigna mine on the Roscommon/Leitrim border lodged a pay claim in May 1921. When the mine owners rejected the claim, the workers occupied the mine and established a workplace soviet on 12 May. The occupation was led by self-described Bolshevik, Geoffrey Coulter. The manager of the mine posted notices throughout the area threatening prosecution against anyone involved in the 'unauthorised' removal of coal from the mine.[113] The soviet lasted for more than two months. The workers continued to mine coal and supplied both local customers[114] and the Great Northern Railway. The workers also made technical improvements to the mine and signed commercial contracts with customers. Along with receiving their demanded pay increase, when the workers handed back the mine to the owners, they insisted that the owners honour all agreements entered into by the workers during the soviet.[115]

While the Bruree Soviet was demonstrating the ability of workers to manage their own affairs in a Co. Limerick village, workers in Cork Harbour began a strike for a wage increase. Harbour pilots and dockers in what was then Queenstown (Cobh) walked out in solidarity. Several vessels were detained in the harbour under the control of the workers. When, on 2 September, the Harbour Board refused to back down one hundred and fifty workers marched into the harbour and took over the offices of the board, raised a red flag and installed Robert Day as the leader of the soviet. Attempts were made by the ITGWU leadership to have permits issued to allow the ships to depart, but the workers refused permission for them to leave. On 5 September Robert Day was elected as the 'Chief Commissioner of the Port'. Subsequently the engineers, caretakers and telephonists agreed to join the strike.[116]

The Cork Examiner reported on Robert Day addressing a mass meeting of workers in the harbour, with Day calling his fellow workers 'Friends, comrades and Bolshevik. The Examiner continued outlining the comments by Day:

'He did not think there was a better title for them than Bolsheviks for that word meant to him an anxiety that the bottom dog should go up and the top dog come down... When they raised their Red flag, people laughed at them and said they were a pack of sillies. They had proved that whatever flag they had faith in, the workers had faith in the Red flag, and the Red flag only... we the workers will have to fight the Republicans harder than we ever fought the bosses for a just share of the government of the country... He told Alderman Higgins... that no power on earth would take it (the red flag) down except the power that put it up, the power of the workers... If the IRA are going to make blacklegs or strike-breakers, there is trouble in store for them'.[117]

While the ITGWU leadership were instructing their members on the docks around the country to accept pay cuts, the dock workers in Cork secured a pay increase of £1 per week after a five-day occupation of the harbour.[118] Robert Day was elected as a Labour TD in Cork in the general election of June 1922.

In mid-September 1921 more than seven hundred workers occupied several foundries in Dublin and Drogheda. In relation to Drogheda the *Freemans Journal* reported that 'The responsible section of the community regarded the position gravely'. The workers in Drogheda had been on strike for six weeks before they occupied the foundry.[119] The establishment were now terrified with what they viewed as the increasing pace of workplace occupations. Once the workers in the foundry began discussing with workers at the Drogheda Chemical Manure Company, the Drogheda Brewery and the Irish Packing Company about occupying those workplaces, the state decided to act. Several lorryloads of RIC arrived, arrested the strike leaders and suppressed the soviet removing all the workers.[120]

Throughout the first half of 1922 numerous soviets emerged around the country. On 18 January 1922 the Dublin Council for the Unemployed occupied the Rotunda Hall (now the Gate Theatre). The occupation was led by renowned writer Liam O'Flaherty, a member of the Communist Party. The occupation was suppressed after five days by the IRA following an attack by a clerically incited mob.[121] The CPI leadership condemned the occupation as a 'childish stunt' resulting in O'Flaherty leaving the country. After the publication of his novel *The Informer* in 1925, regarded as a thinly veiled attack on Roddy Connolly and the CPI, *An Phoblacht* attacked O'Flaherty describing him as someone who liked to 'hover among the prostitutes, thieves and murderers of Dublin'. [122]

The land seizures that Sinn Fein had succeeded in dissipating in 1920 through the use of the Dail courts re-emerged in 1922 and this time were closely linked to the ongoing workplace occupations. The most significant of these occurred in South-East Clare with a land seizure that became known as the Broadford Soviet. A group of landless labourers and cottier tenants occupied the estate of absentee landlord James Going in February 1922. The soviet was inspired by the Castleconnell soviet, a few miles away, that had ended a couple of weeks previously. The workers established "The Committee of Farmers, Tenants, Workers and Transport Union Workers on the Going Estate". The committee entered negotiations with the landlord's agent about the purchase of the estate but rejected what they considered an outlandish price. The committee issued a proclamation stating that they would retain the lands for six months at a valuation of £100. They ordered the landlord to remove all his animals from the land or else he would be charged for the grazing. Subsequently the soviet was left to its own devices. The cooperative nature of the soviet began to dissipate after nine months leading to secretary of the soviet, Michael Collins, contacting the agent to explore a return of the lands to the landlord. The offer was rejected, and the 'soviet' continued in a much looser form until 1925. As late as 1925 the Redemptorist priests in Limerick in charge of the Arch Confraternity were warning workers in Limerick 'to eschew the Bolshevik movement and not to be led away by the specious arguments of men who were associated with the Soviet doctrine'.[123]

The North Cork railway was taken over by railway workers in January 1922 and that was followed by the take-over of two flour mills in Cork during February. The occupations were suppressed by pro-Treaty IRA elements under orders from the Provisional Government. During March the gasworks in Waterford were occupied, followed by an occupation of the gasworks in Tipperary.[124] The Farmers Union in

Meath and Kildare engaged in fund-raising for the IRA as they protected people scabbing on the farm labourers strike. The Cappaquin soviet confiscated the cattle of the leader of the Waterford Farmers Association and milked the cows for distribution to the local community. When they returned the cattle, the soviet included a payment of £3 10s stating: 'The Cappaquin soviet did not run the cows for profit'. The approach of the workers in Cappaquin demonstrates that the soviets were not just about pay, but on the wider issue of workers control over industry.

On 25 April the soviets in Tipperary were extended. The creamery and the flour mills were already under occupation as part of the dispute against Cleeves. Along with the soviet in the gasworks, a further occupation occurred at Tipperary coachbuilders. Two days later three hundred workers occupied the previously closed sawmills at Ballinacourty and began production under workers control. Throughout the South and West of the country, workers were responding to the deepening recession and the breakdown of administration by occupying workplaces in defence of jobs and conditions.[125] Occupations also took place at the Quarterstown Mills and the Ballingarry mine in Limerick.

The Munster Soviets

During December 1921 the Cleeve's owned Condensed Milk Company of Ireland sought lay-offs and wage cuts of one third among its workforce in Limerick, Cork and Tipperary.[126] On 22 December 1921 the ITGWU held a conference in Limerick Junction comprising twenty-three delegates representing the workers in sixty eight creameries owned by Cleeves. Jack McGrath used the meeting to remind the delegates of the divisions that occurred amongst the workforce during the strike against Cleeves in 1919 and Sean Dowling outlined the current level of attacks by employers on dockers, railwaymen and farm workers all over the country. He called on the workers to stand solid and win the dispute. The workers unanimously rejected the proposed cuts in jobs and wages and a 'Workers Committee of Action' was formed.[127]

On 3 January 1922 a national conference was organised by the Department of Labour and held at 18 Parnell Square in Dublin. The workers and bosses were located in separate rooms and no progress was made during negotiations. Divisions did appear amongst the ranks of the workers. James Carr, the President of LUTLC, who was attending as a representative of the Irish Engineering Union stated that they were willing to do a deal with the Limerick Federation of Employers.[128] Other craft unions followed suit and it was left to the ITGWU, the ICWU and the IADMU to oppose the employers. All three unions opposed arbitration and the meeting ended with Cunningham, the company secretary of the Condensed Milk Company of Ireland, questioning why the workers would not trust the government?[129]

Later in January the Minister for Defence received a letter from Messrs. Cleeve complaining of a soviet occupation of one of their factories.[130] The Ministry for Labour supported the employers' position that wage reductions were necessary and put in place two joint councils to arbitrate in the dispute. Cleeves claimed that by the end of 1921 the company had debts of £100,000 with net losses amounting to £274,555.[131] The Union claimed that the company had made £3/4 million between 1918-1919 and were suspicious of the claims of the company.[132] The arbitration system came down on the side of the employers and submitted the proposals to the unions for ballot.[133] At the end of March the Dail Cabinet was getting worried about the situation with the company 'owing to labour disputes' it was decided that 'the Ministers for Labour, Local Government and Agriculture should interview the Provincial Bank with a view to negotiating an extensions of M. Cleeve's overdraft'.[134] When the Workers Committee of Action re-assembled on 31 March the result of the ballot showed a very large majority against the proposals. In the national interest a temporary compromise proposal was made that included a one month's reduction in wages while a new buyer was sought for the Cleeve's company, after which the wages would revert back to previous levels. These proposals were subsequently passed by a small majority.[135]

Despite these efforts to broker an agreement a strike broke out at the Cleeve's plant in Landsdowne in Limerick on 13 April.[136] After four weeks members of the ICWU accepted a wage cut but the ITGWU continued to refuse.[137] As the situation deteriorated two hundred workers in Clonmel occupied the Cleeve's plant on 12 May. Workers in Carrick-On-Suir occupied the Cleeve's creamery and the Condensed Milk factory the following day and before the weekend was out the Cleeve's premises in Kilmallock and Knocklong were also under the workers control.[138] Under direction and co-ordination by Sean Dowling, Jack McGrath and Jack Hedley, the Workers Committee of Action now organised widespread occupations.[139] Dowling and McGrath had been sacked by William O'Brien in the aftermath of the defeat of the farm labourers strike in Kilmallock but continued to organising workers and to defend jobs and conditions. Their sacking was part of a strategy by the leadership of the ITGWU to remove the radical industrial organisers who they were unable to control.

The reaction of the Dail Cabinet was swift. In order to prevent striking workers occupying the Landsdowne plant, a detachment of fully armed Free State troops were placed on guard.[140] Farmers demanded immediate action. At a meeting in Geary's Hotel in Limerick, Mr B. Laffan, then a Sinn Fein chairman of Limerick County Council said that 'this struggle threatened the very lives and liberties of the farmers'. He claimed that all lawful government was being ignored and he proposed a resolution stating that 'we forbid our members to supply the red flag, which is the flag of revolution and anarchy...we look for protection from our government to assert our right as free citizens'.[141] A meeting of the Executive of the Irish Farmer's Union on 18 May took up the demands. The meeting stated that they did not want communism in Ireland and delegates claimed that acts of sabotage were being carried out and that farmers were being forced to supply the creameries at gunpoint. Mr. M. Doran stated that 'if the government would not govern, they should be told to get out', while Rev. Father Maguire from Co. Monaghan made an appeal to those responsible for social order to expel those who had invaded private property.[142]

It must be remembered that these events were occurring precisely at the time that the country was sliding into Civil War. In the initial stage of the occupations farmers did supply the creameries with full production continuing.[143] Butter was sent to Scotland and Wales to co-operative stores. The expelled manager at Carrick-on-Suir, Nolan, claimed that the pro-treaty administration requested the British Authorities to send a gunboat to intercept the Welsh cargo, but it has never been possible to substantiate this claim.[144] In the early hours of 19 May machinery worth £3,000 was destroyed at the Cleeve's creamery in Grange, while the Oakleigh Creamery at Caherconlish was burnt down after receiving milk diverted from other plants.[145] The workers expected that the farmers would continue to supply the occupied creameries as workers at unoccupied creameries were refusing to handle diverted milk.[146] However the farmers boycott was beginning to bite. Diverted milk being delivered to Bridgetown was being guarded by Free State troops.[147] Conflict broke out in Clonmel when women workers from the Cleeve's plant attacked 'women of the farming classes' who were selling butter at a local market, scattering produce all over the road.[148] At the end of May the workers offered to accept a pay cut of 12%, but the offer was rejected by the company. After repeatedly been forced to back down against the determination of the union Cleeves wanted a final victory.[149] In reality the company had little choice. The company was in serious difficulty with repeated problems supplying markets as a result of military, political and class conflicts of the period. The financial viability of the company was at stake.[150] Officially the strike committee called off the strike at the end of June 1922. The workers in Bruree handed back the flour mills at this time.[151]

Despite the official ending of the strike, the occupations were to continue. One of the first of the soviets to be suppressed was that at Knocklong. Within days of the attack on the Four Courts, Liam Lynch ordered Frank Ryan and the anti-Treaty IRA unit under his command, to suppress the soviet in Knocklong. Ryan himself climbed onto the roof of the building to remove the red flag while the workers were being evicted from the premises.[152] This wasn't the first occasion that Lynch had ordered such action. Several months earlier Lynch and his IRA unit ejected workers occupying the Mallow Sawmills. In appreciation the owners of the sawmills paid Lynch £50 for helping with their 'recent labour trouble'.[153]

The most determined soviet was that in Tipperary. Repeated attempts were made by the anti-Treaty IRA to suppress the different workplace occupations in the town.

On one occasion the workers arrested the former manager of the creamery and locked him in an office in the building after he attempted to get local businesses in the town to boycott produce from the creamery. In response the anti-Treaty IRA demanded his release which was refused by the workers. This was followed by a short gun battle between the IRA volunteers and the occupying workers which resulted in the IRA being forced to withdraw. Around this time the anti-Treaty IRA succeeded in suppressing the soviet in the Ballinacourty sawmills and ejected the workers.[154]

While the necessity existed for the workers to extend the soviets, the leadership of the ILPTUC were washing their hands of the crisis. Thomas Johnson declared that 'Labour had nothing to do with it and had no general policy of the kind'. Not only did the trade union leadership abandon the workers, the CPI did the same. The CPI had a base of support in Tipperary and local members established a support group for the soviets in the town. But the nationalist leadership of the CPI convinced their membership to abandon the soviets and joined the anti-Treaty forces. As the anti-Treaty IRA retreated from Tipperary, they burnt the gasworks and blew up the water main so that the fire could not be put out. When the Free State forces entered the town, they immediately suppressed the soviets and ejected the occupying workers.[155]

For a large part of 1922 illegal direct action by workers kept employer ambitions to cut jobs and wages in check. In excess of one hundred and twenty soviet occupations occurred during the year and with such minimal capacity for compromise given the economic conditions, the soviets acquired serious revolutionary intent. The leadership of the ITGWU gave nothing more than lip-service to these struggles and disputes emerged within the union as a result.[156] As the Civil War progressed, and Free State troops advanced into Munster the Government was anxious not only to suppress armed resistance to the Treaty but also to deal decisively with 'bolshevik' agitation. One of the first acts of the troops when they arrived in a village or town was to immediately suppress any soviet they found and arrest the strike leaders.

Factory occupations ceased as a tactic and the ITGWU struggled to maintain its presence and impact on the local industrial scene. Questions have been asked about the role of Dowling, McGrath and Hedley. Why had they supported the leadership in the aftermath of the Limerick 'Soviet'? And what efforts were made to politicise the members of their union.[157] O'Connor Lysaght contends that Sean Dowling was a union organiser rather than a socialist propagandist and as such the politicisation of his members was secondary to industrial organisation.[158] Certainly the commitment of these ITGWU organisers to the syndicalist ideal would have emphasised industrial organisation over political action. At the time of the Limerick Soviet, Dowling could have accepted the rhetoric emanating from Liberty Hall at face value. With the lesson of the struggles that developed in the following years his syndicalist instincts led him to engage with the membership of his union in class struggle.[159] As Dowling has not left any written material dealing with his experiences in Limerick it is not possible to know his political outlook and orientation.

[1] Greaves, *Liam Mellows and the Irish Revolution,* p. 189
[2] O'Connor, 'War and Syndicalism 1914-1923', p.59.
[3] *Watchword of Labour*, 29 May 1920, & *Freeman's Journal*, 22 May 1920.
[4] *Freeman's Journal*, 22 May 1920.
[5] David Lee, 'The Munster Soviets and the Fall of the House of Cleeve', in David Lee & Debbie Jacobs (eds), *Made in Limerick, History of Industries, Trade and Commerce, Volume 1,* (Limerick, 2003), p. 296.
[6] *Freeman's Journal*, 22 May 1920.
[7] Lee, p. 296.
[8] *Watchword of Labour*, 30 October 1920.
[9] *Watchword of Labour*, 20 November 1920.
[10] *Watchword of Labour*, 21 August 1920
[11] O'Connor Lysaght, 'The Munster Soviet Creameries', p.42.
[12] Greaves, *The Irish Transport and General Workers Union,* p. 262.
[13] *Watchword of Labour*, 9 October 1920.
[14] Laffan was later Sinn Fein Chairman of Limerick County Council
[15] *Watchword of Labour*, 14 August 1920.
[16] Crean, *The Labour Movement in Kerry and Limerick 1914-1921,* p. 371
[17] *Watchword of Labour*, 23 October 1920.
[18] O'Connor, *A Labour History of Ireland,* p. 100.
[19] *Dail Eireann Secretariat Files 1919-1922*, DE 1/3, Document No. 95, 6 April 1921.
[20] P.S. O'Hegarty, *The Victory of Sinn Fein*, (Dublin, 1998), p. 28.
[21] *Limerick Leader*, 12 May 1920.
[22] *Limerick Leader*, 12 May 1920.
[23] *Limerick Leader*, 11 June 1920, 19 July 1920, & *Watchword of Labour*, 12 June 1920.
[24] *Munster News*, 23 June 1920.
[25] Greaves, *The Irish Transport and General Workers Union,* p. 272, & *Munster News*, 8 May 1920.
[26] L.M. Cullen, *An Economic History of Ireland Since 1660*, (London, 1987), p. 172.
[27] O'Connor, *A Labour History of Ireland,* p. 109.
[28] *Limerick Leader*, 24 October 1921.
[29] *Limerick Leader*, 14 November 1921.
[30] *Dail Eireann Secretariat Files 1919-1922*, DE 2/483, Minister for Labour, Economic Policy, Document No. 247.
[31] R.F. Foster, *Modern Ireland 1600-1972*, (London, 1988), p.514.
[32] Lee, 'The Munster Soviets and the Fall of the House of Cleeve', p. 298-300.
[33] *Freeman's Journal*, 31 August 1921, *Limerick Echo*, 3 September 1921, *Limerick Leader*, 31 August 1921.
[34] *Limerick Leader*, 5 September 1921.
[35] O'Connor Lysaght, 'The Munster Soviet Creameries', p.43..
[36] *Limerick Leader*, 5 September 1921.
[37] *Watchword of Labour*, 16 October 1920.
[38] *Watchword of Labour*, 13 November 1920.
[39] *Voice of Labour*, 10 December 1921.

[40] *Voice of Labour*, 29 October 1921.

[41] *Voice of Labour*, 5 November 1921.

[42] *Voice of Labour*, 12 November 1921.

[43] *Voice of Labour*, 19 November 1921.

[44] *Voice of Labour*, 10 December 1921.

[45] *Dail Eireann Secretariat Files 1919-1922*, DE 2/5, Document No. 180, List of Decisions at Meeting of the Ministry, Economic Affairs, Friday 2 December 1921.

[46] *Voice of Labour*, 17 December 1921.

[47] *Voice of Labour*, 4 February 1922.

[48] Trevor Anderson, 'The Dail Courts in Limerick', *North Munster Antiquarian Journal*, (Volume 49, 2009), p. 111

[49] Ibid., p. 113

[50] *Voice of Labour*, 29 October 1921.

[51] *Voice of Labour*, 19 November 1921, & 10 December 1921.

[52] *Voice of Labour*, 10 December 1921.

[53] *Voice of Labour*, 10 December 1921.

[54] *Voice of Labour*, 12 November 1921.

[55] *Voice of Labour*, 29 October 1921.

[56] *Voice of Labour*, 29 October 1921.

[57] *Limerick Echo*, 27 August 1921.

[58] *Voice of Labour*, 22 October 1921, & 12 November 1921.

[59] O'Connor, *A Labour History of Ireland*, p. 109.

[60] O'Connor, *Syndicalism in Ireland*, p.23.

[61] O'Connor, *A Labour History of Ireland*, p. 100.

[62] O'Connor, *Syndicalism in Ireland*, p.53.

[63] *Voice of Labour*, 12 November 1921.

[64] *Munster News*, 9 November 1921, & *Limerick Leader*, 11 November 1921.

[65] *Voice of Labour*, 12 November 1921.

[66] *Voice of Labour*, 12 November 1921.

[67] *Limerick Chronicle*, 12 November, 1921.

[68] *Voice of Labour*, 12 November 1921.

[69] *Limerick Leader*, 14 November 1921, & *Munster News*, 19 November 1921

[70] *Freeman's Journal*, 22 November 1921, & *Limerick Chronicle*, 22 November 1921.

[71] *Freeman's Journal*, 23 November 1921.

[72] *Limerick Echo*, 3 December 1921.

[73] *Limerick Leader*, 16 December 1921, & *Limerick Echo*, 17 December 1921.

[74] *Limerick Leader*, 16 December 1921.

[75] *Limerick Leader*, 30 December 1921.

[76] *Limerick Leader*, 25 January 1922 & *Munster News*, 28 January 1922.

[77] *Limerick Leader*, 16 January 1922.

[78] *Limerick Leader*, 16 January 1922, & *Munster News*, 21 January 1922.

[79] *Limerick Echo*, 21 January 1922.

[80] *Limerick Leader*, 18 January 1922.

[81] Mainchín Seoighe, *The Story of Kilmallock*, (Kilmallock, 1988), p. 287.

[82] *Munster News*, 21 January 1922.

[83] Seoighe, p. 287.

[84] *Limerick Chronicle*, 26 January 1922, & *Munster News*, 28 January 1922.

[85] *Limerick Chronicle*, 26 January 1922.

[86] Seoighe, p. 287.

[87] *Limerick Leader*, 25 January 1922, & *Munster News*, 28 January 1922.

[88] Seoighe, p. 287.

[89] *Munster News*, 25 January 1922.

[90] *Limerick Echo*, 25 February 1922.

[91] *Limerick Echo*, 11 March 1922.

[92] Emmet O'Connor, 'Agrarian Unrest and the Labour Movement in County Waterford, 1917-1923', *Saothar,* Volume 6, (1980), p. 43

[93] *Munster Express,* 28 January 1922

[94] O'Connor, 'Agrarian Unrest', p. 43

[95] *Munster Express,* 28 May 1922

[96] O'Connor, 'Agrarian Unrest', p. 44

[97] Ibid., p. 44

[98] Greaves, *Liam Mellows and the Irish Revolution,* p. 324

[99] Michael Gallagher, 'The Pact General Election of 1922', *Irish Historical Studies*, Vol. 22, No. 84 (September 1979), p. 408-409

[100] Ibid., p. 409

[101] Arthur Mitchell, *Labour in Irish Politics, 1890-1930,* (Dublin, 1974), p. 145-146

[102] Ibid., p. 148

[103] Gallagher, p. 411

[104] Matt Treacy, *The Communist Party of Ireland 1921 – 2011*, (Dublin, 2012), p. 11

[105] National Library of Ireland, MS 15,673/8/17, MS 15,676/1/72, MS 15,673/8/11

[106] Mitchell, *Labour in Irish Politics, 1890-1930,* p. 163

[107] Brian Hanley, 'The Irish Citizen Army after 1916', *Saothar,* Volume 28, (2003), p. 40

[108] Mitchell, p. 163

[109] Hanley, 'The Irish Citizen Army after 1916', p. 40

[110] Ibid., p. 40

[111] By 1936 Roddy Connolly had become a member of the Labour Party Administrative Council. By that time Labour was firmly playing the role of a mudguard for the implementation of right-wing policies in Ireland.

[112] For further information on the Monaghan Hospital Soviet see: Ciaran Mulholland & Anton McCabe, 'The Red Flag over the Asylum: the Monaghan Asylum Soviet of 1919', in Pauline Prior (ed.), *In Asylums, Mental Health Care and the Irish. Historical Studies, 1800-2010,* (Dublin, 2012)

[113] *National Library of Ireland*, MS 15,674/6/15

[114] Mitchell, p. 139

[115] Greaves, *Liam Mellows and the Irish Revolution,* p. 189

[116] Kostick, *Revolution in Ireland,* p. 163-164

[117] *Cork Examiner,* 7 September 1921

[118] Kostick, p. 164

[119] *Freemans Journal,* 15 September 1921

[120] *Drogheda Independent,* 17 September 1921.

[121] Kostick, p. 176

[122] Treacy, p. 10-11

[123] Michael McCarthy, 'The Broadford Soviet', *Old Limerick Journal,* Volume 4, (September 1980), pp. 37-40

[124] Kostick, p. 78

[125] Ibid., p. 188

[126] *Voice of Labour*, 7 January 1922, & Lee, 'The Munster Soviets and the Fall of the House of Cleeve', p. 300.

[127] *Voice of Labour*, 7 January 1922.

[128] The Irish Engineering Union was formed as a result of a conscious attempt by Michael Collins to split the trade union movement along nationalist lines. Collins specifically targeted the British based Amalgamated Engineering Union which had 30,000 members in Ireland. He planned to use the IRA to facilitate the split in the union. The Irish Engineering Union was formed under the direct control of Sinn Fein, its officers were all appointed by Collins and were Sinn Fein members. The IEU developed a reputation as a scab union during this period.

[129] *Voice of Labour*, 14 January 1922.

[130] *Dail Eireann Secretariat Files 1919-1922*, DE 1/4, Document No. 22, 16 January 1922.

[131] Lee, p. 300.

[132] *Voice of Labour*, 5 November 1921.

[133] *Dail Eireann Secretariat Files 1919-1922*, DE 2/5 Documents No. 191 & 192, The Ministry for Labour, Report on Activities of the Labour Department During the Period 11 January 1922 – 18 April 1922.

[134] *Dail Eireann Secretariat Files 1919-1922*, DE 1/4, Document No. 122, 31 March 1922.

[135] *Dail Eireann Secretariat Files 1919-1922*, DE 2/5 Documents No. 191 & 192.

[136] *Munster News*, 19 April 1922.

[137] *Limerick Leader*, 15 May 1922.

[138] *Freeman's Journal*, 15 May 1922.

[139] David Lee, 'The Munster Soviets and the Fall of the House of Cleeve', p. 301, & Greaves, *The Irish Transport and General Workers Union*, p. 312.

[140] *Limerick Leader*, 17 May 1922.

[141] *Irish Times*, 18 May 1922.

[142] *Irish Times*, 19 May 1922.

[143] *Voice of Labour*, 27 May 1922.

[144] O'Connor Lysaght, 'The Munster Soviet Creameries', p.45.

[145] *Freeman's Journal*, 20 May 1922.

[146] *Freeman's Journal*, 20 May 1922.

[147] *Limerick Leader*, 17 May 1922.

[148] *Limerick Leader*, 31 May 1922.

[149] *Freeman's Journal*, 9 June 1922.

[150] Lee, p. 305.

[151] *Munster News*, 28 June 1922.

[152] Adrian Hoar, *In Green and Red, The Lives of Frank Ryan*, (Dingle, 2004), p. 18

[153] Kostick, *Revolution in Ireland*, p. 164

[154] Ibid., p. 189

[155] Ibid., p. 190

[156] O'Connor, *A Labour History of Ireland*, p. 112.

[157] Crean, 'From Petrograd to Bruree', p.157.

[158] D.R. O'Connor Lysaght, County Tipperary: Class Struggle and National Struggle 1916-1924, William Nolan & Thomas G. McGrath, (eds), *Tipperary, History and Society: Interdisciplinary Essays on the History of an Irish County*, (Dublin, 1997), p. 400.

[159] Crean, p.157.

THE WORKERS MOVEMENT DEFEATED

'It looked as if it was going to wreck the whole union and we had a consultation with the executive about it and they said that it was all over now and we will have to end it, We decided we would stop the strike on a certain date, but we could not afford to give any notice of it because that would give trouble in a variety of ways...'
—William O'Brien, leader of the ITGWU explaining the abandonment of striking farm labourers in Waterford. 1923

The Post Office Strike 1922

In recounting the events of this period many years later, the *Limerick Chronicle* commented that 'at this period law and order were practically non-existent. The workers appeared to get out of hand and became most aggressive to the proprietors'.[1] The defeat of this period was total and the impact on the ITGWU significant.

The new Provisional/Free State government were intent on imposing their rule and wiping out the potential of the trade union movement. After the suppression of the Munster Soviets, the first national confrontation came in September 1922 when ten thousand post office workers engaged in nationwide strike action. The government broke a pay agreement from the previous March by imposing cuts in bonus payments.

The Provisional Government were intent on the total defeat of the strikers. Military police were used to guard post office vans and scabs. Strike leaders in Galway and Dundalk were arrested and interned without charge. Pickets were pistol whipped by the police to force them off the picket line while armoured vehicles were used to intimidate striking workers by deliberately driving at speed directly at picket lines. Police opened fire on striking workers staging a mass picket at the Rotunda, wounding one female worker.

On 25 September Thomas Johnson and four other ILPTUC officials met with the President of the Provisional Government, W. T. Cosgrave. Johnson warned Cosgrave that the trade union leadership were being bombarded with demands from members of the ITGWU and the railway union to engage in solidarity action with the post office strikers. The leadership were having extreme difficulty restraining workers from supporting the strike. Johnson was not making this statement as a warning or threat to Cosgrave that the trade union leadership were intent on acting in support of the post office workers, but rather that they were doing their best to prevent such action. The approach of Johnson gave the Provisional Government the green light to increase the repression against the strike, including raiding the offices of the strikers' union. The national media became open propaganda pieces for the government. By the end of September, the postal workers had been forced to abandon the strike.

Farm Labourers 1923

James Larkin returned to Ireland from the USA in April 1923. Just prior to Larkin's return, O'Brien held a conference of the ITGWU and changed the constitution. The new constitution limited the rights of membership, an attempt to curtail the independence and militancy of the rank-and-file. Removed from the constitution was the union's aims of workers control and internationalism.[2] As always, William O'Brien focused on the short-term interests of the bureaucracy in the ITGWU.[3] O'Brien was attempting to ensure that his plans weren't derailed by Larkin's militant approach after his return to this country. The conflict was to lead to a major schism within the trade union movement, and the ITGWU in particular. The demoralisation of the working class in the aftermath of the defeats of 1922, coupled with a counter-revolution by the bourgeois-nationalist forces in Ireland mitigated against Larkin gaining an echo among workers.[4]

The counter-revolutionary offensive by the new Free State government was seen in its sharpest form in the treatment of the farm labourers strike in Waterford that began on 17 May 1923. The strike was against attempts to impose significant cuts in wages and working conditions. It involved over 1.500 workers, lasted for seven months and turned into probably the most bitter and violent dispute in the history of the country. Crucially, the strike illustrated the balance of class forces in Ireland at the time and demonstrated the utter betrayal of workers by the leadership of the trade union movement. It was a strike that had revolutionary significance.

By the beginning of the strike the new Free State government was firmly in control of the country with the civil war ending. The government was determined to quash any threat to its authority and the threat that now existed came from the organised labour movement. Immediately that the strike began the Waterford Farmers Association enlisted the support of the government, support that they were only too willing to provide.

The workers began the strike with confidence that they were capable of successfully defending their position. The aggressiveness and determination of the strikers almost broke the resolve of the farmers within the first two weeks. Road blockades proved effective preventing farmers moving produce. Sympathetic action came from creamery workers who blacked farmers produce, dockers, railwaymen, shop assistants, carters, domestic servants and factory workers who refused to assist the farmers in any way. Even the boatmen of Bonmahon and Boatstrand, though non-union themselves, supported the labourers. Several employers locked out the workers engaged in sympathetic action, but this only served to strengthen the resolve of the workers.[5]

When dock workers in Waterford refused to load a consignment of butter onto the Fishguard ferry, armed troops with fixed bayonets were drafted in to protect scabs. The crew of the ship then refused to operate the vessel while the blacked cargo remained in the hold. Faced with the prospect of the ship being forced to remain in port, the captain ordered the consignment removed from the ship. As a result of the action, the Clyde Shipping Company and the Great Western Railway refused to accept consignments from strike bound farmers. Workers from the ITGWU, the National Union of Seamen and Firemen and Waterford Trades Council set up a workers committee to enforce this blacking of goods.[6]

By the end of May farmers were reliant on armed troops to protect the transportation of farm produce and supplies. Goods were moved in columns with armed units travelling in support. In one incident, on 29 May, a large protest confronted farmers who were loading supplies from a ship in Waterford. The army dispersed the crowd and while the convoy was passing 'the Sweep' it was ambushed, with gunshots from a rifle and a revolver fired at a detachment of troops. The soldiers returned fire and gave chase and one soldier was slightly wounded.

Farmers willing to accept the demands of strikers were threatened. Several farmers were reported to have suffered reprisals for reaching an agreement with the ITGWU. As the strike continued into the middle of June it was losing its character as a conventional industrial dispute, evolving instead into a semi-insurrectionary class conflict. This was sparked by the full military backing given to the farmers by the Free State government and the arrival of 250 members of the newly established quasi-fascist Special Infantry Corps. The Specials were an armed police corps and specifically set-up by the government to break strike action and smash the trade unions threatening the primacy of private property.[7]

Within two weeks the Specials numbered 600 and had put the county into an iron grip. On 4 July martial law was declared in East Waterford and a curfew imposed. An internment camp was established in the grounds of Waterford Court House and striking workers were rounded up. Union offices were raided, flags and emblems were impounded, and documentation and union records confiscated. The Specials threatened to shoot union officials distributing strike pay. In the village of Fenor, between Dungarvan and Tramore, nine strikers were arrested, the Specials planted a shotgun, and the workers were charged and tried in court. A mass picket blockading the transport of pigs in Ballybricken was baton charged by police and the Specials. Demonstrating the open support of the government, the Specials were deployed throughout the county as requested by the farmers.[8]

With the support of the Specials, farmers were now actively scabbing in support of urban businesses who had sacked their workers for blacking strike-bound goods. The employers in Dungarvan formed a 'Protection Association' pledging support for the WFA and issuing a warning that all employees who refused to handle 'tainted' goods would be immediately dismissed. Dock workers in Dungarvan were sacked after refusing to unload a ship with eighty tons of cargo for strike-bound farmers. The ship was unloaded by local traders and farmers under the protection of the Specials. The workers in Dungarvan called a general strike in the town and Red Guards patrolled the streets. The Specials confronted pickets with fixed bayonets to drive them away from in front of local businesses. Several incidents of fighting broke out between strikers and scabs with the Specials arresting the strikers when they arrived on time. After the general strike was suppressed clandestine attacks were carried out to ransack supplies destined for farmers.[9]

Both James Larkin and Thomas Johnson visited Waterford and participated in a Labour Party public rally. Johnson was heckled to such an extent that he was forced to abandon his speech. L.J. Duffy, General Secretary of the Irish Distributive Workers Union, condemned those who heckled as 'political scabs'. Larkin engaged in rhetoric, but after ten years out of the country appeared to lack understanding of the changed political and industrial situation. He made little impact on the workers who attended the rally. There was clear hostility among workers towards both factions fighting for control of the ITGWU.[10]

Seeing the divisions within the ITGWU the WFA went on the attack, condemning comments from James Baird, the ITGWU industrial organiser in Waterford for calling for the nationalisation of farm land. On 18 June twenty labour meetings were held throughout Waterford with Baird and Larkin the main speakers at several. Larkin was now getting a more positive response but lacking any organised revolutionary force around him was unable to impact the situation. Noteworthy was the effort made by Larkin to appeal to rank-and-file soldiers who were going to face unemployment as a result of upcoming demobilisation as a result of the ending of the civil war.[11] Unfortunately, in Waterford it was the 'Specials' who were the controlling military force in the county. The ITGWU national leadership attempted to engage in negotiations. Thomas Foran wrote to the WFA offering arbitration. This was rejected out of hand by the farmers.[12]

Attacks on pickets intensified while the striking workers engaged in increased clandestine attacks, felling trees, burning haybarns, smashing machinery knocking fences and gates and driving off cattle. In addition, there were sporadic sniper attacks on farmhouses, convoys and outposts of the Specials. The attacks were having a significant impact on farmers and were threatening to force a breach in their ranks.[13]

The 1923 general election took place in August, three months into the farm labourers strike. Labour was facing a different situation than a year earlier. More the 800 farm labourers had left the ITGWU after the defeat of the strike in West Waterford in 1922. The union organisation was considerably weaker as a result. There was also a significant level of demoralisation because of the defeat the previous year. The strike leader who had been elected in 1922, Nicholas Phelan, exemplified this demoralisation and didn't defend his Dail seat. The second Labour TD in Waterford, John Butler, was now a firm supporter of the ITGWU leadership. Instead of Phelan, John Baird stood as a candidate. Representing the striking workers Baird was the radical candidate in the election. The election was a major setback for Labour throughout the county, including Waterford. Butler's vote dropped from 6,288 to 2,710. Baird outpolled Butler with 3,186 votes but Butler secured the seat on transfers. Butler was to lose his seat in 1927 and later stood as a Fine Gael candidate. The defeat for Labour in the election was significant. Radical candidates, like Robert Day and Patrick Gaffney lost their seats. However, the defeat also included high profile bureaucrats like William O'Brien, whose vote in Dublin South collapsed from 4,734 to 933 (just 2%).

The struggle in Waterford entered its most crucial phase in August. The farmers were intent on securing the harvest which would allow them to holdout well into 1924. The farmers, with the support of the 'Specials', organised themselves into armed vigilante 'White Guards'. They engaged in a systematic campaign of terror against striking labourers and union activists. Labourers' cottages were attacked and burned to the ground. Pickets were attacked and beaten up, many of them pistol-whipped. The WFA declared that if the strike continued into 1924 then an All-Ireland fund would be established to fund the farmers campaign against the union.[14]

The outcome of the strike was not definitively determined in either direction. The striking workers demanded that the national trade union leadership call a general strike in support of the labourers. They demand fell on deaf ears. James Baird put forward the proposal to stage the widespread occupation of factories and farms in Waterford. It was clear that the workers recognised the serious nature of the dispute, but it is an open question whether the Waterford labour movement would have had the ability to embark on such a largescale endeavour. Either way William O'Brien was to act to sabotage the strike. In his memoirs he declared:

'It looked as if it was going to wreck the whole union and we had a consultation with the executive about it and they said that it was all over now and we will have to end it, We decided we would stop the strike on a certain date, but we could not afford to give any notice of it because that would give trouble in a variety of ways. Foran and I went down and we saw the representative body and we told them that was the last week they could be paid. You can imagine how they took that. Our boilerman (Baird) was there and he got up and ... his own union - the Boilermakers - had unsuccessful strikes and they went so far as to mortgage their head office premises to pay for their members. I told him that was alright for a Boilermakers' Society, but that only a small number of our members were agricultural workers. We had to take a different view of it. That ended that and we did not try to organise the agricultural labourers afterwards'.[15]

O'Brien stopped the strike pay of the labourers, called off the strike and abandoned the workers to the mercy of the 'Specials' and the 'White Guards'. The defeat of the strike was complete and the ITGWU collapsed in Waterford.[16] Not only that, the demoralisation of the workers was profound. Activists were blacklisted and workers were rehired by the employers and farmers on their terms. Gone was the prospect of negotiating wages and working conditions. Furthermore, the defeat undermined the notion of class solidarity and sympathetic strike action. Class consciousness was completely thrown back and undermined.[17] The prospect of building and promoting support for socialist policies was setback a decade. The parliamentary Labour Party shifted dramatically to the right under the leadership of Thomas Johnson culminating in 1930 with the splitting of the joint industrial and political movement when the Labour Party was to operate independently of the Irish Congress of Trade Unions.

---

[1] *Limerick Chronicle*, 29 September 1951.
[2] D.R. O'Connor Lysaght, 'The Rake's Progress of a Syndicalist: The Political Career of William O'Brien Irish Labour Leader', *Saothar*, Volume 9, (1985), p. 54
[3] O'Connor, *A Labour History of Ireland*, p. 102.
[4] O'Connor Lysaght, 'The Rake's Progress of a Syndicalist', p. 54
[5] O'Connor, 'Agrarian Unrest and the Labour Movement in County Waterford 1917-1923', p. 48
[6] Ibid., p. 49
[7] Ibid.
[8] Ibid., p. 50
[9] *Munster Express*, 16 June 1923
[10] *Munster Express*, 2 June 1923

[11] *Freeman's Journal*, 19 June 1923

[12] O'Connor, 'Agrarian Unrest', p. 51

[13] Ibid., p. 52

[14] Ibid., p. 53

[15] O'Brien, *Forth the Banners Go*, p. 113-114

[16] Like other left-wing activists, James Baird was sacked as industrial organiser by O'Brien during this dispute. He emigrated to Australia in 1924.

[17] O'Connor, 'Agrarian Unrest', p. 54

CONCLUSION

*'A picket becomes too large for legality as soon as it becomes large
enough to be effective'.*
*—Charlie Donnelly, following his conviction for organising a mass
picket of a strikebound department store in Dublin. 1933.*

Connolly's prediction of a carnival of reaction on the island of Ireland if partition was imposed came to fruition as a result of the compromise reached between the nationalist movement in Ireland and British Imperialism. The Northern State emerged as an openly sectarian state with widespread discrimination of the Catholic population. During a debate in the Northern Ireland parliament in Stormont in 1934, James Craig, the Prime Minister of Northern Ireland, stated 'All I boast of is that we are a Protestant Parliament and a Protestant State'.[1]

In the Free State the situation was not much different. In a largely homogenous state where ninety-three percent of the population were regarded as Catholic the government of WT Cosgrave handed over control of health, education and many other aspects of Irish society to the Catholic hierarchy, with all the consequences that have emerged in recent years. For the Cumann na nGaedheal government this served a dual purpose, ensuring the consistent support for his government while at the same time absolving the government of the responsibility for the provision of vital social services. The Free State emerged as a reactionary Catholic state with widespread repression. Internment without trial continued up until 1926 with the Free State taking over and using the former British internment camp in the Curragh.[2] Repressive legislation was introduced, including the Public Safety (Emergency Powers) Act in August 1923. The influence of the Catholic hierarchy was demonstrated, for example, with the widespread use of censorship and the passing of the Criminal Law Amendment Act in 1934 which banned the use of contraceptives.

The ITGWU suffered severely in the new Free State. Between 1922-1931 the membership dropped from 120,000 to just 11,000 directly as a result of the abandonment of workers in struggle by the leadership. In 1925 Limerick faced another major industrial dispute during the building of the Ardnacrusha power station. Once again William O'Brien and the leadership of the ILPTUC effectively sabotaged the dispute and abandoned the striking workers. The building of the Shannon Scheme provoked major controversy as many Cumann na nGaedheal TDs called for the abandonment of the scheme on the grounds that it was the government behaving in a 'communist' fashion. The government were intent on using the building of the scheme to drive wages down across the entire economy. The city rate for labourers was 1s 3d (15d) per hour for a 47-hour week but when labourers were recruited to build a railway line from the city out to the worksite the wages offered were 8d per hour for a 54-hour week.

When members of the ITGWU who were working on converting the Strand Barracks to a supply depot for the worksite, walked off the job, the ITGWU issued a public statement calling on their members to return to work to allow for talks to take place with the contractors, Siemens. The striking workers ignored the call and when Siemens rebuked a national approach by the ITGWU, the union declared a strike. An attempt was made to use the ex-servicemen's association (former soldiers demobilised from the Free State army after the Army Mutiny in 1924) to scab on the dispute, resulting in a split in the association.

With widespread unemployment throughout the country, Siemens advertised for 3,000 workers at a rate of 32s per week. Two weeks later widespread rioting took place outside Strand Barracks. Shortly afterwards the dock workers staged a crucial intervention. Free State troops with fixed bayonets guarded a ship carrying supplies for Siemens and when it was unloaded by German mechanics, the dock workers declared a solidarity strike in support of the striking workers at the Strand Barracks.

On Sunday 4 October, two weeks into the strike, thousands of workers attended a mass meeting at the O'Connell Monument, addressed by William O'Brien and President of the Trades Council, John Cronin. While O'Brien was, once again, promising support to the workers of Limerick, Cronin was declaring: "A man who strikes another in the fight is no friend of the labour movement, Violence will not be tolerated". Cronin was ignored, the following day largescale fighting broke out on the docks in Limerick between striking dockers on one side and the police and scabs on the other. Clubs, rubber pipes filled with lead, iron bars and other weapons were used in a riot lasting several hours. The workers of Limerick were engaged in a life or death struggle, knowing that defeat in this dispute would lead to widespread attacks on jobs and wages throughout the country.

Workers in Germany were contacted, and supplies being sent from Germany to Siemens in Limerick were blacklisted. The German Constructional Workers' Union called on the German workers in Limerick to join the strike. A strike committee comprising of representatives of the leadership of the ILPTUC, Limerick Trades Council and the ITGWU was established. On 22 October the government admitted that they had discussed wage rates with Siemens and gave them information on wage rates they expected to be paid in Limerick. Effectively the government were coordinating with Siemens the wage rates to be paid, serving a political purpose for the government in their policy objectives.

As during the Limerick Soviet, O'Brien and the leadership continuously referred to 'national action' in support of the strike. However, instead of calling national strike action in support of the Limerick strike, at a meeting in Dublin on 9 November, the national leadership merely declared a national blacklisting of all work connected with the Siemens contract. When concrete national strike action was needed, the leadership were once again found wanting. Mass meetings of workers took place in several locations around the country on 22 November, with clear support being expressed for action to assist the Limerick strike. The blacklisting of supplies for Siemens was haphazard at best, even a special conference of the ILPTUC that was held on 30 November made little impact. The blacklisting of Siemens was fully implemented across Limerick, but without national action the strike began to crumble. The strike was unofficially called off on 11 January 1926, although the dock workers remained on strike for several more days.[3]

The conditions on the Shannon Scheme were an expression in microcosm of the lives and conditions for working class people throughout the country. Workers on the worksite were paid 32s per week with a bunk in a timber hut provided by the contractor. The workforce varied over the construction time but peaked at over 5,000 in 1928. However, there were only a high of 720 bunks provided on site. The workers paid 11s 8d per week for food from the site canteen with small rations available. Extra food was provided at an extra cost. When workers attempted to cook their own food, the food was confiscated by camp security. On at least one occasion workers built a small lean-to attached to their accommodation hut to do some cooking, only for the camp security to smash the lean-to and beat up the workers.

Given the shortage of sleeping accommodation on site, hundreds of workers were living in local haybarns, outhouses and pigsties. In one case, at O'Grady's yard in Blackwater, ninety-four people comprising of twenty-one families and including fifty-three children, were living in appalling conditions. Each family were being charged £1 per week, nearly two thirds of the weekly wage of a worker on the Shannon Scheme. Conditions were so deplorable that disease was common, including typhoid fever.

Health and safety concerns were almost non-existent on the worksite. Dozens of workers were killed, and hundreds injured, many suffering life-long disability as a result. The scale of the injuries was so great that Siemens and the government got into a dispute over who was responsible for the care of the injured workers. The Department of Health informed the Clare and Limerick Boards of Health that they could refuse to treat any worker who was not from their locality. The same Boards of Health were responsible for inspecting accommodation, but when a health inspector highlighted the deplorable living conditions he was publicly attacked by the government and sacked from his job.

Regular attempts were made by workers to try and organise on the worksite. However, whenever such attempts came to light, the workers were immediately sacked and the camp security threw them off the site. The company adopted a strategy of only employing workers for periods of three months in order to reduce the possibility of workers getting to know one another well and being able to organise successfully. All through the four years of building work the ILPTUC leadership paid scant attention to what was happening in Ardnacrusha.[4]

From the wages and working conditions, to the attitude of the Free State government, to the role of the trade union movement, the strike and subsequent building of the largest infrastructural development in the state, the Ardnacrusha power station demonstrated the nature of the new Free State. A native capitalist class incapable of funding and building such an venture, a government intent on exploiting this major infrastructural development in order to drive wages down across the entire economy in order to boost profits, an employer willing to use repression to control the workforce and prevent union organisation, a leadership in the trade union movement unwilling to challenge the status quo and a working class forced to eke out a miserable existence in an economy that was incapable of providing for the basic needs of a large section of the population.

The defeat of the Shannon Scheme strike had a profound effect on the labour movement in Limerick. The radicalism of the ITGWU during the revolutionary period had dissipated. By the late 1920s the conservatism of the craft unionism as epitomised by the likes of John Cronin was dominant. By the mid-1930s the Trades council was a bastion of Catholic conservatism. In 1936 the Trades Council passed a resolution condemning the Republican forces in the Spanish Civil War for the 'the burning of churches and the murder of priests and nuns' – a resolution welcomed by the leaders of the Arch Confraternity in the city. John McQuane, President of the Trades Council described the Catholic Church as 'a bulwark between Christianity and Communism'. Among those adding to the condemnation of the Spanish Republicans was former Soviet treasurer, James Casey. The resolution was passed unanimously by the Trades Council delegates.[5]

The Limerick Workers Union added their voice to the condemnation.[6] Members of the Amalgamated Transport and General Workers Union working as clerks for the Electricity Supply Board at Ardnacrusha disaffiliated from their British based union which had raised funds for the Republican forces fighting Spanish fascism.[7] On 15 November 1936 Limerick Labour TD, Michael Keyes, spoke on a platform with Fianna Fail and Fine Gael representatives at a large, rain-soaked, rally at Tait's Clock, organised by the far-right Irish Christian Front. Keyes addressing the crowd of several thousand proposed a resolution 'That we pledge our support to the Irish

Christian Front in its efforts to bring into existence in this country a social and economic system based on the Christian ideals of life as expressed in the Papal Encyclicals and thereby to overcome the evils of Communism and Socialism, which are altogether contrary to Christian principals'. James McQuane, was the official representative of Limerick Trades Council at the rally.[8]

Right-wing propaganda during the Spanish Civil War was commonplace in Ireland. To see condemnations of the Spanish Republican government and the Republican forces would not have been unusual. However, for the Labour TD and the President of the Limerick Trades Council to take an active part in the rally of the far-right Irish Christian Front demonstrates how far to the right the Limerick labour movement had drifted since the Limerick Soviet and the revolutionary period in Ireland. The repeated abandonment of the Limerick working class by the leadership of the ILPTUC led to large sections of workers in Limerick becoming insular and conservative in their outlook. It allowed for the Catholic hierarchy to use the Arch Confraternity to maintain the religious loyalty of workers in the city and it facilitated the dominance of conservative nationalism for several decades after independence.

What can be clearly seen from the events of the revolutionary period in Ireland is the difference between the determination of the Irish working class to defend their interests under the tutelage of radical left-wing activists like Sean Dowling and the weakness of the national leadership of the ILPTUC. Time and again opportunities arose for the ILPTUC leadership to place labour front and centre in the quest for power, in the leadership of the struggle for national self-determination and social, political and economic emancipation. Time and again the same leadership were found wanting. *Ferriter* argued that it was an inability on behalf of the national leadership to play this role,[9] however, a more appropriate assessment was that the national leadership were unwilling to organise for the labour movement to take the lead in the national struggle and, at times, actively sabotaged the potential for a workers revolution.

Even as late as 1922 when the country was hurtling towards a civil war, as the different class interests were pulling Sinn Fein and the IRA apart, the national leadership of the ILPTUC could have facilitated the labour movement stepping into the breach and prevented the carnival of reaction that emerged North and South after independence. Workers were actively taking strike action and organising occupations with revolutionary intent. There was significant support among the ranks of the ITGWU for the establishment of an Irish Workers Army to defend the working class as it was being faced with a brutal civil war. Once again, the ILPTUC leadership could have placed the labour movement front and centre. By adopting a class position on the Treaty and actively organising the labour movement to act in defence of the working class, the leadership could have demonstrated that they served the workers movement and were not coat-tailing what was by then the reactionary wing of Irish nationalism.

Opposing the Treaty on a class basis, outlining that it only served the purposes of British imperialism and the Irish capitalist class, and demonstrating that the workers movement was the only force capable of preventing the emergence of two reactionary, sectarian states on this island could have created the potential for revolutionary action. It would have increased class consciousness, shown an understanding of the processes at plan and demonstrated to workers in struggle that the leadership of the labour movement were acting in their interests.

Unfortunately, the role of the national leadership of the ILPTUC, deprived at the time of its two most influential figures, James Connolly and James Larkin, was one of obfuscation and betrayal. As was demonstrated in their approach to the Limerick Soviet, they repeatedly handed the initiate back to the leaders of the Irish nationalist movement and ultimately led to the division of the island along sectarian lines and defeat for the Irish working class.

---

[1] *Northern Ireland Parliamentary Debates,* Volume 16 (1933, 1934), p. 1095 - 1096
[2] See James Durney, 'The Curragh internees 1921-24: from defiance to defeat', *Journal of the County Kildare Archaeological Society,* Volume XX, Part 2, (2010-2011), pp. 6-24.
[3] For an account of the Shannon Scheme strike see: Michael McCarthy, 'The Shannon Scheme Strike', *Old Limerick Journal,* Volume 5, (December 1980), pp 21-26
[4] see: Michael McCarthy, 'How the Shannon Scheme Workers Lived', *Old Limerick Journal,* Volume 8, (Autumn 1981), pp 5-11
[5] *Limerick Leader,* 24 August 1936
[6] *Limerick Leader,* 5 September 1936
[7] *Limerick Leader,* 19 September 1936
[8] *Limerick Leader,* 16 November 1936
[9] Diarmaid Ferriter, *The Transformation of Ireland, 1900-2000,* (London, 2004), p. 213

BIBLIOGRAPHY

Primary Sources

1911 Census
Dail Eireann Secretariat Files 1919-1922, DE 1/3
Dail Eireann Secretariat Files 1919-1922, DE 1/4
Dail Eireann Secretariat Files 1919-1922, DE 2/5
Dail Eireann Secretariat Files 1919-1922, DE 2/81
Dail Eireann Secretariat Files 1919-1922, DE 2/483
Eighth Report from the Select Committee on the Poor Laws (Ireland), 1849
House of Commons Debates, Hansard.
John Dowling baptismal record, Parish of Cobh
Limerick Chamber of Commerce Minute Book, 1807-1813
Limerick Chamber of Commerce Minute Book, 23 June 1815-28 April 1820
Her Majesty's Commission of Inquiry into the State of the Law and Practice With Respect to the Occupation of Land in Ireland, (Dublin,1847).
Irish Labour Party and Trade Union Congress, Report to the Twenty-Fourth Annual Meeting, 1918
Irish Labour Party and Trade Union Congress, Report to the Twenty-Fifth Annual Meeting, 1919
Irish Labour Party and Trade Union Congress, Report of the Twenty-Sixth Annual Meeting, 1920
Irish Labour Party and Trade Union Congress, Special Conference Report, 1918
ITGWU Annual Report 1918
ITGWU Annual Report 1919
Limerick United Trade and Labour Council Minutes
Minute Book of the Kilmallock Union
National Library of Ireland, MS 15,673/8/17, MS 15,676/1/72, MS 15,673/8/11
Ninth Annual Report by The Chief Labour Correspondent on Trade Unions (1896)
Northern Ireland Parliamentary Debates
Outrage Papers, County Limerick

Report by The Chief Labour Correspondent to the Board of Trade on Trade Unions in 1898
Report on the Strikes and Lock-Outs of 1890
Report on the Strikes and Lock-Outs of 1891
Report on the Strikes and Lock-Outs of 1894
State of the Country Papers
Statement by Witness, Bureau of Military History 1913-1921
The Constructive Work of Dail Eireann, No.1, The National Police and Courts of Justice
Weekly Reports of Scarcity Commission showing Progress of Disease in Potatoes, Complaints and Applications for Relief, March - April 1846.

Newspapers and Periodicals

Anglo-Celt
Belfast Weekly Telegraph
Bottom Dog
Connacht Tribune
Connaught Telegraph
Cork Examiner
Derry Journal
Donegal News
Drogheda Independent
Ennis Advertiser
Evening Herald
Factionalist
Fermanagh Herald
Forward
Freemans Journal
Irish Independent
Irish Times
Irish Worker
Kerry News
Kerry Weekly Reporter
Kilkenny People
Killarney Echo and South Kerry Chronicle

Leitrim Observer
Liberator
Limerick Chronicle
Limerick Echo
Limerick Leader
Longford Leader
Manchester Guardian
Meath Chronicle
Munster News
Nationalist
Nationalist and Leinster Times
Nenagh Guardian
Nenagh News
New Ireland
Offaly Independent
Red Flag
Skibbereen Eagle
Sligo Champion
Sunday Independent
Times
Tuam Herald
Voice of Labour
Watchdog of Labour
Watchword of Labour
Workers Bulletin
Workers Dreadnought

Secondary Sources

Anderson, Trevor, 'The Dail Courts in Limerick', *North Munster Antiquarian Journal,* Volume 49, (2009), pp. 111-124
Boyle, John W., *The Irish Labour Movement in the Nineteenth Century,* (Washington, 1988).
Bradley, Dan, *Farm Labourers Irish Struggle 1900-1976*, (Belfast, 1988)

Bryce, Colm, 'Ireland and the Russian Revolution', *Irish Marxist Review,* Volume 6, Number 17, (2017), pp. 42-54

Burke, Edmund, (ed.), *The Annual Register or a View of the History, Politics and Literature for the Year 1811,* (London, 1825)

Busteed, Mervyn, *The Irish in Manchester C.1750-1921: Resistance, Adaptation and Identity,* (Manchester, 2016)

Cahill, Liam, *Forgotten Revolution, Limerick Soviet 1919: A Threat to British Power in Ireland,* (Dublin, 1990)

Campbell, Fergus, & O'Shiel, Kevin, 'The Last Land War? Kevin O'Shiel's Memoir of the Irish Revolution 1916-21', *Archivium Hibernicum,* Vol. 57 (2003), pp. 155-200

Campbell, Fergus, *Land and Revolution: Nationalist Politics in the West of Ireland 1891-1921,* (Oxford, 2005)

Casey, James, 'A Limerick Challenge to British Tyranny', in Ruan O'Donnell, (ed.) *Limerick's Fighting Story: Told by the Men Who Made It* (Dublin, 2009), pp. 93-102

Clark, Samuel, and Donnelly Jr., James S., (eds) *Irish Peasants Violence and Political Unread 1780-1914,* (Wisconsin, 1986)

Connolly, James, *Labour in Ireland,* (Dublin, 1940)

Crean, Tom, 'From Petrograd to Bruree', in David Fitzpatrick (ed.), *Revolution? Ireland 1917-1923,* (Dublin, 1990)

Crean, Tom, *The Labour Movement in Kerry and Limerick 1914-1921, PhD Thesis,* (Trinity College Dublin, 1996)

Crean, Tom, 'The Socialist Challenge in Ireland', in Cillian Gillespie (ed.), *Ireland's Lost Revolution 1916-1923,* (London, 2016), pp. 148-174

Cullen, L.M., *An Economic History of Ireland Since 1660,* (London, 1987)

Cunningham, John, "'Tis Hard to Argue Starvation into the Quiet': Protest ad Resistance 1846-1847", in Enda Delaney, & Brendán Mac Suibhne, (eds), *Ireland's Great Famine and Popular Politics,* (London, 2016), pp. 10-33

Donnelly Jr., James S., 'The Terry Alt Movement 1829-31', *History Ireland,* Volume 2, Issue 4, (Winter 1994), pp. 30-35

Donnelly, Jr., James S., *Captain Rock, The Irish Agrarian Rebellion 1821-1824,* (Wisconsin, 2009)

Durney, James. 'The Curragh internees 1921-24: from defiance to defeat', *Journal of the County Kildare Archaeological Society,* Volume XX, Part 2, (2010-2011), pp. 6-24.

Eiríksson, Andrés, 'Food Supplies and Food Riots', in Cormac Ó Gráda, (ed.), *Famine 150: Commemorative Lecture Series,* (Dublin 1997), pp. 67-94

Feeley, Pat, 'Whiteboys and Ribbonmen', *The Old Limerick Journal,* Number 4, (September 1980), pp. 23-27

Fitzgerald, Laura, & McLoughlin, Kevin, 'A Stand Against Imperialism and War', in Cillian Gillespie, (ed.), *Ireland's Lost Revolution 1916-1923,* (London, 2016), pp. 49-82

Fitzpatrick, David, 'Strikes in Ireland, 1914-1921', *Saothar,* (Volume 6, 1980), pp. 26-39

Fitzpatrick, David, (ed.), *Revolution? Ireland 1917-1923*, (Dublin, 1990)

Foley, Eugene J., 'Donnellys of Cork Street', *Dublin Historical Record,* Volume 51, Number 1, (Spring, 1998), pp. 74-80

Foster, R. F., *Modern Ireland 1600-1972*, (London, 1988)

Gallagher, Michael, 'The Pact General Election of 1922', *Irish Historical Studies*, Volume 22, Number 84, (September 1979), pp. 404-421

Garnett, R. G., *Co-operation and the Owenite Socialist Communities in Britain 1825-1845,* (Manchester, 1972)

Gillespie, Cillian, (ed.), *Ireland's Lost Revolution 1916-1923: The Working Class and the Struggle for Socialism,* (London, 2016)

Gillespie, Cillian, 'The Life and Ideas of James Connolly', in Cillian Gillespie, (ed.), *Ireland's Lost Revolution 1916-1923: The Working Class and the Struggle for Socialism,* (London, 2016), pp. 17-48

Gray, John, *City in Revolt : James Larkin & the Belfast Dock Strike of 1907,* (Belfast, 1985).

Greaves, C. Desmond, *Liam Mellows and the Irish Revolution,* (London, 1971).

Greaves, C. Desmond, *The Irish Transport and General Workers Union – The Formative Years*, (Dublin, 1982)

Hadden, Peter, *Troubled Times, The National Question in Ireland*, (Belfast, 1995).

Hanley, Brian, 'The Irish Citizen Army after 1916', *Saothar,* Volume 28, (2003), pp. 37-47

Hannan, Kevin, 'The Famine in Limerick, *The Old Limerick Journal Famine Edition,* Volume 32, (Winter 1995), pp. 21-24

Haugh, Dominic, 'The ITGWU in Limerick 1917-1922', *Saothar,* Volume 31, (2006), pp. 27-42

Haugh, Dominic, 'Sean Dowling', in Emmet O'Connor & John Cunningham, (eds), *Studies in Irish Radical Leadership, Lives on the Left,* (Manchester, 2016), pp. 148-162

Hedley, Jack, 'Sean Dowling', *Irish Democrat,* February 1949.

Herbert, Robert, 'The Trade Guilds of Limerick', *North Munster Antiquarian Journal,* 2/3 (1941), pp. 121-134

Hoar, Adrian, *In Green and Red, The Lives of Frank Ryan,* (Dingle, 2004)

Kenna, Shane, *Jeremiah O'Donovan Rossa: Unrepentant Fenian,* (Kildare, 2015)

Kemmy, Jim, 'The Limerick Soviet', *Saothar,* (Volume 2, 1976), pp. 45-52

Kemmy, Jim, 'The General Strike 1919', *Old Limerick Journal,* (Volume 2, March 1980), pp. 26-31

Kemmy, Jim, 'Introduction', in Liam Cahill, *Forgotten Revolution – Limerick Soviet 1919, A Threat to British Power in Ireland*, (Dublin, 1990)

Kemmy, Jim, 'The Seige of Lock Mills', in Jim Kemmy, (ed.), *Limerick Anthology* (Dublin, 1996), p. 236

Kemmy, Jim, (ed.), *Limerick Anthology* (Dublin, 1996)

Kenefick, William, 'Irish Dockers and Trade Unionism on Clydeside', *Irish Studies Review,* Volume 5, Number 19, (1997), pp. 22-29

Kostick, Conor, *Revolution in Ireland: Popular Militancy 1917 to 1923* (London, 1996)

Lane, Fintan, 'P. F. Johnson, Nationalism, and Irish Rural Labourers 1869-82', *Irish Historical Studies*, Volume 33, Number 130, (November 2002), pp. 191-208

Lane, Fintan, 'Rural Labourers, Social Change and Politics in Late Nineteenth-Century Ireland', in Fintan Lane, & Donal Ó Drisceoil, (eds), *Politics and the Irish Working Class, 1830-1945,* (Basingstoke, 2005), pp. 113-139

Lane, Fintan, & Ó Drisceoil, Donal, (eds), *Politics and the Irish Working Class, 1830-1945,* (Basingstoke, 2005)

Lane, Padraig G., 'The Land and Labour Association 1894-1914', *Journal of the Cork Historical and Archaeological Society,* Volume 98, (1993), pp 90-106

Leckey, Joseph J., 'The Railway Servants Strike in Co. Cork, 1898', *Saothar,* Volume 2, (1976), pp. 39-45

Lee, David, & Jacobs, Debbie, (eds), *Made in Limerick, History of Industries, Trade and Commerce, Volume 1,* (Limerick, 2003)

Lee, David, 'The Munster Soviets and the Fall of the House of Cleeve', in David Lee, & Debbie Jacobs, (eds), *Made in Limerick, History of Industries, Trade and Commerce, Volume 1,* (Limerick, 2003)

Lee, David, & Jacobs, Debbie, *Limerick Municipal Elections 1841-2009,* (Limerick, 2009)

Lee, Joseph, 'Railway Labour in Ireland, 1833-1856', *Saothar,* Volume 5, (1979), pp. 9-10

Lenihan, Maurice, *Limerick; Its History and Antiquities,* (Cork, 1866)

Lenin, V. I., *Left-Wing Communism: An Infantile Disorder,* (New York, 1940)

Lenin, V. I., 'Class War in Dublin', *Severnaya Pravda,* No. 23, August 29, 1913, in *Collected Works*, Volume 19, (Moscow, 1977), pp. 332-336

Lenin, V. I., 'To the Central Committee of the R.D.S.L.P.', *Pravda* No. 250, November 7, 1920, in *Collected Works,* Volume 25, (Moscow, 1977), pp. 289-293

Limerick Corporation Commemorative Edition, *Limerick City and The Great Hunger,* (Limerick 1997)

Locker Lampson, Geoffrey, *A Consideration of the State of Ireland in the Nineteenth Century* (London, 1907)

Margadant, Ted, 'Commentary on Charles Tilly's "Social Movements"', *Theory and Society*, Volume 27, Number 4, (August 1998), pp. 481-488

Marley, Laurence, 'Michael McKeown', in Emmet O'Connor & John Cunningham, (eds), *Studies in Irish Radical Leadership, Lives on the Left,* (Manchester, 2016), pp. 71-84

Marx, Karl, *Civil War in France*, (New York, 2005)

Marx, Karl, & Engels, Frederick, *Manifesto of the Communist Party,* (Moscow, 1969)

McCarthy, Michael, 'The Broadford Soviet', *Old Limerick Journal,* Volume 4, (September 1980), pp. 37-40

McCarthy, Michael, 'The Shannon Scheme Strike', *Old Limerick Journal,* Volume 5, (December 1980), pp 21-26

McCarthy, Michael, 'How the Shannon Scheme Workers Lived', *Old Limerick Journal,* Volume 8, (Autumn 1981), pp 5-11

MacCurtain, Margaret, 'Pre-Famine Peasantry in Ireland: Definition and Theme', *Irish University Review,* Volume 4, Number 2, (Autumn, 1974), pp. 188-198

MacLochlainn, Alf 'Social Life in County Clare', *Irish University Review,* Volume 2, Number 1, (Spring, 1972). pp. 55-78

McKay, Enda, 'The Limerick Municipal Elections, January 1899', *The Old Limerick Journal,* Volume 36, (Winter 1999) pp. 3-10

McNamara, Conor, *Politics and Society in East Galway, 1914-21,* (PhD Thesis, St. Patrick's College, Drumcondra, 2008)

McNamara, Conor, *War and Revolution in the West of Ireland: Galway, 1913–1922,* (Newbridge, 2018)

McNamara, Mike, *The Limerick Soviet: When Limerick took on an Empire,* (Limerick, 2017)

Macready, Sir Nevil, *Annals Of An Active Life Volume 2,* (London, 1925)

Milotte, Mike, *Communism in Modern Ireland: The Pursuit of the Workers' Republic Since 1916,* (Dublin, 1984)

Mitchell, Arthur, *Labour in Irish Politics, 1890-1930,* (Dublin, 1974)

Mitchell, Arthur, *Revolutionary Government in Ireland,* (Dublin, 1995)

Moloney, Timothy, *Limerick Constitutional Nationalism 1898-1918: Change and Continuity,* (Newcastle-upon-Tyne, 2010)

Morgan, Austen, *Labour and Partition: The Belfast Working Class 1905 - 23,* (London, 1991)

Mulholland, Ciaran, & McCabe, Anton, 'The Red Flag over the Asylum: the Monaghan Asylum Soviet of 1919', in Pauline Prior, (ed.), *In Asylums, Mental Health Care and the Irish. Historical Studies, 1800-2010,* (Dublin, 2012)

Nevin, Donal, (ed.), *Trade Union Century,* (Dublin, 1994)

Nolan, William, & McGrath, Thomas G., (eds), *Tipperary, History and Society: Interdisciplinary Essays on the History of an Irish County,* (Dublin, 1997)

O'Brien, William, *Forth the Banners Go,* as told to Edward MacLysaght, (Dublin 1969)

O'Callaghan, John, *Revolutionary Limerick, The Republican Campaign for Independence in Limerick, 1913-1921,* (Dublin, 2010)

O'Connell, Michael, *Remember Limerick 1919,* (London, 1994)

O'Connor, Emmet, 'Agrarian Unrest and the Labour Movement in County Waterford, 1917-1923', *Saothar,* Volume 6, (1980), pp. 40-58

O' Connor, Emmet, 'Active Sabotage in Industrial Conflict 1917-1923', *Irish Economic and Social History,* Volume XII, (1985), pp. 50-62

O'Connor, *Syndicalism in Ireland,1917-1923,* (Cork, 1988)

O'Connor, Emmet, *A Labour History of Ireland 1824-1960* (Dublin 1992)

O'Connor, Emmet, 'War and Syndicalism 1914-1923', in Donal Nevin, (ed.), *Trade Union Century,* (Dublin, 1994), pp. 54-65

O'Connor, Emmet, 'The Waterford Soviet: Fact or fancy?', *History Ireland,* Volume 8, Issue 1, (2000), pp. 10-12

O'Connor, Emmet, 'Labour and Politics, 1830–1945: Colonisation and Mental Colonisation', in Fintan Lane, & Donal Ó Drisceoil, (eds), *Politics and the Irish Working Class, 1830-1945,* (Basingstoke, 2005), pp. 27-43

O'Connor, Emmet, & Cunningham, John, (eds), *Studies in Irish Radical Leadership, Lives on the Left,* (Manchester, 2016)

O'Connor Lysaght, D. R., *The Story of the Limerick Soviet,* (Limerick, 1983)

O'Connor Lysaght, D. R., 'The Munster Soviet Creameries', in *Saothalann Staire Eireann*, No.1, (Dublin, 1981)

O'Connor Lysaght, D. R., 'County Tipperary: Class Struggle and National Struggle 1916-1924', in William Nolan, & Thomas G. McGrath, (eds), *Tipperary, History and Society: Interdisciplinary Essays on the History of an Irish County*, (Dublin, 1997)

O'Connor Lysaght, D. R., 'The Rake's Progress of a Syndicalist: The Political Career of William O'Brien Irish Labour Leader', *Saothar*, Volume 9, (1985), pp.48-63

Ó Gráda, Cormac, (ed.), *Famine 150: Commemorative Lecture Series,* (Dublin 1997).

O'Hegarty, P. S., *The Victory of Sinn Fein,* (Dublin, 1998)

O'Neill, Thomas P. 'The Great Irish Famine 1845-1852', *The Old Limerick Journal Famine Edition,* Volume 32, (Winter 1995), pp. 16-20

O Snodaigh, Aengus, 'Remembering the Past: The Limerick Soviet', *An Phoblacht,* (29 April 1999)

The Old Limerick Journal Famine Edition, Volume 32, (Winter 1995)

Pare, William, *Co-operative Agriculture: A Solution of the Land Question, As Exemplified in the History of the Ralahine Cooperative Agricultural Association, County Clare, Ireland,* (London, 1870)

Prior, Pauline, (ed.), *In Asylums, Mental Health Care and the Irish. Historical Studies, 1800-2010,* (Dublin, 2012)

Potter, Matthew, *The Government and the People of Limerick, The History of Limerick Corporation / City Council 1197-2006,* (Limerick 2006)

Power, Joe, 'Terry Alt and Lady Clare', *The Other Clare,* Volume 10, (March 1986), pp. 15-18

Puirseil, Niamh, 'The Democratic Programme and the roots of the Republic', talk delivered at *Law, Revolution and Sovereignty: Reflections on the Legal Legacy of the 1916 Rising & Declaration of Independence Conference*, (9 April 2016)

Queally, Nicola, *Rebellion, Resistance and the Irish Working Class: The Case of the Limerick Soviet,* (Cambridge, 2010)

Randall, Adrian, & Charlesworth, Andrew, (eds) *Markets, Market Culture and Popular Protest in Eighteenth Century Britain and Ireland,* (Liverpool, 1996)

Roberts, Paul E. W., 'Caravats and Shanavests: Whiteboyism and faction fighting in East Munster 1802-1811', in Samuel Clark, and James S. Donnelly Jr., (eds) *Irish Peasants Violence and Political Unread 1780-1914,* (Wisconsin, 1986), pp. 64-101

Rudé, George, *The Crowd in History,* (London 1999)

Rumpf, E., & Hepburn, A. C., *Nationalism and Socialism in Twentieth Century Ireland*, (Liverpool, 1977)

Russell, Ruth, *What's the Matter With Ireland?* (New York, 1920)

Ryan, Tom, 'The 1841 Census', *Old Limerick Journal,* (Winter Edition 1996), pp. 25-26

Seoighe, Mainchín, *The Story of Kilmallock*, (Kilmallock, 1988)

Seoighe, Mainchín, 'Aspects of the Famine in Limerick', *North Munster Antiquarian Journal,* Volume 49, (2009), pp. 73-84

Sheehan, Daniel Desmond, *Ireland Since Parnell,* (London, 1921)

Sheehan, Joseph T., *Land Purchase Policy in Ireland 1917-1923,* (MA Thesis Maynooth, 1993)

Smethurst, John B., & Carter, Peter, *Historical Directory of Trade Unions, Volume 6,* (Farnham, 2009)

Taplin, Eric, *The Dockers' Union: A Study of the National Union of Dock Labourers, 1889-1922,* (Leicester, 1986)

Thompson, E. P., 'The Moral Economy and the English Crowd in the Eighteenth Century', *Past and Present,* Volume 50, (February 1971), pp. 76-136

Tierney, Mark, 'The Great Famine in Murroe', *The Old Limerick Journal Famine Edition,* Volume 32, (Winter 1995), pp. 75-83

Toomey, Thomas, & Greensmyth, Harry, *An Antique and Storied Land, A History of the Parish of Donoughmore, Knockea, Roxborough, Co. Limerick and Its Environs*, (Limerick, 1991)

Townshend, Charles, 'The Irish Railway Strike of 1920: Industrial Action and Civil Resistance in the Struggle for Independence', *Irish Historical Studies*, Volume 22, Number 83, (March 1979), pp. 265-282

Treacy, Matt, *The Communist Party of Ireland 1921 – 2011*, (Dublin, 2012)

Trotsky, Leon, *Terrorism and Communism, A Reply to Karl Kautsky*, (New York, 1922)

Wells, Roger, 'The Irish Famine of 1799-1801: Market Culture, Moral Economies and Social Protest', in Adrian Randall, & Andrew Charlesworth, (eds) *Markets, Market Culture and Popular Protest in Eighteenth Century Britain and Ireland*, (Liverpool, 1996), pp. 163-194

Online sources

Enright, Flan, *Pre-Famine Clare-Society in Crisis* [Available online at http://www.clarelibrary.ie/eolas/coclare/history/prefamine_clare.htm]

Limerick's Life, *Limerick Population Changes* [Available online at http://limerickslife.com/limerick-population/]

John Reed, 'Soviets in Action', *The Liberator*, October 1918. [Available online at: https://www.marxists.org/archive/reed/1918/soviets.htm]

Slater, Sharon, *The Limerick Soviet – Two Weeks of Self Rule*, [Available online at: http://limerickslife.com]

Trotsky, Leon, *What Next? Vital Questions for the German Proletariat*, [Available online at: https://www.marxists.org/archive/trotsky/germany/1932-ger/index.htm]

Workers Solidarity Movement, *Limerick Soviet 1919*, [Available at: http://www.wsm.ie/c/limerick-soviet-1919-notes]

Printed in Great Britain
by Amazon